# Shared Services

## A Manager's Journey

Daniel C. Melchior, Jr.

John Wiley & Sons, Inc.

**Library of Congress Cataloging-in-Publication Data:**

Melchior, Daniel C., 1966-

    Shared services: a manager's journey / Daniel C. Melchior, Jr.

       p. cm.

    Includes index.

    ISBN 978–0–470–14663–7 (cloth)

1. Shared services (Management)    I. Title.

    HD62.13.M45 2007

    658.4'023—dc22                             2007018192

*To Mom and Dad*

# CONTENTS

# FOREWORD

In 1994, I knew Dan as an accountant for one of the divisions of our company. I was corporate controller and had recently received approval to implement our Shared Services vision for the U.S. operations.

My initial task was to surround myself with the best people I could find. My recruitment efforts included looking to prospective customers, those people currently working in our divisions. Their knowledge in designing our processes and delivery services would be invaluable, as they would help us balance the "consultant best practice" with the "real-world pragmatic."

Despite my best efforts, most of the division people I targeted for recruitment were not interested, as the prevalent view was that this Shared Services thing will be like any number of corporate initiatives and eventually go away. Shared Services was not initially considered a good career move within the company.

However, Dan was one of the few brave souls who got it. He understood the vision and the value-creating opportunities Shared Services could deliver. Along with Dan and a handful of other pioneer-spirited folks, we set off on our journey to create value for our organization in ways and means not done before.

And that journey is what Dan's book is all about. Dan has lived these experiences. Reading this book knocked a whole lot of dust off my memories. For those of you who are on your own journey, you will no doubt relate to the challenges as well as the fun and victories that are all part of the story. For those of you who are just embarking or thinking about embarking on your own journey, Dan has presented an easy-to-read story of what is ahead of you.

Shared Services can be transforming to an organization as well as to the individuals involved. I know it has been transforming to Dan, and he has articulated his journey in a fun and easy-to-read manner. Enjoy!

*Ira Fialkow*
*Vice President*
*Shared Services & Human Resources*
*Rinker Group Limited*

# PREFACE

My hope in writing this book is that readers will learn from the experiences that a Shared Services manager encounters while establishing and running a Shared Services center. Readers will join meetings, listen to conversations, and hear the debate for choosing one path or another. Some of the important topics addressed are: location of the center, organizational structure, process steering teams, allocation methodologies, customer service, bonus plans, key performance indicators, and acquisition implementations. I wrote the book as a fictional story detailing the daily responsibilities of Dennis, a Shared Services director who is responsible for establishing a Shared Services center. Many of Dennis's challenges are based on my own experiences managing and directing Shared Services centers over the past 11 years. This book will provide valuable information to any current Shared Services professionals as well as financial professionals considering implementing a Shared Services center. It will also stimulate thought-provoking conversations about Shared Services organizations and the strategies used to make these organizations successful. Because the book is written from the perspective of a practitioner rather than a consultant, it will appeal to all levels of any Shared Services organization. I am confident you will find the book to be an enjoyable read while also providing very practical and proven strategies and methodologies.

# ACKNOWLEDGMENTS

I would like to thank Ira Fialkow for giving me the opportunity to work in a Shared Services organization and for teaching me most of what I know about Shared Services.

I am also indebted to all of my coworkers who made me look good over the past 10 years: "You are only as good as those you are surrounded by."

# CHAPTER I

# BROWN FIELDS, GREEN FIELDS, AND HAZEL FIELDS

Dennis was happy to be driving home at 7:00 pm, which for him was a decent hour. Thursdays were also nice because every Thursday he ate dinner with the entire family since the kids' activities were all scheduled for other nights. Jennifer, his wife, enjoyed dinner with the family and looked forward to hearing about everyone's day. His 40-minute commute usually allowed him to think about things other than work, but lately Dennis was feeling a little uneasy about his job.

Three months ago he had been slated to head up Capp's Shared Services division. Dennis was chosen because he came to Capp from an established Shared Services center, where he worked his way up to director of Shared Services over the course of seven years. Publicly he was hired to be the corporate controller, but only two months into the job he was given the task of analyzing the potential move to a Shared Services environment. The analysis phase proved to be very successful and showed the results Dennis expected. Capp was founded in 1954 as a lumber company and had evolved into a large building materials company selling everything from lumber, drywall, and shingles to cabinets and plumbing fixtures. Because of Capp's numerous plants and geographic spread, a decentralized administrative organization was costly and very inefficient. Capp had 150 wholesale warehouses in 23 states (see Exhibit 1.1).

EXHIBIT **1.1**    *Capp's Geographical Locations by State*

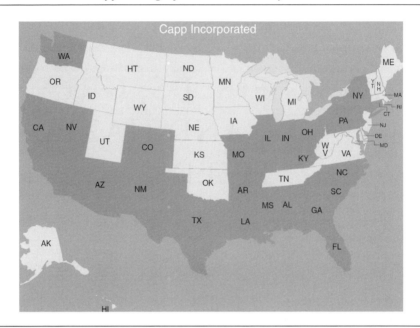

John Phelps, the chief executive officer, and Donna Angelo, Dennis's boss and chief financial officer, agreed to move forward with the Shared Services initiative. Everyone agreed they would begin with the El Paso division, since it was one of the smaller divisions but was as diverse as most at Capp. While they all agreed which division would go first, they could not agree on where to locate the Shared Services division. John wanted to put Shared Services in the corporate offices in Tampa, Florida; Donna preferred a green field (i.e., a center in a city where the company did not already operate) in Des Moines; and Dennis thought they should be in Tampa but not at the corporate office, which would be a hazel field (a brown field would be a center in an existing Capp office). An analysis by a staffing firm suggested that Donna was correct; Capp would get quality employees at a very fair price in Des Moines. The analysis also mentioned that while Tampa could be a viable site, it was not as economically advantageous as Des Moines. Being in a hurricane zone also did not help Tampa's rating. If nothing else, John, Donna, and

Dennis all agreed they would not consider setting up an offshore center. Deciding on the location seemed to be taking longer than it should, and Dennis was not sure if they could agree. Most likely John would simply listen to their arguments for one more week and then make a decision. He hoped it would be made soon.

Dennis rounded the corner of Palm Avenue and slowly made his way up the street. Some of the neighborhood children were usually playing kickball, Wiffle ball, or tag, so he drove extra slowly. As he pulled into the driveway, he noticed Samantha, his youngest daughter, sitting on the stoop playing with Shorty, the family beagle. Seeing both of them made Dennis forget all about green fields, brown fields, or hazel fields.

Walking in the door, Dennis was followed closely by Shorty as he held Samantha in one arm and hugged his youngest son, Danny, with the other. He looked around for Jackie, his oldest daughter, but did not see her. He assumed, like most times, she was in her room. The smells of homemade spaghetti sauce and garlic rolls reminded Dennis why he liked eating with his family so much. Andrew, their oldest son, was a senior in high school and was talking on the phone. Dennis was not sure if Andrew enjoyed the family dinners at his age, but he sure ate plenty and never complained.

Jennifer gave Dennis a kiss on the cheek. "Dinner will be ready in a bit. How was work?" "We are three weeks late in making a decision on the location of the Shared Services center, but I'm sure John will either press us or make it himself this week." "Well, let's not worry about that tonight, we just need to enjoy dinner. Besides, you have to help Jackie with her homework tonight, so you'd better reserve your brainpower," Jennifer said with a chuckle. After Andrew hung up the phone and Jackie came out of her room, they all sat down to eat.

"Andrew, so two more months and you'll be eating mac and cheese and frozen pizzas every night," said Dennis. Andrew was two months from going away to college.

"Well, at least I'll be able to come home on weekends so you and Mom can do my laundry," Andrew replied with a grin.

"Not if our service center ends up in Des Moines," Dennis replied, reminding the family that they might have to move.

"Why can't you just have the center here? I don't understand why you would want to move everyone to Des Moines," said Jackie.

"Well, it's complicated, honey, but it really comes down to money. The cost of living is cheaper in Des Moines, and it's not in a hurricane zone, so we can save some money on the redundancy of our infrastructure." As he spoke, Dennis realized that he was starting to buy into Donna's argument.

"What about the people who work here in Tampa: are they all going to move? They must have a lot of sun and beaches in Des Moines or else everyone wouldn't want to move," Danny said. Everyone smiled at his naiveté.

"Dad," Andrew said. "We've talked about this before and I still don't get it. When I was looking at colleges, you always told me it's not the college that makes you, it's what you make of the college."

"Yeah, I remember saying that."

"Well, doesn't the same thing apply here? No matter what city you choose, your success is going to come from the people you hire to run it and the way you actually run it. I'm sure there are just as many qualified people here in Tampa. What is the actual difference in wages? Let's just say you have 200 employees and the average pay is $45,000 versus $55,000, the savings is $2 million."

"So Mr. Math Major or is it Charley Money Bags? Two million isn't a lot of money?"

"I'm not saying that, but remember you said you are going to start small and then bring in other businesses. If that's the case, then you won't be up to the $2 million difference for more than two years. Also, won't it be easier for the owners to make sure things are going as planned when the center is in the same town? You say it's going to be cheaper in Iowa, but isn't that all you are really saving? I mean, what about the people who are going to be out of work? I assume you'll have to pay a severance."

"You make good points, and we've considered all of them. I'm just not sure which way John is leaning. I tend to agree with you though."

Dennis was proud that Andrew gave him something to think seriously about. He was feeling pretty good as he drove to work the next day because Andrew reminded him that the ultimate success factor was not in choosing the proper location but in choosing the right people. After last night's discussion, Dennis felt John and Donna were not putting enough emphasis on the people, especially those who were already working for Capp. John and Donna usually arrived around the same time as Dennis, and it would be pretty easy to have a quick chat about his new thoughts regarding the location of the Shared Services center.

Dennis pulled into his assigned parking space and noticed that John and Donna were already there. Of the 300 employees in the building, only 10 had assigned parking spaces. It was a nice perk, considering that it rains frequently in Tampa and the 10 spots were not only covered but also very close to the door.

Dennis got in the elevator and pushed the button for the fourth floor. Since he had arrived at Capp and was assigned to analyze Shared Services, some of the employees were a little uptight when they saw him. He figured it was a natural reaction: The employees did not know if they were even going to have a Shared Services center, much less where it was going to be located.

As he got off of the elevator, he noticed John and Donna were having a discussion in John's office. Dennis walked there. "Morning, guys."

"Hey, Dennis, come in here. We have some thoughts about the location," said John.

Dennis sat down at the round table where Donna was drinking her coffee. John had the consultant reports spread on the table.

"You know, we spent a decent amount of money on this study for a good reason. We are new to this, and the consultants cover all aspects and are objective. It seems a bit silly to spend the time and money to get their opinion and then not use it. I agree with the consultants and Donna and think we should go with Des Moines."

As John was talking, Dennis was looking at the reports. John was right in saying they at least covered all of the variables. Each location was evaluated on eight criteria:

1. Quality of workforce
2. Cost of workforce
3. Cost of real estate
4. Convenience of travel from current locations
5. Local taxes
6. Government assistance or grants
7. Probability of natural disasters or emergencies
8. Time zone relative to the other business units

Because Capp would not consider going out of the country, criteria such as language compatibility and political stability were not evaluated.

Dennis looked at Donna and then John before speaking. "I agree that we should definitely consider the evaluation, but I've been giving this a lot of thought as well. Quite honestly, I think we're overevaluating and overthinking the issue. I ate dinner with my family last night and had an interesting discussion with my son. I was talking about the location and how important the decision was, and he asked one question: Why? Why is it so important? He reminded me that when he was evaluating colleges, I told him the college he chooses will not make him, he will make the college. By the same token, the people we choose to operate the center will determine our success. It will not come down to location or even the difference we might have to pay in Tampa versus Des Moines. Our success will simply be a product of the people we hire."

Dennis waited for a response. Neither John nor Donna said anything immediately, which meant either that they were considering what he had said or they were trying to figure out how to tell him it was too late, they had made their decision.

"Having said that, does that mean you are okay with any of the proposed sites, or do you have a preference?" Donna asked.

"I do have a preference, but it's not based on any of the criteria listed. We've considered all of the labor costs, including severance if necessary, and we've talked about, but not quantified, the cultural impact on our current staff if we displace workers."

"Well, that is a little tough to quantify," said John.

"I agree, but that doesn't mean we can discount it. Remember, our success depends not only on our center but also on the cooperation and assistance of our divisions. While we are mandating Shared Services, we will get a lot of mileage out of selecting Tampa as a site and hiring some employees from the Tampa business unit."

Donna and John looked at each other and said, "So you're saying we should locate the center in Tampa?"

"It's important to have people in our organization who understand some level of the day-to-day operations that are completed in the divisions and why it is being done a certain way today. Also, one of the biggest statements that each division will make as we bring them on board is 'we did it better, cheaper, and never had any problems.' Without someone who was involved in the day-to-day on our side to defend us, we won't be able to counter that argument."

"But, Dennis," John said forcefully, "this is not about sides. We aren't here to divide our company. Shared Services will allow us to be more efficient and allow our divisions to concentrate on sales and operations. This is not an option, and everyone will fall in line."

"With all due respect, John, just because you mandate something doesn't mean that every person will embrace it. We have to attack it on multiple fronts, and your mandate is the most powerful and best way to do that, but we also need front-line soldiers, so to speak, to combat propaganda and rumors. There is no one better to have on our side than a former division employee who believes in what we are doing and will help sell it."

Dennis and John were used to debating issues forcefully; that is what helped them make good decisions. Neither man took these discussions personally. John sat back for a second thinking. "Donna, so what do you think?" he asked.

"Well, as we were discussing before he came in, we did pay good money for this study, but we also pay good money for Dennis," she said with a little laugh. "He's been working in the Shared Services world for some time, so we should probably pay a bit more attention to him than a consultant with a study."

She looked at Dennis and said, "Let me ask you something, and I need an honest answer. We decided to undertake this study before we hired you. If we had hired you first, would you have agreed to hire a consultant to complete this study, or would we have just made the decision ourselves?"

"We would have made the decision ourselves. I mean, if we were really at odds over this, maybe we bring in someone to help us, but I would not bring them in at the beginning. Of all of the Shared Services operations I have looked at, the location ultimately had very little to do with the success or failure of the operation. I've seen brown field, green field, and hazel field operations all succeed and I've seen them all fail. I've also seen them everywhere in between."

John started to laugh. Donna and Dennis both looked at him in surprise. "Dennis, that actually sounded a bit poetic." John started to sing "I've seen brown fields, green fields, and hazel fields. . . ."

All three started to laugh. The one thing Dennis liked about working at Capp was the fun nature of both John's and Donna's personalities. Even though they worked very hard and were very driven, they knew enough to not take everything too seriously.

After the laughter died down, John made a decision, sort of. "I'll tell you what. Let me think for one more night and I'll come in tomorrow morning with a guaranteed decision. Just do me a favor, whatever it is, all three of us have to walk the walk and talk the talk. Agreed?"

Donna and Dennis looked at each other and in unison said "Agreed!"

# CHAPTER 2

# FINALLY

Dennis arrived at work a bit earlier than yesterday and noticed that neither John nor Donna had arrived yet. As a matter of fact, his was the first car in the parking lot. This was a bit unusual, so he looked at his watch. He was surprised to see it was only 7:05 am. Maybe subconsciously he had arrived early because he couldn't wait to hear John's decision.

Dennis could not really concentrate on any of the work he needed to get done, so he surfed the net reading about the recent Space Shuttle launch. He was so engrossed in the article that he didn't hear Donna come in until she said good morning.

"Good morning, Donna, how are you?"

"I can't complain, all is well," Donna said.

"Well, today's the big day. I can't wait to hear what John has decided. At least then we'll be able to really move on to getting this project rolling," Dennis said with a smile.

"I agree we've beaten this thing up enough. So, what do you think it will be?"

Dennis furrowed his brow and said, "You know, I really can't say. I'm having trouble reading him on this. Two days ago I definitely believed it would be Des Moines, but now I'm really unsure. Either way, I'm ready. I'm looking forward to the next steps."

Just then John's assistant Terri walked into Dennis's office and said, "John will be coming in a bit late today. His son had a few issues at school, and his teacher wants to talk to John. I think it has something to do with trying to feed the class fish the sandwiches that John made him for lunch."

9

"Sounds like a smart kid," Donna said. "I wouldn't eat anything John fixed either."

The three of them had a good laugh even though Dennis was disappointed he would have to wait to hear John's decision. Dennis reminded himself to tell John that he should stick to his core competencies and outsource the sandwich making.

In the meantime, Dennis decided to call Oscar Harris, the director of the SAP implementation project. Oscar had been with Capp for 12 years in various accounting functions and was chosen to head up the SAP project because he had led many of the acquisition efforts over the years and was very well respected by the divisions. The project team set up shop in a temporary office across the street from the El Paso division. Oscar had chosen not to spend much on furnishings other than a pool table that also converted to table tennis and a foosball table.

Everyone involved in the decision to implement Shared Services and SAP felt it was important to not be too dependent on consultants or accounting firms as the project progressed. Since the project was going to last three years, Oscar and the team leads had been chosen because they were mid- to long-term loyal Capp employees who had a significant amount of business knowledge and expertise.

Each team leader was sent to months of training on the particular module he or she was responsible for implementing. Leaders were chosen for specific modules because their business experience at Capp related to that functional area. For example, Robert, who was responsible for the Order to Cash team, led the Accounts Receivable department at Capp's largest division. Each person chosen to be on the project was responsible for backfilling his or her own position until the project was completed. They all knew that most likely they would move to other positions within the company once the Shared Services center was rolled out because their departments would be eliminated.

Three years seemed like a long time, and everyone on Oscar's team was excited about learning new software and being involved in such an important initiative. Besides that, the bonus structure was very lucrative, with a payout for every successful implementation and a final payout once all divisions had been converted. The final payout made up 60 percent of the bonus, so everyone was heavily incentivized to remain on the project until completion.

Even though it was only 5:30 am in El Paso, Dennis knew he had a decent chance of catching Oscar in the office. Oscar was one of the hardest workers he had ever met. Once Oscar took on a project, he routinely worked 80 to 90 hours a week.

"Oscar, do you ever go home?" Dennis asked when he heard the man's voice.

"Only during fire alarms," Oscar answered. "How is everything in Tampa? Did you ever figure out where we're going to put this center?"

"Well, John is supposed to tell us this morning, but right now he's explaining to his son's teacher why he insists on making his son a lunch that he won't eat," Dennis said.

"Is he still feeding his lunch to the fish? Tell John to stick to what he knows, which is not making lunch."

"I've got a note on my desk to talk to him about it," Dennis said, laughing. "So how is everything in El Paso?"

"We're making good progress in all areas, but the consultants we're using are not doing a good enough job at knowledge transfer. I'm a bit concerned that we'll be more dependent on them than we really want to be. My team leaders are fairly busy, and they don't always get to spend enough time with the consultants."

"Well, once I get the managers hired for the Shared Services center, I'd like to send them to El Paso to work with your teams and assist where they can in the implementation. Hopefully this will free up some time for your team and also give everyone a chance to get to know each other. We're going to be heavily dependent on each other for the next three years, so we better get acquainted," said Dennis.

"That's a great idea. We're a long way from Tampa, and having our people not know each other could be detrimental to teamwork."

"Okay, once I get my team together, which will probably take the next few weeks, we can get together and figure out the schedules and such."

"Sounds good," said Oscar. "Talk to you soon."

As Dennis hung up, he heard John talking in the hall. When he looked up, both John and Donna were standing in the doorway of his office.

"I'll bet I can guess what you are talking about, and I don't want to keep you in suspense any longer than necessary, so here it is. Starting today I'm not going to fix my son any more lunches," said John. "Just kidding; well, not really, but we'll talk about that later.

"About our location, I really had made up my mind two weeks ago, but I wanted to really make sure we had it right, so I waited a couple of weeks. It's a good thing I did because now I'm sure. I'm sure that I was not right two weeks ago when I thought it should be Des Moines. I thought a lot about your points, Dennis, and we're going with Tampa and a new facility."

Dennis and Donna looked at each other, a bit shocked. Donna appeared shocked that John's decision was not Des Moines, which was her choice. Dennis thought about the conversation he had had with Andrew that had prompted his discussion with John. He was certainly glad he brought the topic up at dinner; otherwise they might be moving to Des Moines.

Once John made a final decision, he did not like to discuss it, so neither Dennis nor Donna asked for any clarification.

"Okay," John said. "Now we can get down to actually selecting a site and looking for talent. I'll get with real estate manager, Tony Robertson, so we can start to look at office space. I'm not sure yet if we will buy or lease, but we can work on that. We have the space downstairs we talked about that will hold 10 people until we get our new space."

"Sounds good," said Dennis. "I'll develop a communication that we can send to all divisions so we can start interviewing internal candidates now, and I'll get with HR about posting the jobs externally."

When Capp decided to implement Shared Services and SAP, it chose to move Accounts Payable, Accounts Receivable, Document Management, Payroll, Benefits Administration, and General Ledger Accounting into the center. Dennis decided he would structure the team as shown in Exhibit 2.1.

EXHIBIT **2.1** *Shared Services Organization Chart*

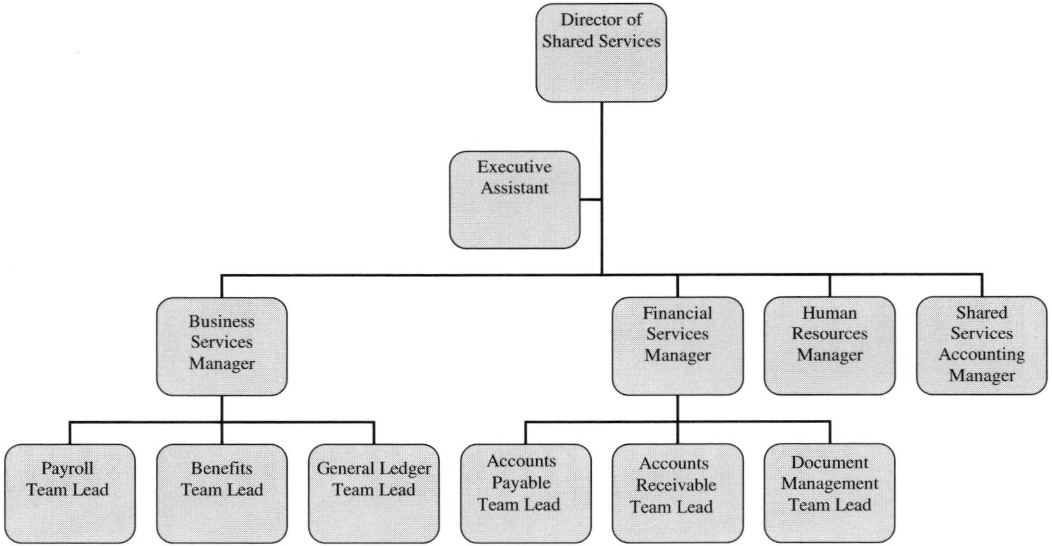

When Dennis had started with Capp, he immediately hired an assistant, Rosa. Now the real work would begin. They had a lot to do, but first and foremost he had to draft a memo to post internally for a Business Services manager, Financial Services manager, Human Resource manager, and Accounting manager. Dennis was excited about building his team. He went to his office, sat down, and looked around. On the wall facing his desk hung a poster with the words "You Are Only as Good as Those You Are Surrounded By." Dennis knew it was time to surround himself with great people.

# CHAPTER 3

# YOU ARE ONLY AS GOOD AS THOSE YOU ARE SURROUNDED BY

Today was going to be very busy for Dennis. The first thing he needed to do was review a memo that John had drafted explaining the decision to locate the center in Tampa. (See Exhibits 3.1 and 3.2.)

Dennis reviewed the memo and was pleased that John said "You are only as good as those you are surrounded by." He knew that many employees were anxious about the center and what it would mean to each of them. Making every employee comfortable about applying and interviewing for the opportunities was a major goal for Dennis.

"Rosa, we need to get started on posting these positions," Dennis said while shuffling through the hardcopies he had on his desk. "Obviously we need to get these positions filled as quickly as possible, but we need to make sure we take our time and get the absolute right candidates. They will ultimately establish the culture, determine the processes, and make up the foundation for our success. Send an email with these four job postings this afternoon."

"Will do," said Rosa. "Are you going to interview the candidates by yourself or will others be joining you?"

"Sandy from Corporate HR will come over and do the screening, then Donna and I will interview them at the same time. I like to do team

EXHIBIT **3.1**   *Internal Memo Announcing the Shared Services Site Location*

## INTEROFFICE MEMORANDUM

TO:             All Employees
FROM:         John Phelps, Chief Executive Officer
SUBJECT:     Shared Services

As many of you know, we have been in the process of evaluating the creation of a Shared Services center for our organization. Shared Services offers an opportunity for our company to continue to streamline our accounting and HR processes and add significant value to each of our divisions. Along with the implementation of Shared Services, we have also chosen to implement SAP as our accounting software. The implementation of Shared Services and SAP will take place simultaneously as we roll out each division (see preliminary schedule attached).

Foremost in everyone's mind is most likely the location of our Shared Services center. We spent a significant amount of time and energy making this decision and sought the expertise of consultants and experienced Shared Services executives. After much thought, we are very pleased to announce that our center will be located in Tampa, Florida, the city where our company was founded and has grown and prospered. While Tampa was not on the list of locations the experts suggested, we feel a great deal of loyalty to Tampa and, most important, our employees in Tampa. We are in the process of locating office space for our center and will let you know as soon as we find a home. In the short term, we will set up our offices on the first floor next to Internal Audit.

Tomorrow you will receive from Dennis Malone a list of opportunities in the Shared Services organization. These opportunities are only the first of many that will become available over the next 30 months as we implement Shared Services across the organization. Dennis is often quoted as saying "you are only as good as those you are surrounded by." He was adamant that the center should be located in Tampa because he wanted to surround himself with the best, and Tampa represents the largest number of current Accounting personnel. We encourage everyone throughout the organization to review the list of opportunities and apply for any position you feel fits your career goals and where you think you can make a difference.

If you have any questions or concerns, please contact me.

EXHIBIT **3.2**   *Preliminary Implementation Schedule*

## PRELIMINARY SHARED SERVICES
## IMPLEMENTATION SCHEDULE

| Location (Divisions) | Date |
|---|---|
| El Paso, Texas | October 1, 2005 |
| Western Division | |
| AZ, CA, CO, NM, NV, WA | March 1, 2006 |
| Mid-West/South Division | |
| AL, AR, IL, IN, KY, LA, MO, MS, OH | January 1, 2006 |
| Eastern Division | |
| CT, FL, GA, NC, NY, PA, SC | October 1, 2007 |

interviews because someone else might get a different read on someone than I do," replied Dennis.

"Don't you think some people will be intimidated by the team interview process?" Rosa asked. "I mean, it's nerve-racking enough to get interviewed by one person, much less two or more."

"I agree, it can be a bit intimidating, but we'll tell them when the interview is set up that it's a team interview. That at least gives them a heads-up and allows them to prepare. The reason I don't like people to interview them separately is they might give different answers to the same question. I like everyone to hear the same answer and then make their determination based on that. Besides, we'll put people at ease and let them know it is more of a conversation than an inquisition. You know my interviewing style. I didn't intimidate you, right?"

"First off, I can't be intimidated, and second off, when you started the interview by telling me that your morning consisted of chasing your dog Shorty down the street because he was chasing a cat and then have that turn into you and Shorty being chased back down the street by a bigger dog, you kind of lost your bite, no pun intended," Rosa shot back with a laugh.

"Boy, you and Samantha love telling that story, but anyone being chased by a Rottweiler would have been running just like I was."

"Well, I believe Samantha said it was the friendly neighborhood Lab and he was wagging his tail as fast as you were running."

"Well, I'm sticking to my version. And by the way, I'm leaving a bit early today to go by the market and pick up some steaks and shrimp. I haven't told my family that we're locating the center in Tampa, so I'm going to break the news and then we're going to celebrate with a cookout. They will be excited that we don't have to move so I'm going to treat them to my special version of surf and turf."

"I thought you wanted to celebrate, not punish them," Rosa said with a laugh.

Driving home, Dennis was looking forward to telling his family they would be able to stay in Tampa. He was also happy knowing that the decision was not just good for him and his family but for Capp. After all, his job was to help make these types of decisions, and he was very confident they had made the right one.

Dennis and his family did not always eat together, but he called Jennifer and told everyone to be home. They probably knew what he wanted to talk about.

As he rounded Palm Avenue and pulled into his driveway, Dennis noticed Samantha, Shorty, and a big Lab playing in the front yard. He could not help but laugh. He was glad Rosa could joke with him and that the office environment was such that everyone enjoyed coming to work. Keeping that type of environment as the center grew would be tough, but he was sure going to try.

First things first, though, and that meant grilling the steaks and shrimp. Even though it was late June, the temperature was just around 70 degrees, a bit cooler than normal, and that made for a perfect night to grill. The breeze was refreshing as he and Jennifer enjoyed a glass of wine. Dennis loved these times, especially watching the kids play in the pool as he grilled. Tonight Andrew stayed poolside to talk, and Dennis figured this was because he was very interested in what had been decided.

"So, Dad, I assume we're here because you're going to tell us where we're going to live for the next few years?" Andrew asked.

"I always knew you were a smart boy. We did make a decision. I was going to wait until we eat to tell you but since you and Mom are here, I'll tell you now. We're staying in Tampa."

"Yes!" Andrew exclaimed, pumping his fist as if he'd just hit a game-winning shot.

Jennifer looked at Dennis with a very satisfied smile on her face. It appeared that she could not be happier.

"So did my argument about this being the same type of decision as deciding on college help?" asked Andrew.

"Certainly it did," replied Dennis. "We also talked a great deal about what it would mean to the culture of the company to displace workers who have been at Capp for many years. It is important that we have some people in our center who have worked at the divisions and understand the history of the company. I'm sure we'll be able to find the right people to run our center with some coming from Capp and some from the outside. And if we have to get some external candidates from outside of the Tampa area, it's not a tough sell to ask them to move to a beautiful spot like this."

"Honey," said Jennifer, "the steaks are burning!"

"Holy cow!" Dennis rushed to the grill, lifted the lid, and smoke poured from the grill. Quickly he grabbed the tongs and flipped the steaks. His eyes were watering and burning from the smoke facial. Once his eyes and the smoke cleared, though, he could see the steaks were fine.

"I did that on purpose to get that good smoke flavor," he said with a laugh. "They're okay."

"That's the main reason I was going to tell you while we were eating, not while I was grilling. Now let me concentrate."

"Please do," Jennifer and Andrew replied at the same time.

Dennis and his family enjoyed dinner and lots of laughs as they played a game of Monopoly. Dennis always lost as everyone else teamed up to beat him. As much as he hated to lose, he liked the fact that his family displayed good teamwork. It was either that or he was a lousy Monopoly player.

Two weeks had passed since the job postings were emailed. Dennis had 12 internal and 7 external candidates to interview. They had received many more resumes, but Dennis and Donna narrowed the list to the 19 candidates who seemed best qualified based on their resumes. Nineteen qualified candidates for four jobs was a pretty good ratio. Sandy posted the jobs online with the local newspaper and also used a couple of national job search Web sites. Capp preferred not to use recruiters since their fees were usually around 20 percent of the annual salary, and there were no guarantees the employees would stay after 90 days. The only guarantee was a credit for future placements, but this just seemed liked a way to keep having to do business with the same recruiters. The corporate approach, which Dennis agreed with, was to use recruiters only as a last resort.

Dennis and Donna decided to schedule the interviews over Monday through Thursday. That would give them a chance to interview everyone, and then on Friday they could either make their selections or bring back candidates for second interviews if necessary. Sandy would initially greet the candidates and provide an overview of Capp, if the candidates were external, and a brief overview of Shared Services for everyone.

The first candidate Monday morning was Sara Mitchell, who applied for the Business Services manager position. Currently Sara was working at Capp in corporate headquarters as an Accounting manager. She had been with the company for four years and had a good reputation in both corporate and at the divisions.

Donna and Dennis were waiting in a conference room for Sandy to bring Sara over. The room was small, which would make the interview process seem less intimidating. They each had a list of questions they were going to ask. Dennis believed they should ask each candidate the same general questions, which would allow them to more fairly compare candidates. Dennis was going to ask the behavioral questions and Donna would cover the more technical or accounting-related questions. The questions were mostly situational, meaning the candidates would be asked to describe

EXHIBIT **3.3**    *Applicant Assessment Form*

| Applicant Name: | | Date: |
|---|---|---|
| Position: | | Interviewer: |
| Attribute | Rating (1–5) 5 highest | Notes |
| Initiative | | |
| Teamwork | | |
| Problem Solving | | |
| Communication | | |
| Leadership | | |
| Average Rating | | |
| Recommendation | | |
| Hire | Second Interview | No further interest |
| | | |

actual work situations they encountered in their previous experiences, since these questions usually provided more insight into the candidates' management style, team skills, problem-solving ability, and past behavior. Once the interview was finished, Dennis and Donna would complete an assessment sheet based on the questions asked. (See Exhibit 3.3.) This would help ensure that all candidates were judged on the same criteria. While technical skills were important, both Donna and Dennis felt that values, character, teamwork, and attitude were the key elements that would make someone a successful Shared Services employee.

Sandy slowly opened the door to the conference room.

"Donna and Dennis, I think you already know Sara," she said.

"Yes, of course," said Dennis. "We met a few months ago. Nice to see you again."

"Nice to see you," replied Sara.

"I don't think we've ever met in person, but I know we've talked on the phone a few times," said Sara to Donna.

"That's right, nice to finally put a face to the voice."

"Thanks, Sandy, we'll take it from here," Dennis said.

"Sit anywhere you like." Dennis motioned to the empty chairs. "We're pretty informal here so anywhere is fine. I know Sandy told you this would be a team interview, and for right now, Donna and I are the team, but we hope to change that pretty soon. Both of us will ask you a number of questions, but this is really just a conversation because you need to learn as much about us and what we are trying to do, just as we are trying to learn about you. So having said that, if you think of a question you want to ask us, please feel free to interrupt because I would rather have you interrupt than forget the question. Sound fair?"

"Sure," replied Sara.

"What do you consider important for getting a group of people to work well together?" asked Dennis.

Sara thought for a few seconds. "To me, the number-one way to get a group of people to work together is to provide them with a common goal. There should be a common overall goal, and then all other goals should relate to accomplishing the overall goal. To use an analogy, I'm a big football fan, and obviously in any sport the goal is to win the game. A football team might realize that if they run for more than 150 yards in a game, they win 96 percent of the time. If that is the case, then they should have a goal of rushing for 150 yards or more. That goal might mean that they need to have 40 rushing attempts in a game, so that would become a goal. I think sports provide great examples of what it takes to get everyone to work well together, and we can follow some of the proven methodologies that teams employ to win. So, first and foremost, getting everyone to work together is a common goal."

"Okay," Donna said. "Can you provide an example of a time that you provided a common goal to your team at work?"

"Well, as you know I supervise the Corporate Accounting team, and we as a team are responsible for all balance sheet reconciliations. When I started, we were not as up to date as we should have been in completing these reconciliations. On average, we completed reconciliations 90 days after we closed a particular month. I felt we should be able to do this in 45 days, so we put together a program called the Drive for 45. We set a date to get all reconciliations completed within this time frame and provided an incentive if all reconciliations were completed within this time. Essentially the team had 90 days to get everything up to date. We displayed our progress graphically and publicly within the department and covered the results in a weekly meeting. I'm proud to say we met our goal in 80 days, and to celebrate the team enjoyed a small bonus and a very fun lunch."

"Sounds impressive," remarked Dennis. "I hope you've been able to maintain it."

"Actually, it's gotten a bit better. We now have all reconciliations completed within 38 days. We still display the graph and we still talk about it in our meetings, although we usually only talk about it monthly since we are doing so well."

Dennis and Donna continued to ask questions, and Sara provided very positive examples of her work. She asked many questions, all related to Capp's strategy, vision, and Shared Service philosophies. While Capp was good at communicating their overall strategy, the Shared Service concept was new, so Dennis understood why Sara asked so many questions related to the new concept.

Dennis concluded the interview, stating "We'd like to make a decision by early next week. We might require a second interview, but that has yet to be determined. Sandy will contact you regarding the next steps."

"Thank you both very much," Sara said. "I really look forward to hearing from you, and I'm very excited about this opportunity. I've read a great deal about Shared Services. Many successful companies have implemented it and are thriving because of it. I'd very much like to be involved in the creation of our center and think this is a very exciting time for our company. If you need any additional information from me, just let me know."

Sara shook hands with Donna and Dennis, who opened the door, and Sara left.

"Well, that was certainly a good start," said Donna.

"No offense, but let's not talk about the candidates before we complete the interview assessment," Dennis said.

"You're a real stickler for the details." Donna smiled.

"Hey, you never know, we might get just as lucky on the next one. If that happens, the selection process would get really tough. We need to fill out the assessment form and we'll make our decision once we've seen all the candidates."

"Fair enough, it's your show," Donna said.

Dennis and Donna interviewed two more candidates that morning. Then it was time for lunch, and Dennis was hungry.

"How about we go out for a bite to eat? I need to get out of this little room and into a place that's a bit more casual," he said.

"Sounds good to me. Let's see if John is available."

The three decided to go to their favorite neighborhood oyster bar.

"How are the interviews going so far?" John asked.

"Well, we definitely have some good candidates, but we're going to wait to comment until we've met them all," Dennis replied.

"Fair enough; I'll wait until the verdicts are in."

During lunch, they talked about nothing in particular. Dennis was looking forward to the afternoon interviews.

The group arrived back at the office at 1:15 pm, which gave Donna and Dennis 15 minutes before their first interview for the Financial Services manager.

Dennis spent a few minutes at his desk looking over George Ramos's resume. George was an external candidate who applied for the position based on the posting Sandy placed on a national job search Web site. He lived in Tampa and was probably familiar with Capp.

Sandy screened George prior to Dennis and Donna's interview. Afterward, she opened the door to the conference room and introduced John to Dennis and Donna.

"George, nice to meet you. Did you have any trouble finding our place?" asked Dennis.

"Nice to meet you as well. No, it was pretty easy since I'm familiar with the area."

Dennis repeated what he had said in earlier interviews about it being a conversation and that he wanted George to interrupt if he had any questions.

Then he asked: "What do you consider important for getting a group of people to work well together?"

"Well, I think if everyone is a professional, they will know what needs to be done. We all come to work to do our job, and it is up to everyone to take responsibility for their area. I don't like to micromanage my people. I know if given the latitude, they'll get the job done. My job is to strategize the next steps in our evolution and make sure we're poised to provide the services the company needs."

"How do you make sure teams don't have conflicting goals?" Donna asked.

"Each team should know what they're trying to accomplish and how it relates to the other teams. A good organization is structured in a way that one team does not step on another team's toes."

"Okay. How would you compare and contrast the best supervisor you've had with the worst?" asked Dennis.

"Wow, that's a loaded question," George replied. "I'll start with the best supervisor who I still talk to frequently. When I first got started in the accounting field, my supervisor took the time to teach me not only about the technical aspects of my job, but also mentored me about management, business, and general life skills. Much of what he taught me I still use everyday."

"When you say general life skills, can you give specifics?" asked Donna.

"Well, when you're young, you need some guidance, and he reminded me not to spend too much time partying and having a good time, if you know what I mean." George laughed.

"And the worst?" Donna asked.

"I really would not say the worst, because all of my supervisors have been okay, but I did have one that micromanaged just about everything and would not let me make a decision. I sometimes wondered what I got paid for."

Dennis and Donna continued to ask questions, and George had a number of his own.

This pattern of interviewing continued for the rest of the week until they had interviewed all candidates.

Friday morning Dennis and Donna both pulled into the parking lot at the same time. The sky was a perfect blue, and the breeze was just slightly bending the palm fronds.

"Boy, I hope it's like this tomorrow," said Dennis. "I need to get a chance to enjoy the weather with my kids."

"No kidding! I wish we could do that today, but we have to finish our selection process."

"Well, at least we don't have to interview anyone today. I mean, I don't mind doing it, but 19 interviews in 4 days is brutal."

"I agree, but at least we have some really good candidates for three of the positions," replied Donna.

They walked into the building and got on the elevator. Neither said a word, but Dennis was feeling like the weight of the world was on his shoulders. He knew that choosing the right candidates was going to be absolutely crucial to the success of the center, and the choices were not easy. In his mind he felt that Donna was thinking the same thing. The choices they were going to make today would determine their destiny.

As they exited the elevator, Donna turned to Dennis and said, "I've got a few things to do this morning, so let's meet at 10:30 to discuss the candidates. Hopefully by the end of the day we'll have our choices."

"Sounds good to me, I'll meet you in your office."

At 10:30, Dennis walked into Donna's office. She was on the phone and typing an email at the same time. She looked at Dennis as if to say sit down, I will only be a minute. Dennis checked his BlackBerry as Donna talked and typed.

"Sorry," said Donna.

"That's okay."

They both opened folders that contained assessment forms for each candidate. They had interviewed these candidates for each position:

| Business Services Manager | Source | Rating-Donna | Rating-Dennis |
| --- | --- | --- | --- |
| Sara Mitchell | Internal | 4 | 3.5 |
| Cathy Van Horn | External | 2 | 3 |
| Rick Becker | Internal | 3.5 | 3 |
| Tom Oliver | External | 2 | 2 |
| David Rice | Internal | 3 | 3 |
| Luis Ortiz | External | 2.5 | 3 |
| James Howard | Internal | 3.5 | 3.5 |

| Financial Services Manager | Source | Rating-Donna | Rating-Dennis |
| --- | --- | --- | --- |
| George Ramos | External | 2 | 2.5 |
| Yvonne Lee | Internal | 3.5 | 4 |
| Ron Brown | External | 3 | 2.5 |
| Steve Chappell | Internal | 3 | 3 |
| Jerry Schaefer | Internal | 3.5 | 4 |
| John Morton | Internal | 4 | 3.5 |

| HR Manager | Source | Rating-Donna | Rating-Dennis |
| --- | --- | --- | --- |
| Tammy Raines | External | 4.5 | 4 |
| Clarence Middlebrook | Internal | 3.5 | 4 |
| Terri O'Neal | Internal | 2.5 | 3.5 |

| Accounting Manager | Source | Rating-Donna | Rating-Dennis |
| --- | --- | --- | --- |
| Tanya McDonald | Internal | 4 | 4 |
| Susan Reid | External | 4 | 4 |
| Rick Mitchell | Internal | 2.5 | 3.5 |

# CHAPTER 4

# DECISION TIME

"Well, Donna, let's start with the Business Services manager," Dennis said. "Tell me what you think."

"In my mind, it's obvious that Sara is clearly the best candidate. She has extensive experience with Capp, has been successful in her current position, and has good internal references. I'm not sure anyone else even compares given all of that."

"I agree completely," said Dennis. "That was easy."

"Okay," said Donna. "Let me ask you this, what're we going to do about offers?"

"First, let's get all of the candidates chosen and then we'll talk about money. Fundamentally I think we should work with Sandy to determine the base salary. I'd also like to provide a consistent bonus schedule for all managers, and it should somewhat mirror what Oscar is doing with his SAP team," said Dennis.

"I never really got involved in that. What's he doing?" asked Donna.

"Each manager has a total bonus potential for the overall project, and it's paid out in increments based on milestones. For example, they get 15 percent of their potential 90 days after El Paso is live. After that, they're paid between 5 and 10 percent for the remaining implementations, and once all existing divisions are live they get 60 percent. It's designed to keep them motivated as we progress but also to hold out enough of a carrot to keep them around for the duration of the project. As you know, when people get a good bit of software knowledge, they are often targeted by recruiters. We want to head that off as much as possible."

"It sounds good, but we'll have to see if it actually works once we get going. I do agree that both the functional and technical teams should have fundamentally the same type of structure. But you're right, let's deal with that later," Donna said.

"Who's next, financial services?" she continued.

"Yeah, let's talk about that. I had two candidates that rated the same: Yvonne Lee and Jerry Schaefer."

"Really? I rated both of those as 3.5, but I have John Morton as a 4."

"Okay, so this won't be as easy as choosing Sara," replied Dennis.

"Can we definitely say these are three candidates and at least eliminate the others?" Donna asked.

"Yes, because we need to stick with the process. We rated them for a reason, and we should utilize that," said Dennis.

"Okay, so talk to me about Yvonne and Jerry."

"Well, first, they're all internal, including John, so they are known quantities. As Yvonne said, she works in Corporate with Sara, and it was obvious that she has many of the same traits. She is Sara's peer and supervises the Cash Management team. It's a smaller team, but she's been just as successful in getting her team to perform. I'm sure she and Sara have collaborated on their initiatives."

"I agree," said Donna, "but that also scares me a bit. I don't want to get too many people who think alike. Also I don't think we want to put too many people from Corporate on the team so early. It could hurt buy-in from the divisions."

"You're right, but she's a strong candidate."

"Agreed, what about Jerry?" asked Donna.

"Being the controller of a large division has given Jerry a lot of insight into the inner workings of our entire accounting process. But what I liked most about him is that he gave most of the credit to his team. He certainly praised their efforts and talked about how much he allowed them to make decisions. It seems he gives them a lot of latitude. We're going to need that type of manager if we're going to make this center successful. Also, there's no doubt in my mind that he has the technical skills and knowledge to do the job. He seemed excited about the changes happening and knows a lot about Shared Services concepts. I think he'll do really well."

"Would you choose him over Yvonne?" asked Donna.

"Well, I did rate them the same, but after hearing myself talk and factoring in your points about Corporate and division buy-in, I'd have to say yes," replied Dennis. "Jerry is my choice. Tell me what you think about John Morton."

"Well, I like the fact that not only is he from a division but he's worked in multiple divisions. He is very well known throughout Capp, and having him on our team will give us a lot of credibility with the divisions. He is also very technically sound, so he has that covered."

"Do you think he's really excited about this project and the upcoming changes, or is he just doing this because he knows ultimately many of the functions he's responsible for now will be in Shared Services?" asked Dennis.

"Well, if your job responsibilities were being reduced, wouldn't you do the same thing?"

"I'm not saying that I wouldn't, but I just get the feeling he's not convinced that Capp should be making this change," said Dennis. "He seems very competent to me and I'm sure he is a good manager, but I'm not convinced that he can lead a team through change, especially when there are going to be naysayers and doubters. Being a good leader during change requires you to embrace the changes and be able to convince everyone that the changes are going to be successful."

"You're saying he should blindly follow our vision?" Donna asked with a note of sarcasm.

"Of course not," Dennis snapped. "One should certainly challenge tactical decisions, but you can't challenge the overall idea of change. You can argue that the car should have two or four doors but you can't argue that we need to build a better car. I don't think he's sold on this concept, and at the first point of less-than-stellar success he might be inclined to say "I told you this wouldn't work." He seems like a nice enough guy and a good manager, but I feel I might have to spend too much time convincing him we're doing the right thing."

"And you won't have to do that with Jerry?"

"I don't think so. I mean, he researched other companies that have implemented Shared Services, gave specific examples, and seemed as if he has completely embraced the idea. I think if you asked him today to sell it to his division, or for that matter any division, he could do it. I'm not so sure that John Morton could. And that's important because our team needs to be as effective at selling Shared Services as they are at practicing accounting."

"Okay, so we're down to Jerry Schaefer and John Morton. "What else about these guys?"

"What do you mean?" asked Dennis.

"What are their current salaries, will they relocate, how soon can they leave their current positions? You know, those kinds of things."

"I don't think we should worry about that now. We have to agree on who the right candidate is based on qualifications, management style, and the like; then we can worry about getting them to accept the position," said Dennis.

"Well, you know I give you latitude to make decisions, especially when it comes to hiring people who are going to report directly to you, so if you're convinced Jerry is the right candidate, I will fully support you."

"Okay then, Jerry is the one. Let's move on to the HR manager. I rated Tammy Raines and Clarence Middlebrook both as 4s.

"I rated Clarence as 3.5 but I had Tammy as a 4.5. I rated Terri O'Neal as 2.5 so I don't think we need to discuss her," said Donna.

Dennis explained, "Both Tammy and Clarence are strong, but I rated them the same because I'm a bit biased toward Clarence since he is an internal candidate. I think they would both do a fantastic job recruiting employees and being an advocate for employees. I do know Clarence is well thought of in his division and at Corporate. Why did you rate Tammy higher than Clarence?"

"For one I like the fact that she's currently working in a Shared Services environment, so she knows what it takes to recruit employees to Shared Services. She also has very established contacts, and I think she'd be able to hit the ground running."

"Don't you think we'll get most of our candidates internally? Those contacts might not be as valuable as if we were going to rely heavily on outside recruiting."

"You might be right," Donna replied.

"Clarence has been with Capp a long time, and he has that down-home spin that everyone really relates to. I think he'll be a great advocate for us as we try to recruit internally, and he can also relay to anyone we hire externally his business and industry knowledge. I'm confident he'll do well."

"I do believe we should give opportunities to internal candidates when possible, so I can go along with Clarence," Donna agreed.

"Okay, three down and one to go."

"We rated Tanya McDonald and Susan Reid the same, but based on the internal versus external argument, we should probably go with Tanya, don't you think?" asked Donna.

"Yeah, in this case especially because Tanya understands the organization and the accounting structure, and that's going to be important when it comes to allocations. They both seemed to have the same type of styles and qualifications, so the only real differentiator is, as you said, internal versus external. Tanya it is.

"Well, that wasn't so hard," Dennis said as he looked at his watch. It was 2:30 pm, which meant they worked right through lunch and never noticed it.

"Time flies when you're having fun, but now I'm hungry," Donna said.

"Maybe we can have John make us some sandwiches." Dennis laughed.

Dennis went back to his office after stopping by the vending machines and buying a bag of pretzels and a diet soda. He realized that he'd better get used to eating these kinds of lunches because the next three years, getting the center up and running, were going to be busy.

# CHAPTER 5

# THE JOURNEY BEGINS

Eight weeks had passed since Dennis and Donna chose Sara Mitchell, Jerry Schaefer, Clarence Middlebrook, and Tanya McDonald as the Shared Services managers. Since then Sara, Jerry, and Clarence had been given the same task of posting and filling the positions needed to support the initial implementation of the El Paso division and to help establish policies, procedures, and processes for the center. Since Tanya was a one-person department, she did not need to hire anyone at this time. Dennis insisted they utilize the same process he and Donna had used to interview and select candidates. He gave authority to make the hiring decisions to each manager, just as Donna had given to him. These positions were filled:

- Payroll team lead (1)
- Payroll team member (2)
- Benefits team lead (1)
- Benefits team member (1)
- General Ledger team lead (1)
- General Ledger team member (1)
- Accounts Payable team lead (1)
- Accounts Payable team member (2)
- Accounts Receivable team lead (1)
- Accounts Receivable team member (1)
- Document Management team lead (1)
- Document Management team member (2)

Tomorrow was Monday, and the last team member was scheduled to start then. Clarence was going to take her through orientation, and then the entire team was going to meet for the next two and a half days to establish a mission statement, values, and vision, and form teams that would help develop governance and policies and procedures. Dennis was looking forward to the meeting because it was his chance to set forth his vision and to start laying the foundation for what he hoped would be a successful journey, a journey that would be personally very rewarding and one that would add significant value to Capp, Inc.

"Daddy, what are you doing?" Samantha asked, watching Dennis write on a notepad.

"I'm getting ready for work tomorrow, Sammie."

"Well, why do you have to get ready for work now? You should only have to work when you're at work, not when you're home."

"Sometimes there just isn't enough time in the day to get everything done when I'm at work. Besides, isn't it about your bedtime?"

"You're right, Daddy. Sometimes there just isn't enough time in the day. We didn't get to play hardly at all today. I like it when my shoes are dirty because that means I was outside having a lot of fun. Today they're not very dirty."

"Well, I'll tell you what: I'll make sure we get to play next Sunday. That's a promise. Now, why don't you get ready for bed?"

"Okay. Mommy will get me ready for bed now."

"Goodnight, sweetheart. See you in the morning."

It was 11:30 am Monday morning, and Dennis had been at the office since 6:30. He wanted to make sure he had everything covered for the meeting. Rosa had made sure there were plenty of flip charts, markers, and pads for everyone in the conference room. She also got some snacks and ordered lunch from the local deli.

"Rosa, is everything ready for the meeting?" asked Dennis.

"Yep, I have all of the supplies, snacks, and sodas we'll need. Even if you bore everyone to tears, they'll have enough sugar and caffeine to keep them awake for days," she joked.

"Okay then, but I promise they'll not be bored because I'm not going to do most of the talking, they are. This is going to be an interactive meeting, and everyone is going to participate."

Dennis and Rosa walked to the conference room together. Dennis was thinking about his opening words, and Rosa was unusually silent. Maybe she just didn't want to disturb his thoughts. He appreciated that.

By noon, everyone was there except Sara. "Don't be shy," said Dennis. "Grab a sandwich and some chips. We're going to spend the first half hour eating and going over the agenda. We have a lot to cover in the next two and a half days, and I want you to know what to expect."

Everyone got something to eat, then sat down and began to eat. Most started to talk among themselves. Finally around 12:15 Sara walked in.

"Sorry I'm late," Sara said as she got herself a sandwich and chips.

Dennis let the group continue to talk for a few more minutes before getting started.

"Okay, let's get started. I hope everyone enjoyed their sandwiches. Before we get to the agenda for the next two days, I want to tell you a story. When I was a kid, my parents both worked in blue-collar jobs. My mother pressed clothes at a dry cleaner and my dad worked in a warehouse. They both got paid hourly and got very little vacation time or sick days. Essentially if they did not show up for work, they did not get paid. Therefore, neither of them was ever late for work. If my mom thought it was going to rain or snow in the morning, she would make everyone get up a little bit earlier because she knew it was going to take longer to either get ready or actually get to work or school. In all my days of going to school, I was never late because my mom was not going to let us make her late for work, nor was my dad. They taught me that being late was not a circumstance; it was a choice. I just wanted to share that with everyone."

Dennis was sure that Sara felt the entire room looking at her. He hated to start like that, but he would not tolerate anyone being late to such an important meeting, a meeting that was going to set the foundation and culture for the next three years.

Everyone was paying attention as he continued. "The next two days are going to establish our culture, our mission, our vision, and set the foundation for our success. I've never been more confident that I am surrounded by the right group of people: a group of people who will work together, challenge each other, and ultimately decide on a course of action that will result in a stronger, quicker, and more competitive company. Each of you has chosen to be a part of something that not everyone in this company believes in. And the people who do not believe in our strategy will challenge, oppose, argue, and I'm sure in some cases make you mad as hell. That is all going to be a part of our story, a story that we will write over the next three years. There is one thing I can assure you of, though, and that is that we have the absolute support of the one person who really matters, John Phelps, our CEO. The most effective Shared Services organizations all have the support of executive management, and in our case I can unequivocally say that John has always supported me and given me the latitude to do my job. That's not to say that he hasn't challenged me and debated some of my decisions, but that is what he is supposed to do."

"You're darn right that's what I'm supposed to do," said John.

Most people hadn't noticed that John had come in as Dennis started to speak. Everyone turned around and looked at John. Those people who were hired externally had never met him; even some of those from the division had never met him.

"How is everyone doing?" John asked. "Hey, Clarence, nice to see you again. Sara, how are you?

"Dennis asked me to drop by, and I thought this meeting would be a great opportunity to meet everyone," John explained.

He went around the room, shaking hands and introducing himself. It was evident to Dennis by the look on everyone's face that they were glad to meet him. It meant a lot that he had taken the time to show his support for Shared Services.

After he'd met everyone, John said: "I don't want to hold up your meeting, but I want to reiterate what Dennis was saying. We've chosen to create a Shared Services division that will ultimately service all of our divisions. We're committed to implementing this strategy along with SAP over the next three years. While that may seem like a long time, I'm confident it will go quicker than you can anticipate today. I'm looking forward to the results that you will deliver and want you to know that you have my full support and the support of my executive team. Dennis is right when he says you will have doubters, but in the end everyone will embrace the change and we will be, as Dennis put it, a stronger, quicker, more competitive company. So I wanted to personally come here and thank you for choosing to be part of this team, and I want to thank you in advance for the effort I know you will put forth. Good luck and have fun. Thanks."

The team gave John a quick round of applause.

"Thanks, John, for coming over to speak with us," Dennis said.

After John left, it was time to get down to business. Dennis could feel the increased energy in the room after John's speech.

"Okay, I want to cover the agenda for the next two and a half days. We have a lot to accomplish, but the agenda does have some flexibility in it if we need to spend some extra time on a particular area."

Rosa passed out the agenda.

"As you can see, we'll spend this afternoon creating a mission statement and values. Then we'll sleep on it and come back tomorrow morning and see if it needs to be tweaked, or we might decide we don't like it at all and need to redo it. You never can tell what thoughts a good night's sleep will bring. After we've completed the mission statement and values, we'll cover governance, which in this case means internal Shared Services governance. In other words, how we govern ourselves. We'll cover items such as conflict resolution—not that we'll ever have any conflicts," Dennis said with a chuckle.

The team's laughter seemed a bit nervous to Dennis.

"Don't worry. I'm sure we'll get used to having conflicts with each other. Remember, many times it's very healthy to disagree. That's how you develop and think of the best ideas. If we all have the same thoughts and ideas, then we really don't need more than one leader. We would just need one leader and a bunch of followers. And I don't believe anyone in here is just a follower, or else you wouldn't be here. You are leading simply by being on a team that's going to change the way Capp does business. You could have easily sat back and waited for the changes to happen; instead you chose to influence, shape, and determine the change. That makes each of you a leader."

Dennis continued, "Under governance, I didn't list the items that I think we should address because we need to determine that as a group. And finally, we'll talk about our interaction with the SAP team and the divisions we are supporting. Does anyone have any questions?

"Okay, since there are no questions, we'll get started. Oh, one more thing: We'll take breaks every 90 minutes to make sure we stay fresh. If I was going to simply stand up here and talk, we'd take a break every 30 minutes so you don't fall asleep." Dennis laughed.

"Now we're going to go around the room, and I want you to introduce yourselves. I also want you to state why you think we are here, meaning what is the goal of the Shared Services center.

"Rosa has graciously volunteered to be our scribe, which is important, because if I was the scribe, we would all have trouble reading my writing, so thank you, Rosa."

"Let's start with Debbie."

"My name is Debbie and I am a Payroll processor. I believe we're here for just the reasons you and Mr. Phelps said, to make Capp a stronger, quicker, and more competitive company."

Rosa was busy writing down her response on a flip chart. She did not write a name next to the statement. Dennis did not want any ideas or statements to be attributed to any one person, but rather to the team.

"I'm Anna, and I am the Payroll team lead and I agree with Debbie, but I'm sure you want to hear something else other than to make Capp a stronger, quicker, and more competitive company."

"You're right, let's come up with as many as we can, but Debbie was right in mentioning that because we definitely need to capture it," replied Dennis. "So what else?"

"To help the divisions. To allow them to concentrate on things that are more related to their markets, like sales and inventory," said Anna.

"Okay," said Dennis. "Pam?"

"Hi, I'm Pam, and I work with Debbie and Anna in Payroll. We are here to do things more efficiently and better than they're being done today."

"Good. Stephanie?"

"We are here to provide service to our vendors, suppliers, employees, and benefits providers."

"Good, but you forgot to say your name and department." Dennis smiled.

"You said my name but I'll say it again. I'm Stephanie, and I am the Benefits team lead."

"Sara?" asked Dennis.

"I'm Sara, as everyone knows, and I'd prefer to hear what all the team members say before giving my opinion as to why we are here." Sara's tone was sharp.

"Okay, we'll save you for last," said Dennis.

"Hi, I'm Aiko, and I work with Stephanie on the Benefits team. I think we are here to reduce costs, right?"

"We certainly are," replied Dennis.

"Isn't that the same as making us a stronger, quicker, and more competitive company?" asked Drew, the Accounts Payable team lead.

"Well, it's a part of that, but at a more granular level. But it is definitely worth capturing. Let's get down everyone's thoughts and then we can discuss all of the responses," Dennis explained.

Steve, the General Ledger team lead, looked around and pointed at himself. "Am I next?"

"Sure."

"We're here to provide consistency. You know, to make sure that each division accounts for their revenues and expenses in the same way so that the executives can better compare divisions and business units. Oh yeah, and I'm Steve, the General Ledger supervisor."

"I'm Dave, and I work on the General Ledger team. I think we're here to automate and use technology."

Dennis was happy to see the quick momentum the team was gaining. Obviously everyone was thinking about what they were going to say and trying to participate.

"Nelly?"

"I'm Nelly, and I am the Accounts Payable team lead. I know I'm here to learn, and I think we'll all learn a great deal over the next few years."

"Interesting," said Dennis. "I know I said we would not discuss these and just capture them, but tell me who you think you'll learn from."

"Everyone. We all have different backgrounds, and so do the people in the divisions and the SAP consultants, so we will all learn from each other."

"Like I said, interesting; that is a very good point."

"I'm Kim, and I work with Nelly and Donna on the Accounts Payable team. First I can say that I've already learned a few things from both Nelly and Donna, so Nelly is correct. Well, if she said we are here to learn, then that means someone has to teach, so I'll say we are here to teach."

"Okay," said Dennis.

"I'm Jerry, and I am the Financial Services manager. I think we're here to make each division our partner and to make them individually stronger but also to help them work a bit more together, which will make them stronger as a whole, not just individually."

Rosa looked as if she was not quite sure how to summarize Jerry's words.

"How about partner with our divisions to make them stronger individually and as a whole," said Dennis. "Does that capture it, Jerry?"

"Perfectly."

"Hi, I'm Donna, and like Nelly and Kim I work on the Accounts Payable team. How about we are here to earn a paycheck? That's important, right?"

"I think we can all agree that getting paid is pretty important to each of us. Thanks for being very honest," replied Dennis.

"All of you know me, I'm Clarence, the Human Resources manager, and I think we are here to help our teams grow and for each individual to advance in their career. In other words, to develop our employees so they can be successful and in turn they can help Capp remain successful."

"Hello, I'm Tanya, the Accounting manager, and I think we're here to help make sure Capp follows accounting principles, complies with Sarbanes-Oxley, and accurately represents our financial status to our stakeholders."

"I'm Drew, and I am the Accounts Receivable team lead. One reason we are here is to increase the quality of the work currently being done in our areas."

"My name is Amy and I am an Accounts Receivable team member. We're here to come up with new ways of doing things."

"You mean like new ideas?" asked Dennis.

"Yeah, come up with new ideas."

"Dolores is my name, and I am the Document Management team lead. I think we're here to help each other. If work needs to get done, we can all chip in and help each other out."

Rosa was on her third page of the flip chart. She was sticking the finished pages to the wall so everyone could review them.

"I'm Jessica, and I work on the Document Management team and everyone took my answers."

"I'm sure you can come up with another one," said Dolores.

"How about to work, we are here to do our jobs?" replied Jessica.

"That's true," said Dennis. "We are definitely here to do that."

"I agree with Jessica, but we're also here to have fun. We'll spend enough time here that we need to make sure we enjoy ourselves, within reason of course. And by the way, I'm Greg from Document Management."

"Good. So we went around the room and everyone gave us their thoughts on what we are here for. Is there anything else anyone wants to add to that list?" asked Dennis.

"I think that about covers it," said Drew.

"Okay, let's take a 15-minute break. When we come back we'll divide up into teams to start working on the mission statement," Dennis said.

No one seemed to have noticed that Sara did not get to mention her goal for Shared Services. Everyone got up and left—everyone except Sara.

# CHAPTER 6

# THE JOURNEY CONTINUES

Sara walked up to Dennis after everyone had left, and the look on her face told him she was not happy. He was pretty sure he knew why.

"Dennis, I do not appreciate you chastising me in front of the team like you did," she said, looking him straight in the eye.

"We should probably talk about this in my office, just in case someone walks back in the room."

"Okay."

They both walked back to Dennis's office, neither saying a word.

Dennis walked into his office but did not sit down. Sara closed the door behind her.

Dennis started. "I understand you probably did not appreciate what I said, but you have to see it from my point of view. This is the first meeting we have with the entire team, and you did not send a good message by being late. It's disrespectful to make everyone wait for one person who is not on time."

"You don't even know why I was late," Sara exclaimed.

"To be very honest, in this case it doesn't matter. The team needs to understand that being prompt and respecting each other's time is very important. I also want you to know that I don't feel that I chastised you. I simply told a story about my parents and their beliefs. If anyone else had been late, the story would have been the same. As a matter of fact, that's the same story I use every time someone is late for the first time.

Except in extreme cases, I do believe that being on time is simply a matter of choice. If you are determining what time to leave for work, you should not use the best-case scenario as your benchmark. You should use somewhere between the worst-case scenario and the most likely scenario. That will ensure that you're on time more than 95 percent of the time. I think we've talked about this enough, I simply expect everyone to be on time to meetings, especially ones that are so high profile," Dennis concluded.

"Well, let me ask you this: Why didn't you come back to me regarding why we are here in Shared Services? Is it because I was late?"

"Not at all; to be honest, I simply forgot. We were going around the room, and I forgot that you asked to wait until the end. When you said that, I wasn't sure if you were mad about the story I told or you just wanted to wait. Therefore, I chose not to question it any further. I apologize for forgetting to come back to you."

"Okay, to be honest, I was upset and didn't feel like talking at that point," Sara explained.

"Well, the best thing to do for the team is to show everyone that it did not bother you and to simply put it behind us. Agreed?"

"Agreed," said Sara.

Dennis and Sara walked back into the conference room. They still had a few minutes before the break was over. Sara sat down and Dennis went back to the front of the room. The rest of the team came back in together and sat down. Everyone was back from break on time.

"Okay, now what I would like us to do is break up into groups of four and use the reasons we've listed to start developing the framework for a mission statement," said Dennis.

"Dennis, before we do that, I'd like to add that I think Nelly was the one who said we are here to learn from each other, and I also think we're here to complement each other," Sara said. "We each bring unique strengths to the team, and if we utilize everyone's strengths as well as teach them to overcome their weaknesses, we'll be better as a team and Capp will be a better company. Also, I'd like to apologize to everyone for being late this morning."

"Thanks, Sara, we appreciate that. Okay, we have a good list of reasons why we are here. Now we need to start thinking about our mission statement. Can anyone tell me why we need a mission statement?" Dennis asked.

Sara looked around the room and said, "Well, when you and Donna interviewed me, you asked me what I thought it took to get a group of people to work well together. My answer was a common goal. In order to get everyone working together, they need a common goal, and in my mind that's why we need a mission statement."

"Anyone else?" asked Dennis.

"Sounds good to me," said Anna.

"Yeah, makes sense," said Drew.

"Exactly right," said Dennis. "We need a common goal, and that is what the mission statement will provide. So let's count off 1, 2, 3, and 4. The ones go in that corner, the twos over there, the threes over there, and fours up here. I will count last, which will make me a 4 since there are 20 of us. Hey, my math is still pretty good. Rosa has posted all of the reasons we came up with on the walls, so use those to start formulating your mission." (See Exhibit 6.1.) "Let's take the next hour to do this. Then we'll take another break and present what we came up with. Okay?"

Because most everyone sat next to their teammates at the meeting, counting off would ensure that they would have to work with someone not on their team for this exercise. Dennis wanted the group to get used to working with each other regardless of which team they were on.

"Dennis, usually how long is a mission statement?" asked Steve.

"There are no really hard-and-fast rules, but generally they're between three and five sentences. Right now, though, I want you to use your creativity and imagination more than sticking to a formula."

"You're asking a bunch of accounting people to be creative?" said Stephanie. "I don't think the Sarbanes-Oxley people are going to like that."

"Luckily we're private and don't have SOX people," Steve said, laughing.

EXHIBIT **6.1** *Brainstorming Notes*

*Reasons Listed by Team for Shared Services*

- To make Capp a stronger, quicker, and more competitive company
- To help the divisions. To allow them to concentrate on things that are more related to their markets, like sales and inventory
- We are here to do things more efficiently and better than they are being done today.
- We are here to provide service to our vendors, suppliers, employees, and benefits providers.
- To reduce costs
- To provide consistency. To make sure that each division accounts for revenues and expenses in the same way so that the executives can better compare divisions and business units
- To automate and use technology
- To learn
- To teach
- To partner with our divisions to make them stronger individually and as a whole
- To earn a paycheck
- To help our teams grow and for each individual to advance in their career. To develop our employees so they can be successful and they can help Capp remain successful
- To help make sure Capp follows accounting principles, complies with Sarbanes-Oxley, and accurately represents our financial status to our stakeholders
- To increase the quality of the work currently being done in our areas
- To come up with new ways of doing things
- To help each other. If work needs to get done, we can all chip in and help each other out.
- To work. We are here to do our jobs.
- Have fun
- To complement each other's strengths

For the next hour, each team worked on its mission statement. There was a lot of energy in the room, and everyone seemed to be participating in and enjoying the process.

"Okay, the hour is up," Dennis said, "so let's take a break, but before you do, choose someone from your team to present your initial thoughts or if you developed a complete mission statement present that to us. Take 15 minutes, and I'll see you back here."

When the group returned, everyone seemed eager to see what the others came up with.

"Do we have a team that wants to volunteer to present first?" asked Dennis.

"Team two will go first," said Debbie.

"Okay, and are you the presenter?"

"No, we volunteered Steve to do that."

"Ordered is more like it," Steve said, laughing. "To be honest, we struggled a bit in the beginning because we tried to formulate a mission statement using the statements that were given, but it was coming out too long-winded and without much structure. So we decided to look for common themes among the statements, and we came up with these themes."

Steve flipped to an already completed page on the flip chart. It listed these words:

- Win
- Core competencies
- Innovation
- Customer service
- Cost effective
- Streamline
- Innovation
- Learn
- Teach
- Collaboration
- Provide stability to employees

- Grow and develop employees
- Honesty and integrity
- Quality
- Innovation
- Teamwork
- Work ethic and effort
- Enjoyment and celebration
- Complement and collaborate

The team had taken each statement and written these words next to each statement. (See Exhibit 6.2.)

"We weren't able to come up with a mission statement in the time allotted, but we felt we were able to create the blocks that will build the foundation—the words being those blocks," Steve continued.

"Very interesting. Did any other teams follow that approach or have the same struggles coming up with a mission statement?" asked Dennis.

"Yeah, we struggled as well," said Aiko, "but we didn't try to identify the common themes like they did, but we probably should have. That was an interesting approach."

"We struggled too," said Dave. "I don't think anyone in here has ever done this before so it's new to us; maybe if we had some examples."

"That would certainly help," added Amy. "You were on our team, and we didn't come up with much either," she said to Dennis.

"Right now we shouldn't worry so much about the end product, what is most important is the process. I don't want to provide examples because then the tendency is to take what has already been done and simply use that."

"But isn't that what learning is about: taking what someone else has done and using it for your processes or making it work for you?" asked Drew.

"In some cases, yes; but we need to make this mission statement our own. We need to create this together because that's what will provide us with the common goal that Sara mentioned earlier. In all honesty, this is part of a bonding process. I could piece something together or steal one

EXHIBIT **6.2** *Brainstorming Notes with Categorization*

*Reasons Listed by Team for Shared Services*

- To make Capp a stronger, quicker, and more competitive company **(win)**
- To help the divisions. To allow them to concentrate on things that are more related to their markets, like sales and inventory **(core competencies)**
- We are here to do things more efficiently and better than they are being done today. **(innovation)**
- We are here to provide service to our vendors, suppliers, employees, and benefits providers. **(customer service)**
- To reduce costs **(cost effective)**
- To provide consistency. To make sure that each division accounts for revenues and expenses in the same way so that the executives can better compare divisions and business units **(streamline)**
- To automate and use technology **(innovation)**
- To learn **(learn)**
- To teach **(teach)**
- To partner with our divisions to make them stronger individually and as a whole **(collaboration)**
- To earn a paycheck **(provide stability to our employees)**
- To help our teams grow and for each individual to advance in their career. To develop our employees so they can be successful and they can help Capp remain successful **(grow and develop employees)**
- To help make sure Capp follows accounting principles, complies with Sarbanes-Oxley, and accurately represents our financial status to our stakeholders **(honesty and integrity)**
- To increase the quality of the work currently being done in our areas **(quality)**
- To come up with new ways of doing things **(innovation)**
- To help each other. If work needs to get done, we can all chip in and help each other out. **(teamwork)**
- To work. We are here to do our jobs. **(work ethic, effort)**
- To have fun **(enjoyment, celebration)**
- To complement each other's strengths **(complement and collaborate)**

from other companies or provide examples that we could alter a bit, but that would defeat the purpose. Let me ask you this. Do you think that what Steve and his team did was a good idea?"

"Yeah, yes, it was good" were the responses Dennis heard.

"Okay then, that means we've learned from each other, which is one of the themes. We have also taught, complemented, engaged in teamwork, communicated, collaborated, and in my mind we have won. Sure, we don't have a mission statement, but we all struggled with the same issue, and as a team we've decided on a path to overcome that struggle. I'm excited as hell about what we accomplished in the last hour," Dennis exclaimed. "Does everyone agree?"

"I certainly do, now that you put it that way," said Clarence.

"Does everyone else feel the same way?" Dennis asked again, this time a bit more forcefully, pumping his fist.

"Yeah!" they all shouted.

"Okay, let's take the work that Steve and his team did and use those themes to create six sentences for each team. They don't have to touch on every theme, but try to be as creative and comprehensive as possible. We'll then share those sentences and as a group we'll work on developing a mission statement. Let's stay in the same teams and take another hour to do this."

For the next hour the teams enthusiastically worked on the mission statement. No one noticed that they did not start until 4:30 pm, which meant they would not get done with the exercise until 5:30.

"Okay, everyone, the hour is up, but in case you hadn't noticed, the time is now 5:30 pm," Dennis alerted the group.

"Oh no, I've got to go. I didn't realize it was past 5:00 pm," said Pam. "I'm sorry."

"That's okay," said Dennis. "The meeting was only supposed to last until 5:00, and we got a little behind. We'll take up where we left off tomorrow at 8:30 am. Don't worry that we're a little behind. This is very important and we're making great progress. I look forward to seeing what you've come up with tomorrow. Just leave your pads and supplies in here. I'm going to lock the room tonight."

# CHAPTER 7

# MISSION ACCOMPLISHED

Dennis went home around 6:00, which was a little earlier than usual. He felt good about what the team had accomplished during the day, so he decided to treat himself to an early night. When he rounded the corner of his block, he didn't see any of the kids playing, but then he noticed it was raining. He was thinking so much about the day's meeting that he had not even noticed that it was raining. His windshield wipers were on, but he didn't remember turning them on. He had decided not to call Jennifer and tell her he would be early. He was hoping to surprise her. Unfortunately, no one was home when he got there.

He called Jennifer on her mobile phone.

"Honey, I got home early and was hoping to eat dinner with you and the kids."

"I'm sorry, Dennis, you should have called. I just assumed you would be home the regular time. I took the kids to my mom's for dinner. You can come over if you like. We just got started."

"That's okay, I'm pretty tired. I'll just heat up some leftovers or something."

"Do you want me to bring you what Mom made? Its pork chops, mashed potatoes, and peas."

"No, don't bother; I'm not actually that hungry. We had some snacks at the meeting this afternoon. I think I see a piece of meatloaf in the refrigerator though. Hey, that sounds good, I'll make a meatloaf sandwich," he said.

"Okay, well, call me if you change your mind and want me to bring a doggie bag."

Dennis got the meatloaf from the refrigerator and made himself a sandwich. That sandwich and some chips really hit the spot. He never liked his mother-in-law's pork chops. She always overcooked them, and he didn't have the heart to tell her.

By the time everyone returned home, Dennis had fallen asleep in the recliner. Samantha woke him up by jumping in his lap.

"Hi, Daddy," she said. "How come you didn't come with us to Grandma's?"

"I'm sorry, honey, I forgot to call your mom and let her know I was coming home early."

"Well, you should have remembered because it would have been a lot more fun with you there."

If Samantha was trying to make him feel guilty, it was working. Dennis got up and helped get the kids ready for bed. At least he had time to read Samantha a story before she went to sleep.

As he drove to work the next morning, Dennis still felt guilty about not telling Jennifer he would be home earlier than usual. If nothing else, he could have driven to her mother's house, although that would have meant eating a dry pork chop. But he knew it would have been worth it to eat with his family.

Dennis went to the meeting room around 8:15 am and was surprised to see half of the team already there, working on the mission statement exercise. He looked forward to seeing what they came up with. By 8:25 everyone was ready to go.

"Well, since everyone is here, we might as well get started a few minutes early, which is a good thing because I have another quick story to tell you," Dennis started.

Sara gave him a look that said to him "This better not be about me."

"Last night I was so happy with the progress we made I decided to leave a bit earlier than usual and surprise my family. To my surprise, when I got home, no one was there. My wife had taken the kids to her mother's house for dinner. Her mother lives about 30 minutes away, and I didn't feel like getting back into the car and fighting traffic, so I stayed home. I wound up eating a meatloaf sandwich and chips, which was actually very good because my wife makes a mean meatloaf. However, I would have rather eaten my mother-in-law's overcooked pork chop with my family than a good meatloaf sandwich by myself. So why am I telling you this story? Well, if I had just communicated that I was going to be early, I could have eaten dinner with my family. Although my intentions to surprise them were good, communicating would have been better for everyone. So don't let me get away with not communicating. If you want to know something, just ask me. If I can answer the question, I will, and if it is something I can't share at that time, I'll tell you that as well. Either way I will communicate something. And by the way, if you see my wife, don't tell her that story. She loves her mom's pork chops," Dennis finished with a grin.

"Maybe you should communicate that she overcooks the pork chops," Nelly pointed out.

"I'll have to think about that."

For the next hour the teams presented the sentences they developed the day before, and then, as a group, they developed the mission statement.

"So do we think we have a winner?" Dennis asked.

"I like it," said Anna.

"Yeah, so do I," added Aiko.

"I think a mission statement is somewhat like art in that it is never going to be perfect to everyone but it makes its point," said Stephanie.

"So let's take a quick vote. How many people like this mission statement?" asked Clarence.

Thirteen people raised their hands.

"For those of you who do not have your hand up, why don't you like it?" Clarence followed up.

"It just isn't hitting me right," said Drew. "I'm not really sure why."

"What about you, Greg? What do you think?"

"It seems a bit long to me, but I'm with Drew. I can't really put my finger on why I don't like it."

Dennis let the conversation go on for a few more minutes. Everyone who did not raise their hand seemed to have the same opinion. "How about if we do this," he said. "Let's post it on the wall and take a vote at the end of the day. Maybe it will grow on those who are a bit unsure, and hopefully it won't tarnish for those who like it. Sound good?"

Everyone agreed, so Dennis had Rosa rewrite two copies of the mission statement very legibly and put it on each side of the room.

The mission statement read:

> Through effort, teamwork, innovation, honesty, and integrity, we will strive to provide superior customer service to our divisions so that they may provide superior service to their customers. We will create an environment that will allow our employees to grow, collaborate, and take appropriate risks. We will celebrate our victories and learn from our mistakes. We will add significant value and continuously contribute to the outstanding reputation of Capp, Incorporated.

It was already 10:30 am and the team had not even started to look at value statements, the day's topic. Dennis was a bit worried about the pace of progress, but he was very satisfied with the teamwork and collaboration.

"The next item on the agenda is to discuss and develop value statements. Does anyone care to take a stab at why we should develop them?" he asked.

"To be honest," said Anna, "I'm a bit confused about the difference between a mission statement and value statements."

"I'm a little bit confused as well," Jessica added.

"Okay, that's fine. Does anyone want to take a guess at the difference or, if you know, can you tell us? Don't be embarrassed because many people get confused with this," said Dennis.

He was a little disappointed that no one wanted to venture a guess, but that was okay. In his mind, they were doing very well for a group that had been together such a short time. Also, no one in the group had been through something like this before. The divisions at Capp did not go through these types of exercises or use these types of meetings to try to establish buy-in.

"As we stated yesterday and earlier this morning, a mission statement is really just what it says it is, a mission; it's much like trying to win a game or a contest. For example, if you were playing a football game, your mission is most likely to win the game, which means scoring more points than your opponent. That is the mission. I think everyone understands that. Now, think of the values as the rules. My ultimate mission is to win the game, but I won't try to accomplish that mission by cheating. In some way, values can be seen as those things you will not compromise in order to complete the mission; or better yet, they are those things you will actively do as part of the mission. For example, in a football game, one of your values might be that you will always put forth maximum effort. Or something that you will not do is intentionally try to injure an opponent. Those are examples of values as it would relate to football. In our mission statement, we have addressed some of those by mentioning honesty and integrity, but values are a little more specific. I don't want to really get into religion, but the Ten Commandments are in many ways examples of values. Does everyone see the difference?"

Tanya said, "It does make more sense to me now. They're really statements of character and value, much like the Golden Rule."

"I understand it better as well," said Nelly.

"Okay then, get back to your teams and try to come up with at least 5 but no more than 10 value statements. Then we'll post them and go through somewhat the same exercise we did with the mission statement. In the interest of time, let's try to do this in 30 minutes if we can. Is that okay with everyone?"

They had already gotten into their groups and started to work, so Dennis assumed it was okay. Although he was on team four, he tried not to have too much influence over the team. Sara, who was also on that team, seemed to be doing a good job of keeping the team focused and understanding the objectives. For the next 30 minutes there was not much discussion. It seemed as if the teams decided to let each person write their own values. At the end of the allotted time, Dennis had Rosa write down all of the values. As she was writing, Dennis gave the rest of the team a 15-minute break. He could sense people were getting a bit antsy and perhaps trying to rush a bit through the process.

When they came back from break, Dennis assured everyone that they were making good progress and not to worry too much about adhering exactly to the agenda.

"We are about halfway through our two-and-a-half-day meeting and although we're behind in the agenda, I'm very pleased with the progress we're making. Remember what I said yesterday about this being less about the exact output and more about the process. The work we're doing today will lay the foundation for years to come, so there is no need to rush the process. We'd be doing ourselves a disservice if we did that. If we don't get to some of the governance items, we can always work on them after this meeting," Dennis explained.

Working the rest of the morning, the group was able to come up with five core values. There was a great deal of consensus that the values should be very simple. The five core values the team created were:

1. Appreciate our customers.
2. Respect your coworkers.
3. Challenge yourself and your team.
4. Communicate, communicate, communicate.
5. Embrace diversity.

"Okay, so now we have developed our mission and our values," Dennis said. "As I mentioned earlier this morning, we'll let the mission statement breathe a little bit, kind of like a glass of wine, and then take a quick vote this afternoon. For that vote, we'll let the majority rule. If we don't agree that is the mission statement, we'll go back to the drawing board, but otherwise that will be our mission statement. Agreed?"

"Sure," everyone said.

The team seemed to be ready for an extended break, so Dennis was happy it was lunchtime.

"Quickly I want to thank Rosa for ordering lunch again. I'm sure she got us something good."

Once everyone had their lunch, Dennis made sure they spent the time relaxing, not talking about work.

After lunch the group started to work on governance items, such as conflict resolution, budgeting process, authorization of time off, selection process, and coverage of hours of operation. At the end of the day, the group voted to keep both the mission statement and values. Sixteen people voted that the mission statement was complete, and 14 voted that the values were properly reflected in those 5 simple statements. Also the group felt that the selection process used to hire everyone in the room had worked, so they left the process that Dennis and Donna developed in place.

Wednesday morning was spent discussing the interaction with the SAP team that was working in El Paso and the training that was going to take place for the end users at the division. After the first break, Sara asked:

"Before we continue can I bring up another subject?"

"Sure," replied Dennis.

"I'm getting pretty concerned about our new offices. They were supposed to be ready on September 1 and here we are on September 17 and they're still not ready. I'm not sure how we're going to be able to operate once El Paso goes live if we're still in the current space.

"Also," she continued, "I know everyone is starting to get a bit on each other's nerves, which I totally understand. We're working in a space that was meant for 10 people and we have 19. I'm sure you want to be able to sit with us. So I guess my question is, are we going to be moved by October 6?"

"I'm glad you brought that up," Dennis replied. "I spoke to Tony Robertson early last week, and he assured me the building would be ready Monday, September 19. By ready, I mean that over the weekend of the 17th, the IT team will move our computers and the movers will take any files and other items we have to move. Because everyone is still pretty much working out of boxes, the move should be fairly easy. So the answer is yes, we will be moved by October 6, and we should have plenty of time to get set up for business."

"Can we go over to the new building and see where we're going to sit?" asked Aiko.

"You know what, let me go call Tony and see if we can get access to the building this afternoon," Dennis answered.

CHAPTER 8

# LOCATION, LOCATION, LOCATION

Dennis went back to his office and called Tony. As usual, he got his voicemail, so he called him on his cell.

"This is Tony."

"Hey Tony, it's Dennis, how are you?"

"Okay. What can I do for you?" he replied.

"My team would like to go over to the new building this afternoon and take a look around. Would that be possible?"

"How many people are we talking about, because the security in that building can be a real pain. Besides, we don't have the certificate of occupancy yet, so they really should not be in there," replied Tony.

"I understand that, but I've got 19 people sitting in enough space for 10, and we also have El Paso going live in less than 20 days, so everyone is getting a bit antsy. I want them to be confident that we are going to be moved and that we'll be ready for El Paso."

"Look, maybe you can take a few people over there, but the whole team is way too many."

"Tony, I need everyone to go over there. We are a team, and they've only been working together for a few weeks, so I don't want to include some and not others. Just do me this favor and I'll owe you one."

"Let me see what I can do, but you will owe me," replied Tony.

"Okay, thanks. Call me back on my cell when you find out. I'd like to take them over after lunch. In fact, I'll use that conference room that has all of the chairs and hold the rest of the meeting in there," Dennis said.

"Now you're pushing it."

"I know, I know, but I'll pay you back." Dennis hung up, thinking that when most people tell you that you owe them one they're just kidding, but in Tony's case he was sure he meant it.

Dennis went back to the meeting. Sara and Jerry were standing at the front of the room going over the plan to train the end users in El Paso.

"So what's the verdict?" Jerry asked when he saw Dennis.

"I spoke to Tony and he said the new space will be ready the weekend of the 17th and that the move will take place that weekend, so we will be in our new home on Monday the 19th," Dennis said. "He's also going to see if we can get access to the building after lunch. If we can, we'll hold the rest of our meeting over there. Does that sound good?"

Everyone nodded in approval. Jerry and Sara went back to leading the discussion about training and the upcoming go-live. Dennis was excited at the energy in the room and also enjoyed the fact that Jerry and Sara were taking charge of the meeting. For the next hour he just sat back and observed.

Dennis's cell phone rang, but no one noticed because he always had it on vibrate. He hated ring tones, especially the goofy ones. As a matter of fact, he was contemplating making it policy that all cell phones must be on vibrate. No one had brought that up during the governance portion of the meeting, even though phones rang several times. No one answered the calls, but nonetheless in his mind it was still a disruption.

"This is Dennis," he said as he walked out of the room.

"Dennis, Tony. I was able to get you access and even made sure the conference room was cleaned up. There isn't a table in the room but there are plenty of chairs. If you remember, the large wall is a whiteboard, but you'll need to bring markers. Do you need anything else?"

"No, that should do it. I really appreciate it.

"Good news, everyone," Dennis said as he walked back into the meeting. "Tony got us access to the building this afternoon, so after lunch we'll take a trip over there. Bring your folders and pens because rather than come back here to wrap up, we're going to finish our meeting over there."

"Very cool," said Sara.

"Can we go now?" asked Anna.

"Since we're going to finish our day over there, we should probably all drive so we can leave straight from there," said Drew.

"I can't wait," added Nelly.

"Well, unfortunately, we're going to have to wait a few more hours, but time will fly because I know you're having fun," said Dennis.

Everyone ate their lunch quickly, and it was obvious they were eager to see the new building. They were probably also excited just to get out of the building. It was a beautiful 82-degree summer day and there was not a cloud in the sky other than an occasional puffy cloud. Dennis would be happy if everyone made it to the new building rather than take a detour to the park. Everyone drove in separate cars because they obviously wanted to go home straight from the new office. The office was only 20 minutes from corporate headquarters. Dennis left early to make sure all of the arrangements had been taken care of and they wouldn't have trouble getting access to the building.

The new building was a multitenant six-story building. The Shared Services center was going to be located on the entire third floor. The floor was designed to hold 125 people mostly in cubicles, but there were offices for all of the managers and for Dennis. While 125 people was more than the anticipated headcount of a fully staffed Shared Services center, Dennis felt the additional space would be utilized by the SAP team and other technical teams that would eventually move to the center once the full rollout was complete.

The layout of the center was designed to foster an open-door policy. The offices were centrally located, and each contained a glass wall to further create an open environment. The cubicles were constructed at a height that would allow the employees to communicate with one another while sitting and yet still have a bit of privacy. The building had a cafeteria and a gym on the first floor. Each company in the building subsidized the cafeteria, which was run by an outside vendor, so the prices would remain competitive. The gym was available to all employees in the building for a minimal monthly fee.

Dennis decided to wait outside for everyone to arrive. The team arrived in so many cars it looked like a caravan or maybe a funeral procession, which did not leave Dennis with a positive thought. He chuckled to himself at the thought that if he did not get this Shared Services center running, it might end up being his funeral.

A few of the employees had been inside the building before, but this was the first opportunity for everyone to see their new home all at once. Jerry and Sara led the team to the front of the building.

"Good afternoon, everyone," said Dennis. "Welcome to Fantasy Island."

Everyone laughed a bit, probably because Dennis was the boss, not because that line was particularly funny. Dennis enjoyed the laughter anyway.

"Are you ready to see your new home?" he asked.

"Sure, yeah! Let's go!"

Everyone filed into the building. There were four elevators, none of which was big enough to hold everyone. Eventually they all got on an elevator except for two people who asked where the steps were. When they reached the third floor, it was obvious that there was work to be done. Dennis didn't think it was possible that the space would be ready to move into the weekend of the 17th. There was garbage everywhere from the construction, and many of the areas had not yet been carpeted or painted. He had a very uneasy feeling in his stomach.

"Wow, I hope these people are going to work fast because I don't see any way in the world we can be in here by the 19th, and my dad is a contractor so I somewhat know what I'm talking about," said Dave.

"I agree," said Donna. "This place is a mess."

Dennis had not been to the new space in three weeks, and now he realized he should have stopped by before bringing the team over. He was ready to call Tony and read him the riot act. Yet at this point he knew he could not panic and let the team know that he felt the same way.

"Listen, I know it looks like quite a mess, but Tony has assured me we will be moved in by the 19th. Remember they don't paint these places like we paint our house. They can get this place ready much quicker than we could ever imagine." Dennis was trying to reassure himself and the team.

"Yeah, but none of the furniture is put together, and it doesn't even look like all of it is here," Stephanie exclaimed.

"Remember though they only have to be ready for 19 of us to move in, not 125," said Sara.

"So you mean we'll have to work here while they are still doing construction? Isn't that going to be kind of loud and messy?" asked Kim.

"Let's not panic yet, okay," Dennis said soothingly. "I'll talk to Tony again this afternoon and find out their exact plan to make this happen. In the meantime let's go to the conference room and continue our meeting."

"I thought we were going to take a tour," Debbie said.

"Well, there's not much to tour other than maybe the bathrooms. I sure hope those are done," said Steve.

The team headed toward the conference room, which was cleaned up, as Tony had promised. This gave Dennis a little more confidence.

Everyone took the chairs and formed a U without anyone saying a word.

Dennis stood in front of the group and restarted the meeting.

"I know this isn't what you expected to see when you came over here, but I've been assured that we will be ready. I want you to continue with the discussion that Sara and Jerry were leading before lunch. I'll go call Tony again to get further clarification on the timing and get the exact details of the plan to get us in here by the 19th. Okay?"

Jerry and Sara started where they left off, talking about training the end users in El Paso. As Dennis was leaving the room, he noticed that the group energy that had been displayed this morning was no longer there.

Dennis walked over to his future office, which was as unfinished as the rest of the space. He called Tony.

"Tony, Dennis. What in the hell is going on over at the new building?"

"What do you mean?"

"I just took my entire team over there for a tour and found the place to be nowhere near completion. There's not a chance in the world that place will be ready to move into the 17th," he said angrily.

"I've been talking to the general contractor, and he tells me it will be ready. What else do you want me to do?"

"Tell him to get it done. Do they have any penalties if they're not done on time?" Dennis asked.

"They did take a hit for not being ready on the 1st but after that, no, they don't have any other penalties," replied Tony.

"Well, what's their incentive to move fast now?"

"Getting paid, Dennis," said Tony. "They will get it done."

"When was the last time you were over here, Tony?"

"When you and I went over there," he replied.

"Well, you should've been over there since then, but you might want to make a trip now because this is going to effect our go-live. I can't expect my team to go live with the El Paso implementation in an area for 10 people when they have 19. If we go live before the space is ready, it will also mean we have to move in the middle of our first implementation, and that has disaster written all over it. I would advise you to talk to the GC today and find out if this is possible because I need to alert John Phelps that we might have a potential obstacle to our October 6 go-live."

Dennis hung up and called John.

"John Phelps's office, this is Terri."

"Terri, hey, it's Dennis. Is John around?"

"No, he's at lunch. Is it urgent?" Terri asked.

"It is but can you see if he can meet with me when he gets back from lunch. Tell him it is about the El Paso go-live," Dennis said.

"He's open at 2:30 for an hour. I'll put you on his calendar. If for some reason he can't make it, I'll call you. Otherwise, he'll see you then," Terri said.

"Thanks."

Dennis looked at his watch. It was 1:45. He had 45 minutes to figure out how to tell John the go-live was in jeopardy.

# CHAPTER 9

# A TOUGH CONVERSATION

Dennis got in his car and drove to corporate headquarters. It seemed a shame that such a beautiful day was going to be ruined by the conversation he was about to have with John. Just then he remembered that he hadn't invited Donna to the meeting, and she was really the one he should be talking to since she was his boss. He quickly called Donna and asked if she could make it. Luckily she was free. Maybe that was a good sign that his luck was not going to be so bad after all.

During the drive he tried to determine how it had come to this. Everything was going as planned. He'd been able to hire the right group of people for his team. Oscar and his team were in the very final stages of configuration and data upload. His team had completed the training documentation and exercises associated with their particular areas. Jerry and Sara had traveled to El Paso to work with Oscar's team on the final pieces of the SAP implementation. They met with and went over the business processes with the personnel in El Paso, and all of the vendors were contacted regarding the upcoming changes. The only thing he could think of is that he should have been more diligent in monitoring the progress of the new building. He was very angry at Tony for having not communicated more often, but he was even angrier at himself for not following up.

Dennis arrived at headquarters and went to his office to check his email and voice messages. He had plenty of new email, but he didn't have time to check those now. It was time to prepare himself. He headed for the bathroom, where he washed his hands and looked in the mirror. Well, here we go, he thought before leaving.

John wasn't at his office when Dennis reached it. Terri was on the phone but motioned to Dennis to hold on.

"Hi, Dennis, how are you?" she asked as she hung up. "John is running a couple of minutes late. Donna called and said she'd be up in a minute."

Dennis sat down and started leafing through a construction magazine. The outlook for construction in the United States was very good, and according to the magazine, the housing boom didn't show any signs of stopping. Dennis thought at least there was some good news today.

"Dennis, how is everything? How is the first meeting with your new team going?" asked John while he stood at Terri's desk.

"The meeting is going fine," replied Dennis.

Just then Donna got off the elevator and walked over.

"Hey, guys, how is everything?" she asked.

"Interesting," said Dennis.

"Interesting good or interesting bad?" asked Donna.

"How about we go into John's office?" The three walked into the office, and Dennis closed the door behind him. John's office had a round table with four chairs and two chairs in front of his desk. It was a fairly large office but not overly fancy, which Dennis admired. Donna sat in a chair by the desk and Dennis chose to sit on the couch. He reasoned if he was going to have an uncomfortable conversation, he might as well be comfortable.

"So what's going on? Terri said you want to talk about the El Paso go-live," John said.

"Right, well, to get right to the point, I took the team over to the new offices today, and it's not even close to being ready," Dennis explained.

"So what're you saying?" asked John.

"I'm saying we're not going to be able to move into our new offices before the October 6 El Paso go-live. And I don't know if you remember, but the offices were supposed to be ready September 1. I've been speaking to Tony Robertson, and he has assured me all along the office would be ready, but now it doesn't look like that is the case."

"So can't you just operate out of the area you're in downstairs until they're ready?" asked John.

"Well, the problem is the area is only meant to hold 10 people and we have 19. The team is very cramped. Also it will be logistically tough because all of the addresses and phone numbers that we published to El Paso and the vendors are in the new building," Dennis told them.

"So are you suggesting that we postpone the implementation until we're able to move?" Donna asked.

"I'm worried that we're not going to be able to deliver the kind of service that will get us off to a good start with the divisions. I'm also worried that we'll have to move in the middle of our first go-live, and that could be very disruptive. You know the divisions talk to each other, and if we get off to a bad start that will hurt our reputation."

"That might be true, but we're not asking the divisions to participate in Shared Services, we're telling them to. I think our reputation will take a worse hit if we have to inform our divisions and the vendors that we need to postpone at such a late date.

"What do you think, Donna?" John asked.

"I agree that we should not postpone the go-live. Oscar and his team are ready with SAP, the training has been completed or is being completed right now. If we delay this, a lot of the training will be forgotten and we might have to do it again," she replied.

"What you're really asking is to delay a go-live based on some logistical problems that we should be able to overcome and because of a comfort issue," John said. "I don't think we want to do that. We need to find a way to make this work on October 6.

"Let me ask you, Dennis, how did you let this happen?"

"Well, first off, I depended too much on Tony. I should have known better. But don't take that in the wrong way. It is entirely my fault. I should have been to that building every day if that's what it took to make this happen. I've told my teams many times over the years that you have to do whatever it takes to make something happen. And also trust everyone but always cut the cards. I did not cut the cards. It's that simple."

"Well, now you do have to do whatever it takes to make this work," said Donna.

"I agree and I can assure you that my team will not let this deter us from making this a successful go-live," responded Dennis.

"Okay," said John, "make it happen. And continue to push Tony. Who knows, maybe they can get it done before the weekend of the 17th."

Dennis walked out of the office feeling a bit sheepish. He should have known that John was not going to let the go-live be delayed. Now he simply had to find a way to tell his team that at least for the next few weeks, they would have to continue working in the cramped area in headquarters that they affectionately called the Phone Booth.

Dennis got back in his car and headed for the new building. The weather was still beautiful, and he wished he could be doing something besides driving back to tell everyone they just had to be patient.

When Dennis arrived the group was on a break. Most were walking around looking at where their cubicles would be or checking out the views or the bathrooms. He went to the conference room and waited. This was going to be the first bit of bad news he had to deliver to the team. He knew he had to put as positive of a spin as possible on it.

When Dennis saw Clarence, Tanya, Jerry, and Sara walking in, he assumed they had been together during the break and were probably discussing the office situation. The rest of the team walked into the room as Dennis continued to talk with the managers.

"Don't look so glum," said Dennis to the managers. "This is only temporary."

All four of them smiled. "How did it go, did you talk to Tony?" asked Clarence.

"Well, actually I talked to Tony as well as John and Donna. We have a solution."

All of them looked relieved. Dennis walked to the front of the room.

"How has the rest of the meeting been going?"

Although everyone said "okays" and "fines," the energy was clearly lacking.

"Okay, I know that since we've been here, everyone is a bit concerned with our new space and whether or not it is going to be ready. I spoke to Tony and he's still optimistic that it will be completed, but he hasn't been over here in a few weeks, so I'm not so sure how educated his optimism is. I also went to speak to John Phelps and Donna Angelo about the situation. I informed them of the circumstances, and they both agreed that we cannot delay the go-live of El Paso. So what does that mean for us? First it means that we'll cross our fingers and hope that Tony's optimism is well placed. And I'll continue to push him daily to make sure that everything that can be done is being done. Second, it means that if the space isn't ready, we'll have to work out of our current area in corporate headquarters. Now, I know that area is very cramped and that all of the new phone numbers and mailing addresses have been distributed, but we'll just have to make that work if we are unable to move."

"Can we work here even if it is still under construction? That would be better than working on top of each other," said Dave.

"The major issue with that is that we don't have our certificate of occupancy yet. We can't even move our stuff until we get that."

Kim said, "In my opinion, I'd rather work in the current area and wait until this is completely done before moving in."

"I wouldn't," said Debbie.

"Well, I'm not sure we are going to have a choice, but think of this as our first challenge. When John and I spoke on Monday, we mentioned that we'd get challenged and doubted. This challenge might have come along sooner than anyone expected, and it is certainly a challenge that we didn't anticipate, but we need to overcome it. Obviously we know it's temporary, and in the grand scheme of things it's really not too important. Now, I know what some of you are thinking, "That's easy for you to say because you have a nice office to work in," which is true. But, to be honest, I'm probably more upset than anyone in this room because this could have been prevented. I should have paid more attention to what was happening with the new space. I blindly trusted that something was going to happen and it didn't. One thing I often say is 'Trust everyone but always cut the cards.' In this case I did not do that, so if you want to be upset at someone, be upset at me. I also want you to know, though, that I'll do everything in my power to make this happen before October 6. Does anyone have any questions?"

"Why can't we delay the go-live?" asked Nelly.

"There are a number of reasons, but probably the main reason is that we've spent a considerable amount of time training the end users and training everyone in this room. It's important that the training coincide with the go-live as closely as possible because people tend to forget information they don't use. Also we have communicated this change to our vendors and suppliers in El Paso, and we want this to be as transparent to them as possible. Those are just a few of the reasons, but delaying the go-live is absolutely not an option. Any other questions?" asked Dennis.

"Okay, I'll keep you informed of this site's progress every time I get an update so there will be no more surprises."

Dennis let the team go home for the day. It was a pretty down way to end what should have been a great two-and-a-half-day meeting, but he was sure this would be the least of the challenges they'd face in the next couple of years.

# CHAPTER 10

# EL PASO GOES LIVE

Over the next few weeks, Dennis was in constant contact with Tony Robertson. Unfortunately, Tony was unable to keep his promise and get the team moved in prior to October 6. Fortunately, though, Oscar's team did a good job of preparing El Paso for the go-live. They cut checks out of the legacy system for all open invoices and put them in a tickler file so they could mail the checks a couple of days before the due date. Because of this, the Accounts Payable team didn't have too much to do for the first couple of weeks. The Payroll team also was able to make a slower transition because, as part of the SAP implementation, all divisions that went live would convert to a biweekly instead of weekly pay cycle. The rollouts were scheduled so that during the first week of go-live, the Payroll team would not have to process a payroll. The Benefits team, which was responsible for reconciling and paying all benefits providers, was also fairly idle because El Paso reconciled and cut checks for all outstanding invoices. The General Ledger team was busy inputting recurring entries into the system for October. It was also responsible for administering recurring payments, such as leases, so it had a good deal of work. The Document Management team wasn't too busy because there weren't too many invoices yet that needed to be scanned.

Jerry and Sara made sure that although the teams weren't doing much processing for El Paso, they had plenty to do with items related to governance. They were setting up group calendars, documenting time-off notifications and the selection process, and performing other miscellaneous tasks.

"I feel like a football player who's been practicing all summer and has yet to play a game," said Steve. "I can't wait until we start doing some real work."

The only good part about not being too busy was they got the chance to get to know each other a bit better, and this was certainly helping morale.

The one team that was very busy from day one was Accounts Receivable. Most customer payments tended to come near the first week of the month because most of Capp's invoices were due at the end of the month. All cash that was received in October needed to be booked in that month, so any checks that arrived after September 30 were held so they could be processed into SAP. This meant the Accounts Receivable team had a check backlog of four business days, and those four days were some of the busiest of the month. As a matter of fact, Drew, the Accounts Receivable team lead, did some analysis prior to the go-live and found out that 65 percent of the checks arrived within seven days of the end of each month. Drew and Amy made up the Accounts Receivable team, and they were both staying late every night. Today was Wednesday, and they'd have to stay at least a couple of hours late.

"Good night, Drew. Good night, Amy," said Stephanie.

"It must be nice to leave early," said Amy.

"What do you mean, early? They're leaving on time," Drew replied.

"Well, we're paying our dues now, but they'll be in the same boat we're in eventually," she said.

"Yeah, we certainly are learning a great deal—like these customers aren't very good at indicating which invoices they're paying."

"Reconciling the invoices to the checks is the toughest part, for sure," Amy said.

Amy and Drew spent a great deal of time on the phone with the Accounts Payable departments of Capp's customers. Because El Paso was in a different time zone, Amy and Drew couldn't contact any of the customers for the first three hours of every day.

"You know, we probably shouldn't come in until 11:00 am," Drew said. "At least that way we would start work at the same time as our customers in El Paso."

"Do you really want to work an 11:00 to 8:00 shift?" asked Amy.

"Well, we're staying here until 7:00 or 8:00 each night anyway, so what's the difference?"

"Yeah, but we do get things done in the morning. But I agree, we're probably not as productive during those hours."

"Maybe we could take turns so that every other day one of us will come in at 11:00," said Drew.

"That might work." Amy looked thoughtful. "Do you think they'll let us do it?"

"I'll ask Jerry in the morning."

Amy and Drew continued to work and call Capp customers to find out which invoices they were paying. It was very time consuming. Although they expected to have to do this occasionally, they didn't expect to have to do it for more than 50 percent of the checks they received. Finally, at 8:30, they were able to get all of the cash applied. It was a tough day, and they were the last two people to walk out of the building.

When Jerry arrived at work at about 7:50 on Thursday, his voicemail light was flashing. It was a message Drew had left last night at 8:15 pm. He said he wanted to talk to Jerry first thing in the morning. Jerry walked by Drew's cubicle, but he was not in yet. He saw Amy reading her email.

"Hey, Amy, how are you?" he asked.

"Good, and you?"

"Good. Hey, Drew left me a message last night at 8:15. Were you here with him at that time?"

"Yeah, we were still trying to apply the cash from the day. You know, the customers aren't very good at indicating which invoices they're paying, so in many cases we have to call them. And since they're in a different time zone, we can't start calling them until 11:00 our time, so most nights we have to stay late."

"Do you know if that's why he wants to talk to me?" asked Jerry.

"Yes, that's the reason. We have a proposal, but I'll let him tell you. He should be in at any minute. He's always here before 8:00."

As soon as Drew came in, he said hi to Amy and sat down to log on to his computer.

"Jerry came over and wanted to know if we were here together when you left the message, and I told him we were here applying the checks," Amy said. "He also wanted to know if that's why you left the message and I said yes. I told him we have a proposal but I'd let you tell him what it is."

"What did he say?" Drew asked.

"He just said okay. I think he's waiting for you to come see him. He was just here about five minutes ago," she replied.

"Okay, I'll find him."

Drew went over to Jerry's office, but he was not there. Drew went to get a cup of coffee and Jerry was in the kitchen, which the team shared with other teams. Everyone at Corporate seemed pretty interested in how the new Shared Services team was doing, so they would hang around if they saw two Shared Services employees together just to see if they could overhear something.

"Good morning, Drew, how's everything?" asked Jerry.

"Okay. Do you have some time this morning? I left you a message last night."

"Sure, let's go to my office."

Jerry's "office" was really a cubicle, but they were all making do the best they could in their temporary space.

"Amy said you came by to see me this morning and she told you how late we were here last night. Well, that's been the case just about every night. I don't know if you've looked at the amount of overtime she's working, but it's averaging 15 hours a week for the first two weeks. I think that is a bit much for two reasons: (1) it's costly to the company, and (2) she's going to burn out fairly quickly if we have to keep up this pace."

"Well, why are you two having to work so late?" asked Jerry.

"There are two main reasons, the first being that the customers are not very good at indicating on their remittance advice which invoices they're paying and because the customers are in a different time zone than us, we generally can't contact them until around 11:00 am our time. I guess really there is a third reason, and that is we had a four-day backlog of checks when we got started, and it is the busiest time of the month. The day we went live we had over 500 checks to apply. Combined with the lack of quality on the remittance advice, it's been a pretty tough couple of weeks."

"Obviously, Drew, one thing we need to do is improve the quality of the remittance advice coming from the customers."

"I agree completely, but that's a bit more of a long-term goal, Jerry. That isn't going to be corrected overnight."

"Agreed. Amy mentioned that you had a proposal you wanted to run by me."

"Yeah, she and I talked about it last night. I think we should be allowed to rotate one of us coming in every day at 11:00 am and working until 8:00 pm," Drew explained. "This would allow us to continue to make the calls after hours to our customers, but it would also cut down on her overtime and hopefully prevent some burnout. What do you think about that?"

"Well, I'm not so sure we should have special schedules for certain teams, especially so early in the life of our organization. It really wouldn't seem fair to the other teams."

"Do you think it is fair that everyone else leaves at 5:00 and she and I stay until at least 7:30, 8:00, or even sometimes later?" Drew asked.

"I didn't say that, but we need to be engaged in correcting the root cause of the problem first and then make adjustments if that doesn't work," replied Jerry.

"Well, fixing the root cause of the problem is going to involve talking to the customers, and that means talking to them from 11:00 am to 8:00 pm our time. It's a catch-22," Drew said adamantly.

"Well, what if we had some of the other teams help call the customers and try to fix the problems?"

"That would be great, but I think it also points to some of our frustration. Dennis is always talking about being a team and everyone being in this together, but no one asks us if we need any help. They simply say good night and head home. They don't even ask the next morning how late we had to stay. It just doesn't seem to us that we're working as a team. Amy and I definitely are, but I don't feel that from anyone else. We've walked out of this building at the same time every day since we started. We don't leave until the other person is ready. So from that aspect everything is good."

"I can see why you'd feel that way," said Jerry. "I have to be honest; I didn't know you had to work that late."

"Well, to be honest, I think you *should* know that. If nothing else, you should be there with us or at least be aware that we are having issues."

"Drew, you have to let me know these things before they get to this point. We just started working together, and I told you in your interview that I was not a micromanager and that I would give you latitude. Well, with that comes the responsibility to let me know when a problem arises. Now I agree that since we're new to one another, I probably should have been paying closer attention. I will do that going forward. About the schedule: Let me talk to Dennis and get his thoughts on it. I know this is important to both you and Amy, so I'll talk to you today and let you know what he says. Okay?"

"Thanks, Jerry, we appreciate it."

# TEAMWORK

Jerry left his area to go see Dennis on the third floor. When he got to Dennis's office, he could hear Dennis on the phone. Rosa was busy typing.

"Hey, Rosa, does Dennis have a few minutes this morning?"

"For you, I'm sure he does."

Just then Dennis hung up the phone and saw Jerry. Normally Dennis was the type that you could just walk into his office. He assumed Jerry was talking to Rosa because he'd been on the phone.

"What's going on?" Dennis asked.

"This morning Drew wanted to see me first thing about an issue they're having, and I'm looking for a bit of guidance on how to handle it," Jerry replied.

"Okay."

"As you know, we held the checks that were going to be posted in October until we went live with SAP. Essentially that meant that Drew and Amy had a backlog of about four days' worth of checks during the busiest days of the month. Well, needless to say, the combination of that, using a new system, and the customers being a little vague about which invoices they're trying to pay, those two have been working a significant number of hours."

"Yeah, I've seen them leaving late or sometimes when I leave I still see their cars in the parking lot."

"To be honest, they're getting a bit rattled by the fact that they seem to be the only ones working late, and they've asked if they could rotate an

11:00 to 8:00 schedule. They claim they need to get in touch with customers fairly often and since the customers are in El Paso, they can't start calling them until 11:00 our time," Jerry said.

"I know some of the teams are not too busy yet. Is anyone helping them?" Dennis asked.

"Not according to Drew. This is the first day I've been aware of the problem," Jerry replied.

"Let me ask you this: How come you didn't know about this until today?" asked Dennis. "We're just getting started, and you need to have your finger on the pulse, especially when we're this early in the game."

"I try to give the teams latitude to do what they need to do, so I was trying not to step on anyone's toes," Jerry explained.

"You know, it's one thing to give latitude and another to ask how everyone is doing or ask for a status report. We need to make sure that our teams have our complete support and they know that we're all in this together. It sounds like Drew and Amy don't feel that way."

"I can't argue with that," said Jerry. "What do you think about the schedule they're proposing?"

"I don't think it's a bad short-term option, but we need to do more than that. We need to show them that we're all in their corner and that everyone is willing to pitch in and help out," Dennis replied.

"What about proper accounting controls?"

"That shouldn't be a problem. We can start out by having some people on the other teams help by calling the customers and getting the proper remittance information. They can simply note it on whatever advice they're sending back. We don't need to change any permissions in SAP. And since we'll have more people calling, they can take their time a bit and try to determine why the customers are not providing the proper remittance information on their checks. So this will attack the immediate need and help with the root cause a bit. But the most important thing is we need to show them our support. You should be there until all the work is done, and you should be doing some of the actual work as well. They have to know that you have their backs," said Dennis.

"Okay."

Dennis could sense that Jerry didn't like the part about him being there too, but he felt strongly that Jerry needed to lead by example, especially so early on.

"Also, I'd like to have a quick meeting with the team to talk about teamwork and explain the situation. I think if everyone knew what was going on, they'd be more than willing to help," he said.

"I agree," Jerry said. "We have a good group of people, and I think they'll take care of each other.

"Okay, I'll have Rosa send out an invite for this morning. We can meet in the conference room up here."

Dennis followed Jerry out of his office. "Rosa, set up a meeting with the whole team as soon as everyone is available. Hopefully it will be this morning. Let's have it in the conference room up here."

The meeting was scheduled from 11:00 to 11:30. Dennis was looking forward to the meeting because he thought it was a good opportunity to talk about teamwork. He enjoyed these types of meetings.

Dennis walked into the conference room at 10:55 and was happy to see that everyone was there except Jerry. Since Jerry was instrumental in this meeting being called, he was confident the man would be on time. About two minutes later Jerry walked in and sat down.

"Okay, well, since everyone is here, we might as well get started a couple of minutes early," said Dennis. "First, I want to thank everyone for being able to meet on such short notice. Second, I want to let you know that I have really good news. I spoke to Tony, and we're going to be able to move this weekend. And the best news is, we don't have to do anything on the weekend. We're going to have movers come in Saturday morning and pick up your files and whatever you need to take to the new office. The IT team will also be moving all of our computers, printers, copiers, and monitors. So Monday morning we'll be in our new home. What do you think about that?"

The entire team applauded. Dennis knew he should announce this news before going into the real reason for the meeting. He just got lucky that Tony called him before the meeting.

"Well, I'm glad to see that everyone is happy to hear that we're moving. I'm looking forward to moving myself. We have one other subject we need to talk about. As you know, for most of us, going live with El Paso has not been extremely busy during these first couple of weeks. Of course, that's going to change by the end of the month, but for now some of us do have a bit of idle time. However, a couple of people on our team have been extremely busy. Drew and Amy have been staying late virtually every night since we went live because we must post cash every day and they had a backlog of deposits that were received in October."

Everyone in the room looked at Drew and Amy. Dennis could tell they were wondering if the two had complained about the fact that they had to work late and no one else had to. It was apparent that his comments made everyone feel a bit uncomfortable.

"First, I'd like to thank Drew and Amy for their hard work and dedication. Second, I'd like to ask for your help. Essentially we're having a problem with our customers and the fact that they don't provide enough detailed information on their remittance advices. Because of this, Amy and Drew have to call more than 50 percent of the customers and ask which invoices they're trying to pay. Eventually we'll be able to solve the root cause of this problem, but for now we need to make sure the checks get applied.

"Also, because our customers are in a different time zone, Drew and Amy usually can't get in touch with anyone until 11:00 am or after. So I'm asking for your help in calling our customers to get the details regarding the remittance advice. If we have a number of people calling, rather than just two, we should be able to apply the payments much quicker and, more important, without Drew and Amy having to work so many hours. I don't need anyone to answer right now, but we need some volunteers to help us over the next couple of weeks. If you can help out, send an email to Jerry or Sara or give them a call and let them know your availability.

"I want to mention one other thing," Dennis continued. "How many people have heard of Ghalib?"

"Who?" asked Nelly.

"Ghalib. Has anyone heard of a man named Ghalib?"

No one had heard of him.

"Well, to be honest, I am not surprised because he was a Persian poet who lived in the 1800s. So you're probably asking yourself what this has to do with anything. One of the things he wrote was this: 'For the raindrop, joy is entering the river.' Again, 'For the raindrop, joy is entering the river.' Can anyone tell me what he meant by that?"

No one said a word. Dennis had not shown this side of himself to the team, so they all seemed to be a bit bewildered.

"Now, I never read an explanation regarding what he meant, so I interpreted it in my own way and here is my interpretation. If a raindrop falls from the sky and hits your windshield, a wiper will quickly come and make it go away. If a raindrop hits the street on a summer day, it will evaporate in seconds. Essentially a raindrop by itself is completely powerless. It will either evaporate or be wiped away forever, but a raindrop that enters the river will live forever and will have a lasting impact. If the raindrop hits the river, it has a chance to feed our oceans, carry our barges, provide life for fish, or even carve the Grand Canyon.

"The Grand Canyon is nothing more than the result of the trillions and trillions of raindrops all doing the same thing. That's the power of teamwork. And when you think about that, it is truly amazing because each individual raindrop is completely powerless, yet together they can accomplish something that will last forever. We as human beings are individually incredibly powerful, so if you combine the power of the 20 people who are in this room, the potential is almost limitless. That is what I am asking you to do. Combine the power of everyone in this room, and we will do things that no one has ever seen before. We will help our friends Drew and Amy, we will build a world-class center, and we will have a lasting effect on this company."

The team looked at each other, a bit surprised, but they seemed to understand the message. A group of people working together could certainly accomplish more than a person or two working alone.

Dennis looked around the room and said, "Thank you for supporting your teammates. I look forward to conquering this problem as a team and also to moving into our new home."

With that he left the room.

# CHAPTER 12

# END-TO-END PROCESS

It was the second full week of January. It had been three months since El Paso first went live on SAP and began utilizing Shared Services. Everything was operating fairly smoothly, and the Shared Services team and Oscar Harris's team were preparing for the upcoming implementation of Capp's largest division, the western division. Capp closed its financials on a calendar-year basis. The Shared Services team survived a year-end, although Kathy, El Paso's controller, had not yet officially closed the year. A couple of minor adjustments needed to be made. She was planning on completing the final entries this week, which would mean she would complete the year-end closing by January 16. Donna Angelo had anticipated the first year-end close in SAP could take as long as a month, so she told Dennis that she was pleasantly surprised that Kathy was going to be done by mid-January. Dennis had reminded Donna that one of the reasons they chose El Paso to go first was because Kathy was such a strong controller and she embraced the changes that were taking place.

Today was Wednesday, and Dennis had just returned from a meeting with his daughter's teacher. It seems that Jackie had gotten in a fight with another kid at school, and the teacher wanted to talk to Dennis and Jennifer. Dennis thought they were making too big of a deal about it, but he did not say that to Jennifer or the teacher. In his mind, he was proud that his daughter had stood up for herself since she could sometimes be a little timid.

Dennis decided to walk around the center today and see how everyone was doing. It almost seemed like a lifetime ago that the team was cramped in the offices in corporate headquarters and complaining about the new space not being ready on time. At that time it was the biggest crisis they had faced, and today it seemed so inconsequential.

"Nelly, how's everything going?" Dennis asked.

"Okay, I'm just working on some business process flows for the western division implementation," she said. "And how're you doing?"

"Pretty good," he said. "Except for the fact that I just got back from a parent-teacher conference because my daughter got in a fight at school. Although she shouldn't be fighting, and I didn't tell my wife this, I was actually fairly proud she stood up for herself," he said, smiling.

"Standing up for yourself is important."

"Hey, why do you have to redo the business process flows for the western division? They should be the same as the ones we did for El Paso, right?" Dennis asked.

"You would think so, but we've been working with Oscar's team and the controllers out west, and they don't like some of the processes we put in place for El Paso. I don't think it is the right thing to do, but they're pretty adamant that we need to make the changes," she replied.

"Are they suggesting that we go back and change the processes for El Paso? The one thing we can't do is have different processes for each implementation. If we do that, we'll have to double our staff to handle all of the differences and exceptions," said Dennis.

"I don't think so; no one has mentioned it to me."

"Okay, I have just one more question and I'll quit bugging you. Are the processes working for El Paso?"

"There are some minor changes we could probably make, and we've been talking with Kathy about those, but they don't necessarily need to be done now. So, in other words, there's nothing major to be done, and for the most part everything is working well," Nelly answered.

Dennis was happy he chose to walk around this morning because what he learned from Nelly was pretty important. He definitely needed to address this issue.

"Oh, one more thing, Nelly," he said. "How long have you been working on the new process flows?"

"Not yet a week."

Well, he thought, at least this hadn't been going on for too long. He needed to find out from Jerry and Sara if the rest of the teams were dealing with the same issue.

Dennis went to his office and started to read his emails for the first time today. Going to his daughter's school set him back a couple of hours. The first thing he noticed was an email sent by Oscar last night.

> Dennis,
> How is everything going? We need to have a conversation about some of the requests your teams are sending to the SAP team. As you know, we are trying to get the western division implementation completed on time, and we don't have much time for the enhancements your team is looking for. Maybe we can agree to put these requests on hold until after we complete western. Also, we're still spending a good deal of time supporting your team on day-to-day issues. Give me a call when you get a chance so we can discuss.
> Thanks. Oscar.

"Rosa, set up a meeting with Sara and Jerry sometime today so we can discuss business process flows and SAP enhancements and requests. We'll need at least an hour, but you better book it for an hour and a half," Dennis said from his office.

"No problem. By the way, how did everything go with your daughter?" Rosa asked.

"Third-round knockout; she fights for the title next week," Dennis replied, laughing.

Jerry and Sara were both able to meet at 2:00 pm. They arrived at Dennis's office together, laughing and smiling. Dennis was glad to see that everyone's mood had improved so much since moving to the new offices. Even though they had been in the offices for more than two months, the mood had not worn off. He hoped it was more than just the surroundings that made everyone happy to come to work.

"How is everything with your little slugger?" asked Jerry.

"Boy, news travels fast," Dennis replied.

"Well, you're such a big boxing fan we knew you'd be proud. I'm sure watching all of those bouts with her helped her technique," added Sara.

"Hey, I'm not proud of what she did. I don't condone fighting."

"I'm sure you don't condone fighting, but it's pretty obvious you are proud. And you should be: Standing up for yourself is important," said Jerry.

"Agreed," said Dennis. "And speaking of standing up for yourself, I got a note from Oscar this morning about the number of requests and the support he has to provide to our teams. I think they're a bit overwhelmed with the western implementation and the work they still have to do for El Paso. He's asking that we hold off a bit on our requests."

"Well, part of the problem is that there were some things configured in SAP that don't help us with our efficiencies. And since the western division is asking us to change our processes a bit, we need to be more efficient in order to maintain our headcount and still be able to get everything processed," Sara responded.

"And you are talking about the headcount that has been authorized for hire for the western rollout?" Dennis asked.

"Yes. If we're not going to be consistent in our processes, we'll need more people, bottom line," added Jerry.

"By the way, how is the recruiting process going?" Dennis asked. "Are the teams using the selection process as we designed it, and is it working?"

"Yes, that's working fine," Sara replied. "For those teams that don't have enough people or are too busy processing to conduct a team interview, we have someone from one of the other teams sit in on the interview. It's working very well, and Clarence is doing a great job finding both internal and external candidates. We have a very good mix of candidates. That's the least of our worries."

"Great. Okay, so as you know, we can't go over our budgeted headcount, so we need to make this work. I spoke to Nelly this morning when I came in, and she was working on new business process flows for western. Why are we allowing them to change the process? We can't do that," said Dennis.

Sara looked at Jerry. "Do you want me to start?" she asked.

"When Oscar and his team started to work with the western controllers, they went over the process and the controllers simply were not happy. They said that much of what we did for El Paso would not work for their business, so Oscar and his team told them we would make the changes."

"But who gave Oscar the green light to make these changes?" Dennis asked.

"I don't know, I guess Donna did," said Jerry.

"Okay, let me talk to Donna and get the story because this is not going to work. We can't have 50 ways to do things and hope to be efficient. I'll try to talk to her today.

"Anything else I should know about this or anything else?" Dennis concluded.

"Nope, that should do it for now," replied Sara.

Jerry and Sara left, and Dennis asked Rosa to come into his office.

"Rosa, I need to meet with Donna as soon as possible to talk about the western division. See if you can set up a meeting later today or tomorrow morning. Let me know as soon as possible if she can't make it."

Dennis started to read his emails again, and just as he was making progress, Rosa walked into his office.

"I checked with Donna and she can't meet today, but said she'd stop by on her way to Corporate and meet you for breakfast in the cafeteria tomorrow at 8:00. I checked your calendar and you're open. Do you want me to confirm that?" she asked.

"Sure, sounds good. Also, call my wife and tell her I'll be home early tonight. If possible I'd like to eat with the kids."

Driving home, Dennis was happy that Jennifer was able to get the kids together for dinner. He was going to pick up Chinese food so he and Jennifer wouldn't have to cook or do much cleanup. He always enjoyed these dinners, although it still seemed odd now that Andrew was away at college. At least he'd get more than one egg roll, he thought. When Dennis pulled into the driveway, Samantha and Jackie were out front playing with Shorty and waiting for him.

"Daddy, did you bring home a bunch of fortune cookies?" asked Samantha.

"No, they were out of fortune cookies. They said there were no more fortunes to be had," he replied. "Just kidding, sweetie," he said as he handed her a couple of the bags. He always bought too much because he and Jennifer liked to have a late-night snack of leftover Chinese food. They'd eat it in bed while watching one of the late-night talk shows. It always reminded them of when they were just married.

Jennifer came over, took the bags from Dennis, and gave him a kiss on the cheek.

"Get out the plates and utensils and we'll do the rest," she said to Dennis.

The kids ate their food with a fork, but Dennis and Jennifer liked to use chopsticks. As a matter of fact, they had a very nice set, so Dennis got those out instead of using the disposable kind. Everyone sat down and started to eat.

"Jackie, how was the rest of your day at school?" Jennifer asked. "Did you make up with Tracy?"

"No, I mean, they made us apologize to each other, but that was all we said. We did not talk for the rest of the day. I saw her get on the school bus and she gave me a mean look, so I guess she's still mad. I am too really," replied Jackie.

"Well, you should make up with her tomorrow," Jennifer told her.

"So, Jackie, tell me again why you got in a fight with Tracy," Dennis said.

"I told you, it was because of the field trip we took the day before."

"Yeah, but you didn't exactly tell me what happened on the field trip or even where you went," Dennis said.

"We went to one of those parks where you get to rappel from a wall and cross bridges that are up in the trees. We only had time to rappel, but we might go back again before summer break," she said.

"Did I sign a waiver for that?"

"Mom did," Jackie said. "Well, when we got there, we all had different things we had to do. My job was to carry the ropes that we were going to use to rappel. Other kids had to bring the food, the helmets, knee pads, elbow pads, and some even got to bring the video cameras. Everybody had something to do, even Timmy."

"Who's Timmy?"

Jennifer looked at Dennis. "Remember, I told you, he's the kid in the wheelchair. He has muscular dystrophy."

"Oh yeah, I remember. I've seen him before. What did he do?"

"He helped carry the food and drinks," Jackie said.

"Well, it sounds like everyone had a lot of different things to do," said Dennis.

"Yeah, but the instructor told us that we only had one thing to do, and that was rappel down the wall. He said it was only 20 feet but it looked a lot higher to me."

"Did you do it?" Jennifer asked.

"Yeah, because we all had to; he told us that if everyone did it, he would buy us pizza and give us free movie passes, but if one person did not do it, no one would get pizza and movie passes," she said. "I think he probably would have given them to us anyway, but that's what he said."

"So how did you end up getting in a fight over the field trip?" Dennis asked.

"Tracy told everyone that Timmy should not count, and if he didn't do it we should still get pizza and movie passes. I thought that was mean and I told her to shut up. The teachers told us both to be quiet, and they were pretty mad so we didn't do anything. But when we got back to class she kept making fun of me and said I liked Timmy, so I hit her," Jackie explained.

Dennis could tell she was still mad, so he didn't ask her any more questions about Tracy.

"So did he give you the pizza and movie passes?" he asked.

"Yeah, but only after Timmy did it," she said.

"Timmy did it?" asked Jennifer, "How did he do that?"

"The instructor had a special harness that would hold him and Timmy, so both of them rappelled down the wall. Timmy's mom was there, and she almost didn't let him do it, but he was begging her to let him so she said yes. He was laughing and screaming all the way down. He really liked it. Timmy's mom was crying when he got down, but I think it was because she was happy. We were all happy. We ate pizza there and we get to go to the movies next week. Before we left, the instructor reminded us that even though we had different things to do, we really had one goal and it was important that everyone make the goal, no matter what. He was pretty cool."

Dennis looked at Jennifer and could see the tears in her eyes. He was tearing up too. He thought that would be a great story to tell at work, but he wasn't sure he could get through it without getting choked up.

They finished dinner and cleaned up. Whenever they ate Chinese food, Jennifer would make the kids clean up before giving them a fortune cookie. That was their reward. For Dennis, the reward that night was Jackie's story.

# CHAPTER 13

# PROCESS STEERING TEAMS

Dennis arrived at work at 7:00 am Thursday. He wanted to be able to get through his email before he met with Donna. He remembered that he had not responded to Oscar's email about the enhancement requests and the support he was providing to the Shared Services team. Anyway, he needed to have his conversation with Donna prior to responding, so if nothing else, he would contact Oscar later today, he thought.

At 7:55 Dennis went downstairs to meet Donna. He didn't often eat breakfast in the cafeteria, although he'd occasionally eat lunch there. They had pretty good prices, and although the selections were limited, the quality of the food was good. The fact that there was a cafeteria in the building was one of the deciding factors in choosing to locate the offices there. The employees really liked the convenience, especially in the summertime, when midday or afternoon thunderstorms could disrupt lunch plans. Also, because the companies in the building all participated in a subsidy program, the meals were very inexpensive.

There were about 10 people in the cafeteria line to get breakfast. Dennis wasn't very hungry since he and Jennifer snacked on the leftover Chinese food last night. He decided to just get a couple of pieces of toast, bacon, and an orange juice. He knew he should probably not be eating bacon since his cholesterol was approaching 200, but he had some anyway. He didn't see Donna yet, so he continued through the line, paid for his breakfast, and sat down at a table for two. He chose a table that was a bit removed from the rest, just in case the conversation included any confidential subjects.

He was buttering his toast when Donna joined him. She had chosen a full breakfast of scrambled eggs, toast, sausage, coffee, and orange juice.

"You're eating a bit light today, aren't you?" she asked.

"Jennifer and I raided the refrigerator last night, so I'm actually not too hungry. I couldn't resist some bacon and butter though since I'm trying to watch my cholesterol," he said, laughing. "Not to worry, though. I drink plenty of red wine to keep my pipes clear."

"That reminds me," she said. "A vendor sent me a bottle of red wine and since I don't drink, I thought I'd give it to you. I'll send it interoffice to you."

"Thanks."

"So what's up? Rosa said you wanted to meet as soon as possible."

"I want to talk about a couple of things. First it seems we have a bit of confusion between our team at Shared Services and the SAP team. Apparently the SAP team has been allowing business process changes to occur for the western division. It seems that some of the processes that we put in place for El Paso either are not adequate or are simply things that the western controllers don't want to do," Dennis explained.

"Give me an example."

"Well, I was talking to Nelly in AP yesterday, and she was redoing the demand check process to suit what the western controllers want. Now, I've been talking to Kathy in El Paso at least three times a week, and they haven't had any problem with the demand check process, yet we're changing it for divisions that have never even used it. That doesn't make sense to me. We need to be consistent in our processes with each division or the Shared Services center is going to bear the brunt of those inconsistencies. It will be very difficult for us to be efficient, and that only means one thing: more cost, either through additional headcount or overtime or even increased headcount in the divisions. Overall we have to agree on one way of doing things that are so simple like paying a bill. If not, we'll find ourselves not realizing the ROI we presented in the business case for Shared Services," Dennis replied.

"Will the process that is being put in place work for El Paso?"

"That's not the point. It's cutting a demand check. How difficult can that be? I'm confident any reasonable process for that will work. The point is we cannot either continue to change for every rollout or, even worse, let each division dictate how it wants to interact with us. We need to determine how our business receives its inputs, just as a factory determines how it receives its raw materials. I know financial people and accountants don't like to be compared to factories, but in a very simplistic way we are much like a factory. We receive raw materials, such as invoices, check requests, payroll files, sales orders, and the like, and we turn that data or those documents into a certain output, whether it's a vendor check, a payroll check, or a customer invoice or statement. We can't be efficient if we allow our inputs to come in inconsistently or if we have to produce an inconsistent output. It simply is not cost effective. And how we receive a check request or how we send out the check doesn't affect the overall strategy of Capp, so the inconsistencies at best add no value at all and at worst they significantly increase costs. We're going down a dangerous path here," Dennis concluded.

"Well, don't forget," Donna began, "that we've become the powerful company that we are by giving the divisions the latitude to operate the way they see fit."

"I'm not saying—"

"Let me finish," Donna snapped. "We cannot dictate to the business how they are going to operate. That will cause a lot of backlash, not only with the controllers but with the general managers who are used to running their own show. We need to find a way for this to work for everyone, and if that means a bit of inconsistency, then so be it. Your job is to make the Shared Services center as efficient and cost effective as possible, given our environment."

"I'm not saying we have to or need to dictate to anyone," Dennis explained. "We can get rid of these inconsistencies if we can get everyone on the same page. We can show them that it makes business sense to be consistent as a company, and we can let them make the decisions."

"But that's what we're doing, and you're saying it doesn't work."

"No, we're letting them make decisions just for their division or group of divisions. We need to have them make decisions for Capp as a whole," he replied.

"And how do we do that? They don't have time to work on processes for the entire company. They need to concentrate on their own divisions."

"We do that by having process steering teams. Essentially we put together a team of people with representatives from Shared Services, the SAP team, and the divisions. We give them the charter to look at the end-to-end process and determine what's best for the company. It might be that, for example, what the western divisions want to do in Accounts Payable is better than what we have implemented for El Paso. If that's the case, then we'll go with that as long as everyone agrees it's right for the whole country. What these teams will do is allow for the sharing of best practices, the divisions will have buy-in because they were involved in the decisions, and ultimately we'll have consistency. I didn't just come up with this idea, Donna; many companies are utilizing process steering teams, and they're reaping the benefits."

"Okay, let me digest what you're saying and we can talk next week. Speaking of digesting, I haven't even touched my breakfast. Is there anything else?" Donna asked.

"Yeah, there is, but please eat," Dennis replied as he ate a piece of bacon.

"You know, Oscar and his team are pretty busy getting ready for the western implementation in March," he started.

"I know. Didn't we just talk about this, or is this Groundhog Day?"

"No, you are not Bill Murray." Dennis laughed. "The SAP team really has three things they need to work on," he continued. "The western implementation, enhancements for the divisions that are live, which right now is only us and El Paso, and day-to-day support, which includes break-fix.

"Obviously their number-one priority is to get western configured, so unless the other items are business critical they don't get done. The problem is we continue to send them requests, as does El Paso, and when we go-live with western, it will be all divisions that are live, which for them will be overwhelming. We need to be able to filter the requests that are making it to Oscar's team because even if they don't actually work on it, they get distracted by the request and generally they have to do at least some type of research, which is time consuming."

"So I assume you have a suggestion," Donna said.

"Yes, I think the requests should go through process steering teams," Dennis explained. In other words, unless the issue is a business-critical break-fix or enhancement such as a legal requirement, the process steering team should be the ones to validate, approve, and prioritize the request. This will keep the SAP team out of the business of filtering requests. Again, think of the factory: The SAP team is in place to execute or create, and it is up to the business to decide what we will create. So not only will the steering teams decide on what processes we will use throughout the company, but they will also decide which requests that fit within that consistent process get approved and how they get prioritized. This will make the SAP team much more efficient, and it will certainly allow them to focus."

"So what does this team look like, who's on it?"

"The team would ideally have representatives from, if not each of the divisions, at least the grouping of divisions, such as the western division. They would be people who are involved in the process daily. For example, on the Order to Cash team, you would have an AR representative from the division, someone from sales, someone from our AR team in Shared Services, an SAP team member who works on that module, and then someone to facilitate the team. The facilitators could be either Shared Services employees or division employees, but they should not be facilitated by someone from the SAP team." (See Exhibit 13.1.)

"And I say that because you don't want the person responsible for execution to be the one determining the strategy. Soldiers on the ground don't decide who to attack or what hill to defend. They are given orders, and they carry out those orders. Now, in certain situations they might have to make adjustments, but that is the latitude you give them. But the latitude given always fits within the overall strategy."

EXHIBIT **13.1** *Steering Team Organization Chart*

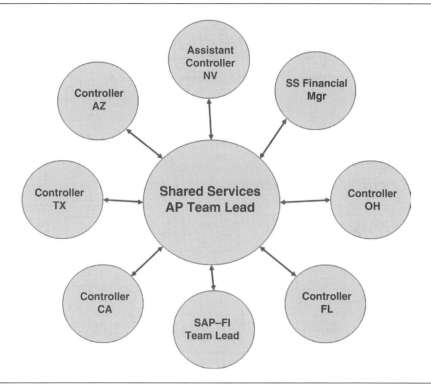

"You make some very interesting points," Donna said. "Have you talked to Oscar about this?"

"No, I haven't, although he did send me an email yesterday regarding the enhancements and support. I'm sure he would be relieved to have steering teams be responsible for the filtering and prioritization of all of the requests he gets. If you like, I can call him this afternoon, or we can both call him."

"Let's both call him; I'd like to have this discussion. Let me ask you this, will these teams require additional headcount?" asked Donna.

"Not at all. They'll meet either in person or via conference call every quarter. They won't have to meet more often because we'll establish a policy that all non–business-critical requests will be put into a queue that will be reviewed quarterly. We'll still allow people to send in requests as often as they like, but we won't allow ourselves to be distracted daily by every request that comes in. Again, we'll focus only on those that have been approved to be worked on, upcoming implementations, and business-critical break-fixes."

"Who determines the criticality of the issue?" she asked.

"The end user, but we'll validate the request and, if need be, we'll educate the users about the criteria used to determine if something is business critical."

"I'm sure I'll have more questions later, but let's call Oscar this afternoon." Looking down at her plate, Donna remarked, "Look at that, I still didn't eat any of my food. Well, it's too cold to eat now. I must have been very interested if I didn't even touch my food. You should offer your services as a diet guru."

They both got up and emptied their trays into the trash. Dennis was looking forward to their call with Oscar.

Later in the day, Dennis went to his office and waited for the conference call. Donna dialed into the call a few minutes after Dennis and Oscar dialed in.

"Sorry I'm a bit late, but I was starving. Remember, you didn't let me eat breakfast this morning," she said.

Dennis and Donna explained the concept to Oscar and got his feedback. Fundamentally he agreed with the concept, but he had concerns that his team wouldn't feel that they were part of the strategic process since they wouldn't lead any of the teams. He understood Dennis's point about not having them lead it and said he would discuss the issue with his team. He wanted to start with just one team and see how it progressed. They all agreed to start with the Procure to Pay process since that was the simplest and the western divisions were trying to change some of them already. Dennis suggested that Nelly lead the team. Everyone was in agreement.

After everyone hung up, Dennis was eager to talk to Nelly about this opportunity. He was sure she'd be excited.

CHAPTER 14

# PREPARATION

It was Monday, February 16. The Process Steering team was set to have its first meeting. Dennis, Jerry, and Nelly had worked together over the past four weeks to determine the exact makeup of the team, had contacted everyone, and set the date for the first meeting. Although the western go-live was only 14 days away and there was still some work to be done by the SAP team, everyone wanted to hold the meeting prior to the go-live. They were worried that if they didn't have the meeting then, it would be delayed another few months. Besides that, they also had to address the issue of the western division requesting changes to some of the business processes that had been established during the El Paso implementation.

Dennis arrived early, as he usually did on Mondays. He liked to get the week off to a quick start, and it was usually fairly quiet on Monday mornings. As he was headed to the kitchen to get his second cup of coffee, he noticed Nelly had just sat down. It was 7:30, and they were the only two in the office.

"Good morning, Nelly. How was your weekend?"

"Very nice; my husband treated me to a special Valentine's dinner of steak and lobster. He grilled it himself. And you?" she replied.

"Ironically, I did the same thing for Jennifer, only I grilled steak and shrimp. Blackened shrimp, Jennifer called it, which was not Cajun blackened but more like burned blackened. She gave me an A for effort though," he replied, laughing.

"So, are you ready for the meeting next week?" Dennis asked.

"Yes, we're all set. I'm flying to Reno Sunday night so that I can spend Monday getting acclimated to the office space that Oscar and his team are using," she said.

"Don't expect anything fancy."

"I know. I heard it's just like the setup they had in El Paso, where they're using long folding tables. I just hope they had the game tables moved to Reno," she said, smiling.

"Well, since everyone uses laptops I don't think they moved anything at all. Although I heard he bought another pool table and table tennis table."

"Why did they relocate to Reno anyway?" Nelly asked.

"Since El Paso isn't really a large division and the Reno and Nevada business is very large, it just made more sense to put the SAP implementation team somewhere in Nevada. We thought about Las Vegas, but office space was much cheaper in Reno, and there are enough flights going in and out. Besides that, the Reno airport is a lot less hectic than McCarron. We had to think of those things since many on the team are traveling every week. We wanted to make it as convenient as possible," Dennis explained.

"That makes sense. I checked with everyone on the team and they all have their flights set. We're staying at a hotel right across the street from the office Oscar is using. I think they're about 10 minutes from the warehouse," Nelly said.

"Yeah, that's about what Oscar said. Let me ask you this, Nelly: Do you think I should tag along for this first meeting since Jerry isn't going to be there?"

"Well, it certainly wouldn't hurt," she replied.

"Yeah, those guys in the West can be pretty tough. I know they're going to be pretty adamant about making some of the process changes before the go-live."

"And what is our stance?" she asked.

"Donna and I have talked about it, and we don't think it will send the right message if we change the processes now. Besides, it doesn't really make that much difference. They just want to keep doing things the way they always have done them," Dennis explained.

"What do you mean, the way they always have done them?" asked Nelly. "If we're going to do the process for them, it will certainly be different than what they're doing today."

"Well, the one we're really worried about is the demand check process. They want to have access to cut demand checks in the division. I'm certain they want this so they can continue to process invoices on their own. If we give them access to cut their own checks, we're going to create duplication of work for one thing. It will be easier for them to just process checks on their own than contact us. If we go down this path, it means that each division will want a check printer, they'll need check stock, and of course they'll need security in SAP to process the transaction. We need to drive our ACH participation so we cut out mail time of checks, and we need to make sure we're able to process the demand check requests they send us in a timely manner. And you know, that's another thing: If we don't do this centrally, it will be tougher to track the number of demand checks that we process. The mere fact that we're doing a demand check means that something broke down in the process to force us to have to do that. Okay, I'm getting off my soapbox now, but our strategy is going to be to listen to what they have to say and stick to our guns. We do not want to be flexible on this one."

"Whew, that was a mouthful. If you're going to be that passionate about it, I definitely would like for you to go," Nelly said, laughing.

"Well, I can guarantee you they're going to be that passionate, so we're going to have to fight fire with fire if it comes to that. I hope not, though."

The office was starting to fill up now. Nelly went back to logging on to her computer, and Dennis went for his second cup of coffee. Along the way, he thought to himself, I should really cut down on the caffeine.

Dennis decided to attend the meeting in Reno with Nelly.

Nelly arrived at the ticket counter on Sunday with one piece of luggage and a computer bag.

"Are you checking any bags?" the ticket agent asked.

"No bags to check," she replied.

"That's a good thing, because I wasn't going to wait for you if you had to wait at baggage claim," said the man behind her.

Nelly turned around and saw Dennis.

"So I take it you're not checking any luggage either?"

"No way; in fact, I try to limit my travel to three days just so I won't have to check any bags," Dennis said.

Dennis and Nelly both checked in and went through security. They were about one hour early for their boarding time.

"I hate to be rushed at the airport," said Dennis.

"I agree; I'd rather sit here than be worried about making my flight," Nelly replied.

"Do you want to grab a bite to eat?" she asked.

"Sure. I could grab a little something and maybe have a beer as well."

They went into a bar that served sandwiches and appetizers. Since most people tend to travel Sunday morning rather than Sunday afternoon, they didn't have much trouble finding a seat.

"Can I get you something to drink?" the waitress asked, smiling.

"Sure. I'll take a glass of zinfandel," said Nelly.

"And I'd like a Killian's," said Dennis.

"Would you like a 12 or 22 ounce?"

"Make it the 22. We have a lot of flying to do."

"Are you going to order food as well? You know, the food on the airplane isn't nearly as good as ours," the waitress said.

"I think we might have some appetizers," Dennis said.

"Okay, I'll get your drinks while you decide. The egg rolls and chicken fingers go very well with the Killian's."

"You don't always get this kind of service in an airport bar. She's very nice," Nelly said.

"Well, she obviously needs the job, so I'm sure she wants to do well and get a nice tip," Dennis replied.

"Why do you say she needs the job?" asked Nelly.

"Anyone who's over 60 and gets up to come to the airport to wait on cranky travelers must need the job. I feel sorry for people who get older and have to do such tough jobs. As far as waiting on people goes, this has to be very tough. We'll make sure we give her a nice tip," replied Dennis.

"Here are your drinks. Are you ready to order?" the waitress asked.

Dennis looked at her name tag and saw her name was Dolores.

"Yeah, Dolores, I think we'll have the southwestern egg rolls and the chicken fingers. Nelly, do you want anything else or an entrée?"

"No, that should be plenty."

"By the way, we have a Dolores who works with us, and she's just about as nice as you. It must be something in the name," Dennis said, smiling.

"Why, thank you. I like to think it is a good name. Is there anything else I can get you?"

"No, that's it. Thanks," said Dennis.

Dennis and Nelly ate the egg rolls and chicken fingers and finished their drinks. Dolores brought them the check, which totaled $28. Dennis paid with his travel card and tipped Dolores 18 percent, the maximum allowed per the company travel policy. As they got up to leave, he reached in his pocket and left a $10 bill on the table. He thought to himself, I'm sure she needs the money.

They got to the gate just as the plane was starting to board. As they walked onto the plane, Dennis wondered why they always put the seat numbers in a place that looks like it could be the row number for one of two rows. To him it was always a bit confusing. Maybe that's how the divisions felt about the new processes and what they were supposed to do. The communication could be a bit confusing at times. Dennis knew that he and Nelly had to do a great job of communicating the purpose of the steering team in order for this concept to be accepted. The next couple of days were going to be fun.

# CHAPTER 15

# DINNER AND A MEETING

Dennis and Nelly arrived in Reno on time and without any complications, other than the rental car agency didn't have the car they reserved, so they had to wait for one to arrive. Unfortunately, the replacement didn't have the navigation system they had requested, so they would be forced to read maps.

"I'm not very good at this," said Nelly, trying to read the map while Dennis drove.

"Yeah, well, I'm not either, but I know how to drive so you're the navigator; that way if we get lost I can blame you," he said, laughing.

"Well, that's okay, I guess, because if we get in a wreck I can blame you, and that's worse than getting lost," she replied.

Fortunately for Dennis and Nelly, the hotel was only about 20 minutes from the airport. With Dennis driving and Nelly navigating, they were happy to make it to the hotel in 40 minutes. They made plans that night to meet Oscar and Scott, the SAP Finance (FI) team lead, for dinner so they could make sure they were all on the same page when they went to the meeting on Tuesday. According to Oscar, there was a steakhouse within walking distance of the hotel where everyone was staying. They all agreed to meet in the lobby of the hotel at 7:30.

"Oscar, nice to see you again," Dennis said, shaking Oscar's hand and patting him on the back. "I don't think you ever met Nelly in person." After everyone was introduced, Dennis said, "So where is this place? I'm hungry. You know they don't serve anything on the planes anymore."

"It's right down the street," said Oscar. "Let's go, it won't even take five minutes."

They walked down the street exchanging small talk about their families. When they entered the restaurant, Dennis could feel his jaws start to ache, he was so hungry. He loved the ambiance of steakhouses. The place was almost entirely lit by candles that were on the tables, hanging on the walls, and in chandeliers. The room was as cozy as a wool blanket on a cold winter night. There were more wine bottles than Dennis had ever seen. This was definitely his kind of place—conducive to good conversation and a feeling of wanting to never leave. He certainly would not mind picking up the tab for this dinner. They all ordered steak, but before they got to that they had a couple of appetizers and a bottle of Chianti.

"So, Oscar, you are pretty much with us on this steering team concept that Donna and I talked to you about a few weeks ago?" he began.

"Sure, it makes all the sense in the world to get everyone on the same page, have them involved in the process of determining what we work on, and setting the two- and three-year strategy for that process. The only thing I'm concerned about is we're going down this path after we've already implemented El Paso. I mean, they're pretty happy with what we did for them, but then again, Kathy is a pretty forward-thinking controller. But now that we're working with the western states, they want some things done differently, and we're going to have to make some decisions," Oscar said.

"I agree, it is a concern, but for me the biggest concern is the fact that they are adamant about processes that are not really business critical," Dennis said. For example, the demand check process; they shouldn't have the ability to cut their own checks, nor should they need the ability."

"Yeah, I agree with Dennis," said Nelly. "We have a process in place that could get money to a vendor the same day if necessary."

"You mean a wire?" asked Scott.

"Yeah, a wire," Nelly replied.

"But we don't want to be doing wires all the time. They're very costly," said Scott.

"Of course they are; we're not suggesting that we do wires in place of every demand check," Nelly said. "What we are saying is that there should never be the need to do a demand check in the division. We have ACH capability, which means that anyone could get the money the next day if they provide us with their bank account information. This, by the way, is a good way to drive up the vendor participation in ACH. If they need a payment that quickly, then we give them a way to get it the next day. The real win is that going forward, every payment they receive will be an ACH payment, which as you know is much more efficient and cost effective than sending a manual check."

"It's not logical to make the argument that they need the ability to cut a demand check at the local level when we have a mechanism in place to get the vendor the money the next day or in dire situations we could get them paid the same day via wire," Dennis added.

"Well, they must think its business critical if they're asking for it, right?" Oscar said.

"To be honest, I don't think it has anything to do with that logic," Dennis explained. "Essentially I think it's a question of losing control. They've always been able to cut checks locally, and if someone needed something right away, they could simply cut it. To me, that's the root of the argument. I understand they might not feel confident in our ability to deliver as timely as they might think they need something, but they have to give us a chance. We really need to solicit the help of Kathy from El Paso so she can put their fears to rest."

"Actually, I don't think they've asked for too many demand checks, if any," Nelly said.

"What time does Kathy get in?" asked Oscar.

"She's supposed to be here tomorrow afternoon, so if she comes to the office, we can talk to her there. If not, I have her cell phone number, so I'll give her a call to ask for her help," Dennis replied.

"Let me ask this," Scott said. "Why is the demand check process worth all of this? It probably doesn't happen that much anyway."

"It's not about the demand checks. It's about the fact that, as a company, we have to decide what type of processes we are going to use and we have to be consistent. Inconsistency leads to inefficiency. It's as simple as that," Dennis explained. "This is only one example of a process that could be different across divisions, and this is a very generic one. Every company in the world has to pay someone at some time, so we're not reinventing the wheel here. If we can't get consistency on something this simple, we won't have much of a chance with the more complex processes. The mistake that we made is we should've put these steering teams in place *prior* to any implementation. Then we could've gotten everyone to agree before the fact."

"We did go over the processes with everyone," said Oscar.

"But not in enough detail," Dennis replied. "We covered most of the process but at too high of a level. For example, we said we were going to pay all bills out of the Shared Services center. We should have said 100 percent, no exceptions. In other words, put the argument out there immediately by saying that under no circumstances will you have the ability to circumvent the system. This would have bubbled the issues to the top of the pot."

"Speaking of bubbling," said Nelly, "the waiter is bringing your soup right now."

"Good, because I'm tired of talking. I'll call Kathy tomorrow, but are we all in agreement that we aren't going to bend on changing processes that were implemented for El Paso, right?" he asked.

"Yeah, we are with you," said Oscar.

"Cool, let's eat."

Everyone enjoyed their meal. Dennis was glad Oscar had chosen a restaurant across from the hotel because they were able to relax, have a few glasses of wine, and have a very open conversation about many issues. He definitely felt that they bonded and were all in agreement that they should stick with the current processes. He was also sure they would need the cohesion, because the divisions could be very tough and were not likely to back down.

On Monday Kathy decided not to come into the SAP implementation offices since her flight was delayed due to weather. She went straight to

EXHIBIT 15.1 *SAP Enhancement Process Flow*

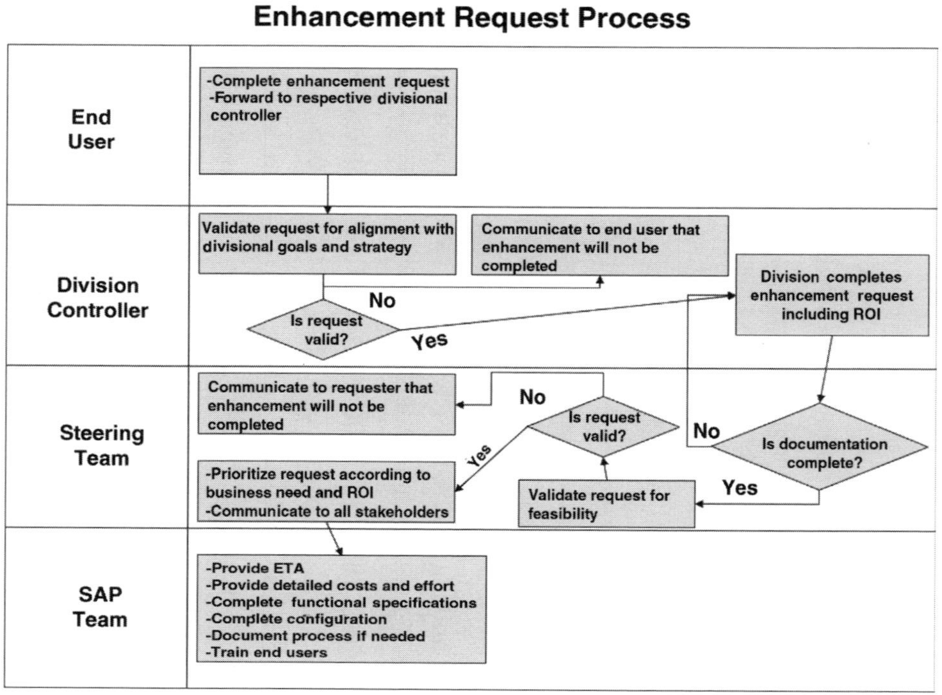

# Enhancement Request Process

| | |
|---|---|
| **End User** | -Complete enhancement request<br>-Forward to respective divisional controller |
| **Division Controller** | Validate request for alignment with divisional goals and strategy<br><br>Is request valid? — No → Communicate to end user that enhancement will not be completed<br>Yes → Division completes enhancement request including ROI |
| **Steering Team** | Communicate to requester that enhancement will not be completed<br>-Prioritize request according to business need and ROI<br>-Communicate to all stakeholders<br>Is request valid? / Validate request for feasibility<br>Is documentation complete? |
| **SAP Team** | -Provide ETA<br>-Provide detailed costs and effort<br>-Complete functional specifications<br>-Complete configuration<br>-Document process if needed<br>-Train end users |

the hotel. Dennis was able to get in touch with her, and she was very happy to provide support to Dennis, Oscar, and their teams. While Kathy had a few issues with the services she was getting, in her mind they were fairly minor and somewhat expected as everyone got used to the new processes and each other. Most of Monday, Nelly and Dennis sat with members of the SAP team as they finished some last-minute configurations and data loads. They helped with auditing some data and running tests in the Quality Assurance environment. This provided a good opportunity for them to bond with the SAP team.

Tuesday morning the meeting started promptly at 8:30. Everyone was on time and seemed eager to get started. Dennis and Nelly welcomed everyone and thanked them for participating. They spent the first part of the morning introducing people and explaining the purpose of the team. This had been covered via conference call when the team had first been formed, but this was the first opportunity to discuss things face to face. Everyone seemed genuinely excited to be involved in the decision-making process and very accepting of the enhancement process and the general purpose of the team. (See Exhibit 15.1.)

As Dennis assumed, the question about current processes that would not work for future implementations did eventually arise. The demand check process was the first example given. Kathy did an excellent job of selling the team on the current process, but some members still fundamentally did not agree with all of the processes they were being given. The discussion went on for the rest of the meeting. In a compromise, Dennis agreed to revisit any process that the western division did not feel was working after 90 days. The processes would be brought up to the steering team just like a new enhancement. Eventually everyone agreed that that approach would work. Dennis was very pleased that at least for now the processes would be the same. He also knew that once a process was established, it could be very difficult to change. He considered the meeting a complete victory for everyone.

# CHAPTER 16

# MEASURE, MEASURE, MEASURE

The western division's implementation went live as planned on March 1. It was now the middle of September. For the most part, the Shared Services center was processing transactions to the satisfaction of the divisions. The entire Shared Services center now employed 44 people. Dennis was fairly happy with the results, which he largely judged as how the center was performing in relation to the business case return on investment (ROI) and the budgets. His teams were under budget, and the divisions had been able to reduce their headcount and expenses as planned. Obviously he could compare the expenses of the center to the budget monthly, and based on the budget he could project the ROI. The ROI was based on the savings that would be realized in the divisions mainly by headcount reduction. The divisions had significantly reduced headcount, and therefore the ROI was being met.

While these numbers were satisfying, it was very difficult for Dennis to see if the center was improving. He needed to figure out a way to measure if every team and ultimately each person was performing satisfactorily. He'd been thinking about this since the center had taken on the western division. Everyone was working hard and things seemed to be getting done, but how did they really know? He would save those thoughts for tomorrow; tonight he was eating with the family.

Jennifer decided to cook instead of having Dennis grill. He had been working a lot of hours since the western implementation, and she wanted him to spend time with the kids. When he got home, Samantha, Jackie, and Danny were already in the pool playing Marco Polo. Shorty was running around barking as if he wanted to play. The kids didn't hear Dennis come in or see him, so he decided to surprise them with a cannonball into the deep end. Unfortunately for Shorty, he happened to be at the wrong end of the pool and ended up looking like a wet rat. He got Dennis back by shaking the water off in his face as he emerged from the deep end. Dennis and the kids continued to play while Jennifer fixed dinner.

"Time to come in and eat," Jennifer yelled.

Like a kid, Dennis knew she was hedging a bit on the time, so they all stayed in the pool about 10 minutes longer. They decided to eat outside rather than have to change out of their bathing suits. Jennifer fixed sloppy joes and macaroni and cheese, which was one of the kids' favorite meals.

"Dad, I got an A on my spelling test today," said Samantha.

"Very good. How many words did you have to spell?"

"Twenty, and I got 19 right," she replied.

"Great," Jennifer said.

"Yeah, so how do you like your new teacher?" asked Dennis.

"I like her a lot. She's an old lady that everyone told me was very mean but she's really, really nice. She told us at the beginning of the year that everyone that said she was mean was right. We were scared for the first couple of days, but then we found out she was just teasing us. She told me today that if I study every time like I did for this test, I'll get an A in spelling. She makes me feel smart. That's why I really like her." Samantha grinned.

"How does she make you feel smart?" Jennifer asked.

"She tells us that learning is simple, and she shows us how we're doing every day," Samantha replied. "We get graded on something every day so we know if we are doing well. I'm pretty sure I'm going to get all A's this year."

Dennis was glad his daughter was happy in school. It was a change; she hadn't liked her teacher last year. He hoped she would be this happy all year.

Sara and Jerry had set up a meeting with Dennis to discuss performance measures. Dennis thought the discussion he had with Samantha last night might relate to the conversation he was going to have at work. He spent the rest of the morning going over the budgets and reviewing the progress reports that Oscar sent monthly about the next implementation, which was for the midwestern and southern divisions.

When Sara and Jerry came to Dennis's office, Dennis asked: "How was lunch?"

"Very good. We went to the Cuban place down the street," Sara answered.

"Thanks for inviting me," he replied wryly.

"Hey, we looked for you and you weren't here," Jerry said.

"I have a cell phone, you know," Dennis said. "Not to worry though. I still taste the sloppy joes I ate last night."

"Yuck," said Sara. "How do you eat those things?"

"My kids like them and actually so do I, just not the second time."

"All right, enough of that. I'm starting to get nauseous," said Jerry.

"Okay, we can talk about how we're going to measure our success. You know, I've been thinking about this. What plan did you guys come up with?" Dennis said.

"Well, essentially we figure we should measure just about everything we do, and obviously we also need to establish some targets. We should establish individual targets and team targets and hold everyone to them," Sara explained.

"When you say measure everything, what do you mean by *everything*?" Dennis asked.

"Well, for example, in Accounts Payable, we should measure the number of invoices processed by person and by the team. We should measure the number of reversals, the number of checks, phone calls, email inquiries, overtime hours, sick days, number of days needed to post an invoice, dollar amount of invoices posted, and everything like that. Essentially there shouldn't be anything we don't look at and measure," Jerry said.

"What do you compare those metrics to?"

"The goals that we establish," said Sara.

"How do you establish the goals?"

"We are going to have to go back to when we started and look at the history. This will give us a baseline to start with, and then we can see if we've improved over time or try to find what we need to do to improve," Sara explained.

"Do you have any idea of the level of effort that will be needed to do this?" asked Dennis.

"It will be significant," said Jerry.

"Who is going to do it?"

"We thought we would assign someone from each of the teams to complete this task," answered Sara. "The reason for that is the person should know something about the subject matter and department if they are going to report on what is being done."

"So do you have a list of everything that you want to measure, by team?" Dennis asked.

"Yeah, here's the list." Jerry handed Dennis the list.

"We're going to measure all of this both individually and as a team every month?"

"Right. And we'll post the results graphically in each department so they can see how they're doing," Sara said.

"Are we sure we want to post individual results publicly?" asked Dennis.

"Why not?" asked Jerry.

"I'm a little concerned that some of the results could be misleading."

"How so?" asked Sara.

"Take Accounts Payable, for example," Dennis explained. "We have some invoices that are very complex and contain a lot of line items and a lot of different coding. Processing those types of invoices takes up a lot of time; the people who process them probably won't process as many invoices as someone else. But the work they are doing is just as important. The point I'm trying to make is you don't want to post a measurement about individuals that doesn't tell the whole story. If one complicated invoice takes 30 minutes to key, people might be reluctant to process it because it will make their numbers look bad. But you need someone to jump on that grenade, so to speak. Measuring individually might discourage someone from doing so. I'm a big believer in posting measures that are completely attributable to the team."

"I hear what you're saying, but doesn't that hide the poor performers?" Sara asked.

"Publicly it does, but they should know that we look at the individual numbers, we just don't post them for everyone to see. We can manage that from the team lead level," Dennis said.

"I'm not totally sure I agree with that," Sara replied.

"I tend to agree with Sara," Jerry said.

"Well, if you can figure out a way to tell the entire story and still post publicly, I might change my mind, but I'm afraid that people will focus almost exclusively on their own individual productivity rather than team productivity. It will create a selfish environment. You know, in the world of professional basketball, they don't give incentive bonuses based on individual scoring because it doesn't necessarily lead to more wins and it would stifle teamwork."

"Well, we're not talking about bonus money here, we're just talking about reporting," said Sara.

"Well, we should be talking about bonuses because I believe we should have some type of bonus plan for all of our employees. And I'm talking about something different than the $500 we give them at the end of the year as a Christmas bonus," Dennis replied.

"So you're saying that every employee should receive some type of performance bonus?" Jerry asked.

"Absolutely, but the bonus would be based on team results, not on individual results."

"Would it be just for their team or for the entire Shared Services center?" asked Sara.

"It should probably be for their team. So in other words, if the team met 75 percent of their objectives, then they would receive 75 percent of their potential bonus. Today we have employees who get paid a

$500 bonus at the end of the year regardless of the type of year we have. That, in my mind, is simply entitlement money. But if we were to put in an incentive program that had a potential of 5 percent of their annual salary, a $30,000-per-year employee would have a potential of $1,500. If they achieved 75 percent of their goals, then they would get $1,125. For them that's better than the $500 they get as entitlement money today, and we get them to focus on the productivity goals. In the long run we'll be much more efficient, and the employees will get a bigger bonus. We can also set the targets so that anything paid above 75 percent is a stretch goal that will result in significant savings."

"So let's take, for example, the transactions per employee metric for Accounts Payable," Jerry said. "What you're saying is we should take the average of that for the entire team and the bonus would be paid on that, if it was the only metric, which it is not but just for argument's sake. Is that what you're saying?"

"Right, that's it," Dennis replied.

"How does that reward the outstanding individual performer?" asked Sara.

"It doesn't. But why would you want to reward the outstanding individual performer? Can that person do it by him- or herself?" Dennis retorted.

"Of course not, but I think it'll be discouraging for someone who works so hard and does so well to know that people who don't perform as well are getting paid the same amount," said Sara.

"But tell me, how are you going to objectively determine who those people are?"

"By the results; it's black and white," Sara said.

"No, it's not. As I mentioned earlier, what if someone is cherry-picking invoices and doing 300 easy ones per day? How are you going to determine that? What about someone who only worries about doing their own work and isn't willing to help others or teach someone new what they know? There are too many scenarios to list, but there are a lot of ways to look good as an individual even when the team isn't succeeding. The ultimate goal is the team wins or loses, not the individual," Dennis answered.

Jerry and Sara looked at each other not saying a word. Finally Jerry spoke.

"Well, maybe that's right, but we still need to have a way to reward the individual performer."

"That's what performance reviews are for. We evaluate our employees on all of the attributes that make them successful and good team players, and then we base our merit increases on that evaluation," Dennis replied.

"But there isn't much of a difference in the increases we give," Sara said.

"Well, how much of a difference were you expecting to give in bonuses? Most likely it's going to be around the same amount," Dennis said. "Last night I was talking to my daughter, and she was saying how her teacher made learning easy for her. We're trying to do the same thing, but we're doing it as a team. School is a very individual thing, but we're talking about getting work done here that cannot be done by one or even a few individuals. It is so much work that it must be done by more than 40 people. The divisions, our customers, don't care about individual results; they're only worried about how we perform as a team."

"I agree, we need a team effort, but I still worry about the individuals," said Jerry.

"I think one thing you'll see is the poorer performers will feel peer pressure from the higher performers and will do better just because of that," Dennis replied.

"You don't think it'll be the other way around?" Jerry asked.

"No, because I believe that high performers will always be high performers, and they don't worry about what others are doing. They want to do well no matter what, and they're not easily influenced by negative peer pressure. It's what I like to call the Michael Jordan effect. Every teammate he ever had worked harder, tried harder, and performed better because they were trying to keep up with him. He led by example, and that's what we need our high performers to do. We can reward them come evaluation time, and we can also point out those who do well in certain situations or by giving them an employee of the quarter award or something like that. But overall, we need to evaluate our results and pay our bonuses based on the results of the team. I fundamentally believe that."

"You're not going to bend on this one, are you?" Jerry asked.

"No, because I believe in it very strongly," Dennis replied.

"Okay, how about if we do this?" Sara said. "Let's take all of the metrics we've listed and tie some goals to them and also calculate potential bonuses based on the current salaries. We'll come back by the end of the week with a proposal for the bonus structure and the final metrics. Sound good? You have the entire list, so if you have any suggestions or see something you don't understand or you think we should add, just let us know."

With that, Jerry and Sara went back to work on their metrics and bonus proposal. Dennis was looking forward to the outcome.

# CHAPTER 17

# BONUS TIME

Dennis walked into the conference room about five minutes before Jerry and Sara were going to present their latest metrics and bonus plan. He had agreed to all of the metrics that were listed on the document they had given him in the last meeting. When starting a bonus plan tied to metrics, he believed it was always best to start with a few simple measures rather than being too complicated up front. The analogy he liked to use was like going to the doctor. When you walk into a doctor's office, they don't take a scalpel and cut you open to find out what is wrong. They weigh you, take your temperature and pulse, and listen to your heart and lungs. In other words, they check your vital signs. In the initial stages of implementing a Shared Services center, it's important to have metrics that are in essence vital signs. Jerry and Sara had done a good job identifying the vital signs at this early stage of the Shared Services implementation.

"We wanted to meet in here," Sara said as she and Jerry entered the conference room, "so we could show you on the screen what we're doing and then if you have any changes we can make them on the fly."

"Sounds good," replied Dennis.

"This should take just a second to hook up," Jerry said as he connected the small projector to his laptop.

"Are you going to plug in your laptop, or do you have enough battery?" Sara asked.

"I should be okay with the battery," he replied as he finished connecting the projector to the laptop.

"Is there anything we can do about the resolution? It looks horrible," Dennis asked.

"You need to change the settings on your laptop to 1280 by 768," Sara told Jerry.

"That looks a little bit better. Maybe I should sit closer," Dennis said.

"Yeah, it's probably your age, not the resolution." Jerry laughed.

"Okay, so we agreed on the metrics you presented last time. What you're going to show me here is the graphics and how it ties into the bonus plan, correct?" Dennis asked.

"Right, and we're going to show you the graphs for the Accounts Payable team. The graphs will be similar for the other teams. Let's start with the production efficiency graph," said Jerry. (See Exhibit 17.1.)

"The columns represent the total number of invoices processed by the team for that particular month," Jerry explained. The asterisk line represents the invoices processed goal. Obviously we can make that anything we want. The diamond line represents the overtime goals in number of overtime hours. The square line represents actual overtime. The beauty of this graph is that you can see the production efficiency very quickly, hence the name. If the asterisk line is in the column and the square line is under the diamond line, then everything is fine because that means the team met its productivity goal and its overtime goal. And obviously that means productivity is good and the variable cost of overtime is within budget."

"So the overtime goal is based on hours?" Dennis asked.

"Yes. What we did is take the average hourly wage on the team and calculate the average overtime wage and then calculate the maximum number of hours that would still keep us under budget by 5 percent. That gives us a little hedge, but it also assumes the overtime will be distributed evenly among the team. But as I said, we can make that number anything we like," Jerry explained.

"Okay, that makes sense."

"So the production efficiency graph will be the same for Accounts Payable, Accounts Receivable, and Document Management since those are very transaction-driven departments," said Sara.

EXHIBIT 17.1 *Production Efficiency: Accounts Payable*

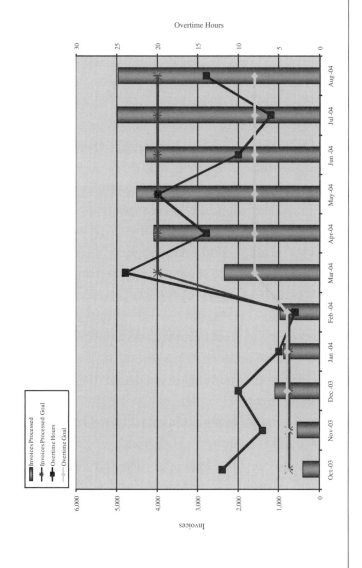

"Okay, I like the metric, but how do you apply a bonus to this particular metric?" Dennis asked.

"Well, you really have to take the entire metric into account when you talk about the bonus, but in this case, let's just say this was the only metric. Since productivity is probably more important than overtime, you could make the productivity worth 75 percent of the bonus and overtime 25 percent of the bonus. Then for every month or every quarter, you can determine if the team made the goal. In the case of Accounts Payable and the graph we're looking at, February and July would be the only months the team made both productivity and overtime. If you look overall, the months the team made the productivity goal are December, January, February, April, May, June, July, and August. The team made the overtime goal in February and July. Does that make sense?" Jerry asked.

"Yeah. So I assume once we look at all of the metrics for a department, we'll determine the percentage that each metric applies to the bonus," Dennis replied. "How often do we pay the bonuses? And what is the potential bonus amount for each employee?"

"I think it will make more sense for us to go through each metric. Then we can talk specifically about the bonuses because once we understand what the metric is about, we can better determine how much of the bonus it should affect," said Sara.

"Sounds good, let's keep going."

"Okay. The electronic invoicing graph is very important because without automation of our work, we'll never become volume insensitive, as you always like to say, Dennis." (See Exhibit 17.2.)

"In this graph, the dark part of the bar represents the number of electronic invoices that would include either EDI (electronic data interchange) or ERS (evaluated receipts settlement) transactions. The light part is the number of manual invoices. By manual, we mean anything that someone has to key. The asterisk line represents the percentage goal we're trying to achieve, and the diamond line represents the actual percentage of electronic transactions," Sara explained.

EXHIBIT 17.2  *Electronic Processing*

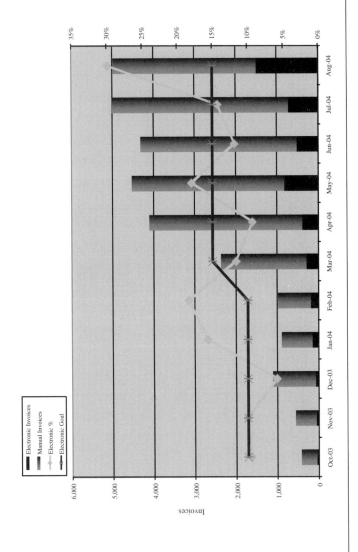

"I know we said we're not going to talk about the bonus, but just one question: Are we going to base the bonus on the number of transactions or on the percentage?" Dennis asked.

"It will be based on the percentage of electronic transactions," Jerry replied.

"How can the team affect the number of electronic transactions? I mean, in particular, the person who is processing the invoice?" Dennis wanted to know.

"On an everyday basis they probably don't much, but remember, everything we're doing is about the team. So they should try to identify those transactions that could be electronic and then they can have either Nelly or a more senior person work with the vendor to convert to electronic invoicing," Sara replied.

"That's exactly the answer I was looking for. This is definitely all about the team, and automation is going to be key to our success. It's funny, you know, I was at a Shared Services conference the other day. Some companies were talking about outsourcing to other countries and the differences in the labor costs and how that has helped to lower their costs significantly. But a few companies were experiencing problems because the countries they outsourced to, particularly India, were experiencing wage inflation at a greater rate than expected, and that was blowing the outsourcing return on investment. They're already experiencing much higher than expected costs, and they've been there less than three years," Dennis said.

"So what's everyone doing in those situations?" asked Sara.

"Some of them are thinking about moving again, but I mentioned that I don't believe that chasing cheaper labor is ever the answer," Dennis replied. "Just like us putting our center in Tampa versus Des Moines. The true answer is not in the cost of the labor but the automation or elimination of transactions. When you chase cheap labor, you are dependent on the labor staying cheap, plus I do believe that in many cases you get what you pay for. When you automate or eliminate, in virtually every case you automate or eliminate forever."

"That's true, but I guess some would say you could also automate, eliminate, and chase cheap labor," Jerry said.

"True, you can do all of that, but you know I prefer to concentrate on a few very important fundamentals and not do too many things at once. I think first you have to do everything you can to make the process as efficient and automated as possible. Then, if you still need cost reduction, you can evaluate lower-cost labor. And besides that, you should certainly never outsource a broken process. I know some people believe that an outsourcer can correct the problem, but I haven't seen too many examples of outsourcers correcting broken business processes. If the company can't fix the problem internally, an outsourcer will have an even tougher time doing it," Dennis said. "We got a little off track there. Back to automation. What about purchasing card transactions—will they be reflected on this graph?"

"They are not now, but I guess they certainly could be," Jerry replied.

"I agree they could be, but I don't think they should be reflected here," said Sara.

"Why is that?" Jerry asked.

"I think here you're trying to represent automation of an invoicing process, and the purchasing card is really automation of the payment process or elimination of the invoice altogether. I think if you were to include purchasing card transactions, you'd be mixing the initiatives a bit. I don't disagree that maybe it should be one of our measures, and it should possibly be considered in the bonus calculation, but we should show it separately," she explained.

"That makes sense to me," Dennis said. "Okay, so we've beat this one up a bit, but let me ask this real quick: How do you determine the goal? It seems a bit tough to determine, especially in the beginning."

"You're right," Sara answered. "In the beginning it can be a bit tough, so we just based the goal on where we are today and then where we want to be. If we didn't know anything and were just taking a guess like when we went live with El Paso, I think it would be hard to bonus someone on a goal that we're just taking a wild guess at. Now, however, we know where we are, and the goal is really driven by where we'd like to be."

"And how do you determine where we want to be?" asked Dennis.

"The thought for the goals really is how many transactions are processed by the average person, and our goal tiers should at least be what one full-time equivalent can process. In some cases it will be many more than that, like for instance, how many three full-time equivalents can process, but if we reach those goals and experience growth, we can remain headcount neutral or become volume insensitive, at least for that many transactions," said Sara.

"So the goals will be at least what one FTE can process?" asked Dennis.

"Right."

"Makes sense."

"The next graph is pretty much the same except it is electronic payments instead of electronic invoices," Jerry explained. (See Exhibit 17.3.)

"If we were going to put purchasing card transactions anywhere, it would be here, but again, I think it's best to put them on a separate graph," Sara said. "Anyway, the same applies here. The dark part of the column represents manual payments and the light part of the column is electronic payments."

"The next graph is reversal percentage." (See Exhibit 17.4.)

"Essentially this is a quality metric," Sara explained. "If we have to reverse a transaction, that means something somewhere went wrong. It might not necessarily be something that our team did, but regardless, an invoice needed to be reversed. If we see this metric trending in the wrong direction, obviously we can dig deeper to get to the root cause of the problem. The goal that we have set is like the others in that it is based on the historical data since we have been live in El Paso. Any questions with that one?"

"No, it's fairly self-explanatory," Dennis said.

"Okay, finally, here is the one the divisions will pay particular attention to—the cost-per-transaction graph," Jerry said. (See Exhibit 17.5.) "The components of this measure are the total cost of the team for a particular month, which obviously includes every expense charged to the team during any particular month. The transactions are the number of

EXHIBIT 17.3   *Electronic Payments*

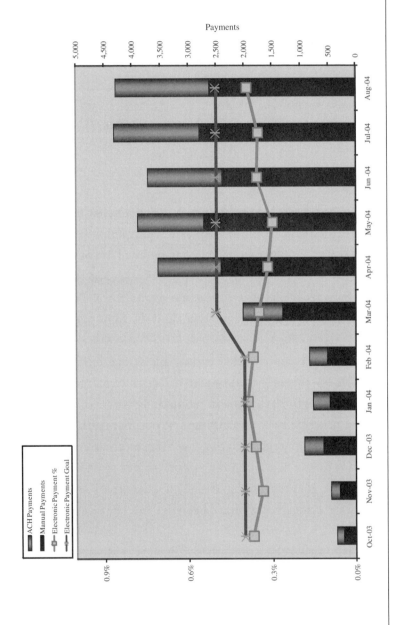

124

EXHIBIT 17.4 *Invoice Reversal Percentage*

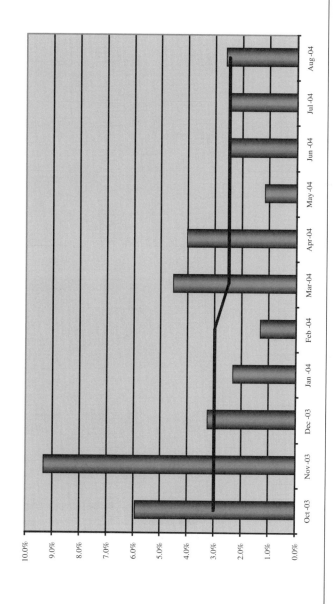

EXHIBIT 17.5  *Cost Per Transaction*

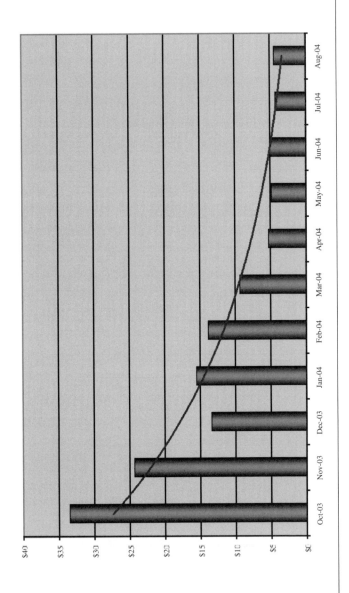

invoices processed. That's an important distinction to point out because SAP has many transaction codes, but this doesn't include every transaction code processed by the team. For example, all invoices are included but payments are not. By that I mean, if we pay an invoice, it requires someone to process a payment as well as process the invoice, but it only counts as one transaction. So keying the invoice and then running the payment job doesn't equal two transactions. Do you understand the difference?"

"Yeah, that makes perfect sense," replied Dennis.

"As you can see," Sara said, "we've been trending in the right direction since go-live, which I assume is typical, because it obviously takes money to start a center and when you initially staff up, you aren't processing that many transactions so the cost per transaction looks very high."

"That's typical, and it does make sense," Dennis said. "The thing we have to be very careful with is when we show this cost, some people, especially in the divisions or Corporate, will want to benchmark it against other companies or outsourcers. The problem is, people will argue that the processing can be done cheaper by someone else if they're unhappy with our service or our costs. I don't have a problem with benchmarking, but it's imperative that we determine what is included in our costs versus what is included in the costs we're comparing ourselves to. Sometimes it can be very difficult to compare apples to apples. So in our case, this is a fully loaded Accounts Payable cost as far as the team goes, but some companies will include the cost of SAP licenses, maintenance, and other types of things in their costs. If that were the case, it would make their cost per transaction higher, but I just wanted to give you an example of how we need to be careful. Okay, so those are the metrics you want to include for the Accounts Payable team, and we want to be able to pay a bonus based on the results. How much weight should each metric carry?"

"Jerry and I talked about that and came up with the following weights," Sara explained. "Productivity should count 30 percent, overtime 10 percent, electronic invoicing 15 percent, electronic payments 15 percent, reversal percentage 5 percent, and cost per transaction 25 percent. The reasons for that are that productivity is really the most important thing we do in that we have to deliver what we promised. Cost is a very big factor as well, and we have two elements there: cost per transaction at 25 percent and overtime at 10 percent. The electronic (payments and invoices) portion of the bonus should be the same since both lead to efficiency that will ultimately drive down cost. Finally, reversal is a quality measure that is important, but if our reversals were really high, we'd see it in our costs and overtime because people would have to work additional hours to make up for the lack of quality. In most cases, if you have to reverse something, you generally have to reprocess it, which leads to more work and overtime. We can always adjust the percentages if we need to after each quarter."

## CHAPTER 18

# PAY UP

Driving to work, Dennis noticed how light the traffic was for a Monday. Then he remembered that school was not in session because of parent-teacher conferences. The traffic would be tolerable for a week since Thanksgiving was three days away, and most snowbirds hadn't returned to Florida yet. Andrew was coming home tomorrow, and Dennis was looking forward to seeing his son. Dennis couldn't believe that Andrew was almost done with the first semester of his sophomore year. Time was moving much faster than Dennis liked, but that's what happens when you get older. At least that's what they say, Dennis thought. Then he wondered, who are they?

Dennis had spent the last three weeks working on the budget for 2007. He attended more meetings in those three weeks than he had in the last three months. The divisions were working on their budgets as well, and a common theme that kept surfacing was they were not very happy with the cost allocation they were receiving from the Shared Services center. Dennis had another meeting this morning with John and Donna to discuss this very topic.

"Dennis, how are you doing?" asked Terri, John's assistant. "I haven't seen you in a while."

"I'm doing well, but I'll be doing a lot better when we get this budget finalized. How're you doing?" he asked.

"Great. I've been getting ready for Thanksgiving. We rotate whose house we go to every year, and this year it's my turn. I enjoy doing it but it's a lot of work," she replied.

"Yeah, I still can't believe it's Thanksgiving already. I'm ready to see Andrew, and I'm looking forward to watching football and eating way too much food." Dennis grinned.

"Sounds like fun. John's running a few minutes late, but go in and have a seat. He'll be here in a minute."

Dennis sat down in John's office and scrolled through his emails on his BlackBerry. He noticed one from the California controller titled "Allocations." What perfect timing, he thought.

"Dennis, sorry we're late. How are you?" John asked as he and Donna entered and sat down.

"Did you see that email from California?" Donna asked.

"Yeah, I was just looking at it. Perfect timing, huh?"

"Definitely," she said.

"Well, it's obvious they don't like the allocation process, so the question is, what're we going to do to change that?" John asked.

"First we have to determine what they don't like about it," Donna said.

"That's a good point. There are many reasons they might mention in their emails or calls as to why they don't like it, but I think they don't like it for two simple reasons. One, they think it simply costs too much and they could do it cheaper themselves, and two, it affects management's bonus. In their minds, the allocation takes money out of their pockets, and for obvious reasons they don't like that," said Dennis.

"That's true, it does take money out of their pockets, but the services you perform for the divisions are part of doing business," John stated. "If Shared Services didn't do it for them, they'd have to do it themselves or pay someone else to do it, and I seriously doubt if they could get it cheaper."

"Part of the reason might also be that they don't have a choice," Donna added.

"Well, I personally told every general manager that Shared Services was mandated for at least three years after go-live," John reminded them.

"Then if they felt they could do it more effectively or outsource it, they could put together a business case and try to prove it. I know that if our Shared Services center runs the way it should, they won't be able to make that case. But if we are less than effective at Shared Services, we have an obligation to look at other alternatives. I think three years is a reasonable time frame to determine if this is going to add the value we think it is."

"I agree, but to be quite honest, they're worried about what it's going to cost them in the short term. Some of them are probably planning to retire within five years, so if they have money taken out of their pockets for three of those years, that won't sit too well with them," Dennis replied.

"But we're not taking money out of their pockets!" Donna exclaimed. "If they were doing it themselves, it would actually cost more. To me the real issue is that they're absorbing a cost they can't control and don't fully understand. I can see why that would bother them. And obviously, since it's budget time, they're overly concerned about it."

"Dennis, do you have any ideas, about how we might allocate the charges differently?" John asked.

"I have a couple of ideas, but we need to work pretty quickly because they only have a couple more weeks to complete their budgets. Let me do this; give me until the end of the week to come up with a couple of methodologies, and then we can sit down on Monday and discuss them. I think we could put something in place fairly quickly if we are able to agree. It's simply one line item in their financials, so for them it's really easy. The hard part is on our side, but I'll handle that. Does that sound fair?" asked Dennis.

"Works for me," said John.

"Me too," Donna said.

"Okay, I'll see you guys Monday morning," said Dennis.

Dennis spent the rest of the day working on issues other than the allocation. He spent a good part of his time talking to Nelly about the Procure to Payment Process steering team. The divisions were satisfied with the team's progress. The team members had been able to prioritize the existing enhancements, and everyone was following the process of requesting new enhancements. This was allowing Oscar and the SAP

team to concentrate on the remaining rollouts and only work on enhancements that all divisions agreed on. They were still having a few
problems with all of the divisions following the same exact processes,
but Nelly was working on heat charts to show which divisions were
consistent and which ones were continuing to resist the process changes.
Dennis was satisfied with the evolution of the team and was strongly
considering creating a steering team for each process. He was hoping to
be able to get these teams established by the end of January. He'd like to
start the first week of the new year, but with budgets and year-end
activities consuming most people's time, he knew this would be almost
impossible.

Dennis left around 6:00 pm, which was becoming his usual departure
time. Jennifer and the kids were happy he was able to come home at a
decent hour most days. On the way home he called Jennifer.

"Hey, hon, do you want me to pick something up tonight, or are you
planning on fixing something?" he asked.

"Since Thursday is Thanksgiving, I really don't want to cook this week
if I don't have to. If you were going to get something, I was going to either
ask you to grill or pick up something myself."

"I agree completely. How about if I just pick up some pizza?"

"That sounds good. Where are you thinking of going?" Jennifer asked.

"How about the coal-fired pizza place? We haven't had that pizza in a
while, and I know the kids love it."

"Yeah, they love the well-done crust."

"Which is why I don't understand why they don't like my grilled
hamburgers," Dennis replied with a grin.

"A mistakenly burned hamburger is a lot different than an intentionally well-done pizza crust," Jennifer said, laughing.

"Hey, I burn them on purpose. I like the smoke flavor."

"You like the smoke and the fire engine showing up."

"That only happened once, but that's in the past. I'll pick up the pizza.
By the way, do you want me to grill the turkey for Thanksgiving?"

"Only if your parents are coming and not mine!"

"Gotcha. I'll see you in a bit."

Dennis phoned the pizza place and placed the order. He reached the pizza place before it was ready, so he decided to sit at the bar and have a beer while he waited. The TV at the bar was showing the evening news, and they were talking about taxes. What a topic to ruin a good cold beer! Dennis thought.

Dennis and Jennifer didn't have any problems getting the family to come to the dinner table for pizza.

"While I was waiting for the pizza, I saw a segment on the news about preparing your taxes and what you need to do to make sure you're ready once the year is over. Do we have all of our documents in one place?" Dennis asked.

"Of course we do. We always do," Jennifer answered.

"Since we always get a refund, we might as well prepare it as fast as possible, although I hate doing the taxes," Dennis said.

"I'll do it this year," Jennifer told him. "If I remember right, you prepared them last year."

"Thanks for remembering. That's right. I feel better already, except when I think about how much we pay in taxes."

"So guys, what's new?" Dennis asked the kids.

They all had their mouths full with pizza, so they weren't talking much. Dennis looked at Jennifer. "I think we found a new way to keep them quiet," he said, laughing.

"So what's happening at work?" Jennifer asked him.

"I met with John and Donna today, and we were talking about our allocations to the divisions. The divisions are not very happy with the allocations."

"Why aren't they happy, too much money?"

"That's part of it for sure. I also think they don't understand how it's calculated, nor do they understand how much money it takes to run a Shared Services center. They also don't understand all of the services they're getting for what they pay."

"Well, to be honest, I wouldn't be that happy either," Jennifer told him.

"For which reason?" Dennis asked.

"For all of them really, but not understanding exactly what they're getting for their money is the biggest problem. Think about it: You just mentioned that you don't like to think about how much you pay in taxes, and a big part of that is you don't understand where the money goes. If you knew where every one of the dollars you pay in taxes was going, you probably wouldn't have as big of a problem with it as you and everyone else does. Don't you think?"

"That's a pretty good point. So you're saying we should have a detailed list of exactly what they're paying for every service they receive?"

"I think that would definitely help," Jennifer agreed. "You could also send them reports about your progress against budget so that they wouldn't be surprised by anything that might happen in the coming years. Really, the issue seems to me to be communication. If everyone knows what they're paying, why they're paying it, and exactly what they're getting for their money, they probably won't have a huge problem. They still might not like it, but at least they'll understand it."

"Can we talk about something else?" Jackie asked.

"We thought you were too busy eating pizza to talk," Jennifer said with a smile. "What do you want to talk about?"

"Anything but what you're talking about," Jackie answered.

For the rest of the dinner the kids talked about school, Andrew coming home from college, seeing their grandparents, and what they were going to do on Thanksgiving break. Dennis was happy that Jackie changed the subject. He'd have time to think about taxes and allocations for the rest of the week. Tonight was family night.

As he drove to work the next day, Dennis thought about what Jennifer had said. He realized that she was right. He was going to spend the day trying to formulate a new allocation methodology that would provide the type of detail that would eliminate any confusion.

He spent the morning talking to Sara and Jerry about the metrics they were using for the bonus program. Those metrics could easily be the foundation for the transaction data needed for allocation purposes. Sara and Jerry also agreed that eliminating confusion in the allocation would solve many of the problems with the current perception the divisions had of Shared Services. Prior to implementing SAP or Shared Services, Corporate agreed to absorb the cost of all SAP software and implementations as well as the start-up costs of the Shared Services center. At this point, Dennis believed that creating a new calculation was going to be fairly easy; all he needed to do was take the budget of each Shared Services team and prorate that budget to each division based on its transactional activity. Today the allocation was simply prorated to each division based on its own revenue. Since Capp didn't share financial information among divisions, no one knew what other divisions were paying.

If John and Donna agreed to use this type of methodology, there would be no reason not to share the allocation detail with each division. Along with the other changes, this would also help eliminate the confusion and lack of understanding. Dennis was looking forward to completing this task. He had a hard time believing that watching a news story about taxes would lead him to talk to Jennifer about allocations. As much as he hated paying taxes, he was certainly glad he saw that story and even happier Jennifer agreed to do their taxes this year. His week was off to a very good start. Life was good.

# CHAPTER 19

# ALLOCATION TIME

A s usual, Dennis was one of the first to arrive at work. When Shared Services first moved into the building, there had been a discussion about whether they should have assigned parking spaces—if not for everyone, at least for Dennis and his direct reports. Dennis certainly was not in favor of this and was glad they had decided against it. If you showed up early, you got a good parking space; it was that simple. Also, just by looking at the parking lot, Dennis could tell who was showing up and when. He sometimes wondered why the people who parked closest to the door were usually the last cars in the parking lot in the evening and why those who parked in the back were generally the first to leave. Dennis wasn't the type of manager to be bothered by these types of things, but he liked the fact that by looking at the parking lot, he knew who he could truly count on to put in a great effort.

Dennis walked up the stairs to get to his office. Unless it was socially unacceptable to leave the people he was walking with, he always took the stairs rather than the elevator. He didn't get a chance to exercise much, and if nothing else, at least he walked up and down the stairs a few times a day.

When he reached his office, he turned on the light and sat down at his desk, which, as always, was covered with papers. To most people it looked messy, but he always knew where everything was, and besides, he was much more about substance than style. His office was probably not as tastefully decorated as some Shared Services directors and he could be a bit messy, but he didn't have time to worry about those things.

As Dennis turned on his computer and entered his password, he noticed the poster hanging on the wall. It said: You Are Only as Good as Those You Are Surrounded By. That was the fundamental belief in both his personal and professional life. At Capp, he worked with good people; he couldn't have gotten the center up and running without them, he thought with a smile.

Dennis opened the files that Jerry and Sara had sent him regarding the bonus program. He would be able to utilize that information to formulate an allocation methodology. He spent the rest of the morning putting together a worksheet that would allocate the entire Shared Services budget to each division based on the number of transactions performed for that division. (See Exhibit 19.1.)

By the end of the day, Dennis had completed the spreadsheet and was ready to present it to John and Donna. Since they were not meeting until Monday, he'd have a chance to let his thoughts breathe for a while. It also meant he could spend the Wednesday before Thanksgiving managing by walking around.

Andrew decided to surprise his family by showing up Tuesday night rather than Wednesday night. Samantha, Jackie and Danny spent the evening talking and playing games with their big brother. Andrew really seemed to be enjoying himself. Dennis sat back, watching TV and enjoying the loud talking and laughter. He thought about the poster he looked at this morning. He knew he was blessed to be surrounded by so many great people in his professional life, but more importantly in his personal life.

Dennis got up Wednesday morning and was surprised when Andrew got up just a few minutes later.

"I'm fixing some oatmeal, do you want some?" Dennis asked.

"Sure, what kind do we have?"

"Brown sugar and cinnamon."

"Okay, but make mine two packets," Andrew said.

"I should have known one wouldn't be enough." Dennis grinned.

EXHIBIT **19.1**    *Allocation Spreadsheet*

| | Total AP Invoices | Percentage of Total Transactions | Accounts Payable Budget | Total AR Invoices | Percentage of Total Transactions | Accounts Receivable Budget | Total DM Documents | Percentage of Total Transactions | Document Management Budget |
|---|---|---|---|---|---|---|---|---|---|
| | | | 496,446 | | | 384,454 | | | 274,993 |
| AL | – | – | – | – | – | – | – | – | – |
| AR | | – | | | – | | | – | |
| AZ | 5,987 | 14% | 70,216 | 6,422 | 14% | 52,974 | 6,422 | 14% | 37,891 |
| CA | 6,459 | 15% | 75,655 | 7,352 | 16% | 60,646 | 7,352 | 16% | 43,379 |
| CO | 4,231 | 10% | 49,558 | 5,012 | 11% | 41,343 | 5,012 | 11% | 29,572 |
| CT | | – | – | | – | – | | – | – |
| FL | | – | – | | – | – | | – | – |
| GA | | – | – | | – | – | | – | – |
| IL | | – | – | | – | – | | – | – |
| IN | | – | – | | – | – | | – | – |
| KY | | – | – | | – | – | | – | – |
| LA | | – | – | | – | – | | – | – |
| MO | | – | – | | – | – | | – | – |
| MS | | – | – | | – | – | | – | – |
| NC | | – | – | | – | – | | – | – |
| NM | 3,987 | 9% | 46,700 | 4,256 | 9% | 35,107 | 4,256 | 9% | 25,111 |
| NV | 7,254 | 17% | 84,966 | 7,865 | 17% | 64,877 | 7,865 | 17% | 46,405 |
| NY | | – | – | | – | – | | – | – |
| OH | | – | – | | – | – | | – | – |
| PA | | – | – | | – | – | | – | – |
| SC | | – | – | | – | – | | – | – |
| TX | 8,697 | 21% | 101,868 | 9,231 | 20% | 76,145 | 9,231 | 20% | 54,465 |
| WA | 5,769 | 14% | 67,573 | 6,469 | 14% | 53,362 | 6,469 | 14% | 38,169 |
| | **42,384** | **100%** | **496,446** | **46,607** | **100%** | **384,454** | **46,607** | **100%** | **274,993** |

"Two isn't either, I'm just warming up for what Mom will fix. I'm going back to bed as soon as I eat this."

"Lucky dog! I have to go to work today."

"How is everything going at work? We don't get much of a chance to talk about that."

"Everything is pretty good. We have a few issues here and there, but for the most part everything is working okay," replied Dennis.

"So staying in Tampa ended up being a good decision?"

"It was a very good decision. I was looking at a poster I have in my office—the one that says 'You Are Only as Good as Those You Are Surrounded By.' We've been able to hire a lot of good people, so things

| Division Head-count | Percentage of Total Head-count | Benefits Budget | Division Head-count | Percentage of Total Headcount | Payroll Budget | Total Trans-actional Allocation | Total Transac-tional Percen-tage | GL, OH, Mngmt & Admin Budget | Total Allocation |
|---|---|---|---|---|---|---|---|---|---|
|  |  | 302,960 |  |  | 409,848 | 1,868,701 |  | 1,244,842 | 3,113,543 |
| – | – | – | – |  | – | – |  |  | – |
|  |  |  |  | – |  | – |  |  | – |
| 723 | 18% | 54,352 | 723 | 18% | 73,529 | 288,872 | 15% | 192,433 | 481,306 |
| 1,252 | 31% | 94,121 | 1,252 | 31% | 127,327 | 401,127 | 21% | 267,212 | 668,339 |
| 426 | 11% | 32,025 | 426 | 11% | 43,324 | 195,822 | 10% | 130,448 | 326,270 |
|  |  | – |  |  | – | – |  |  | – |
|  |  |  |  | – |  | – |  |  | – |
|  |  |  |  |  |  | – |  |  | – |
|  |  |  |  |  |  | – |  |  | – |
|  |  |  |  |  |  | – |  |  | – |
|  |  |  |  |  |  | – |  |  | – |
|  |  |  |  |  |  | – |  |  | – |
|  |  |  |  | – |  | – |  |  | – |
| 426 | 11% | 32,025 | 426 | 11% | 43,324 | 182,267 | 10% | 121,418 | 303,686 |
| 568 | 14% | 42,700 | 568 | 14% | 57,765 | 296,714 | 16% | 197,657 | 494,372 |
|  |  | – |  |  | – | – |  |  | – |
|  |  |  |  | – |  | – |  |  | – |
|  |  |  |  | – |  | – |  |  | – |
| 323 | 8% | 24,282 | 323 | 8% | 32,849 | 289,610 | 0 | 192,924 | 482,534 |
| 312 | 8% | 23,455 | 312 | 8% | 31,730 | 214,288 | 0 | 142,749 | 357,037 |
| **4,030** | **100%** | **302,960** | **4,030** | **100%** | **409,848** | **1,868,701** | **100%** | **1,244,842** | **3,113,543** |

have worked very well. I'm sure we would have hired good people no matter where we located, but it was a bit easier in Tampa because so many people from headquarters applied. Obviously it's easier to make decisions on known people rather than unknown ones."

"I helped make that decision, you know," Andrew said.

"I know you did. I remember the night we talked about that and compared it to you deciding on a college. Let me ask you the same question: How is everything going at school, and are you happy with your choice?"

"I'm very happy, but like we were saying almost two years ago, you'll make the school and the experience, not the other way around. You can't know the outcome of a decision not made, but you can certainly influence the outcome of decisions that are made. I believe you control your own destiny, and a big part of that is just what you said: You're only as good as those you're surrounded by," replied Andrew.

"I think we both made good decisions, and we'll continue to do well. I remember you mentioned that you didn't think the cost of the center would be that much more in Tampa than in Des Moines. Right now I'm in the middle of developing an allocation that will be acceptable to the divisions. They're not happy with the cost, but I don't think they'd be happy no matter where we put Shared Services or what amount they paid—unless of course it was free." Dennis grinned.

"Well, since it's not free, you better go develop that allocation, and I'm going back to bed," Andrew said.

"Oh, to be young again!"

With that, Dennis grabbed his computer case and headed out the door. Today he arrived at work much later than usual. There were many more cars than normal in the parking lot. Kim from the Accounts Payable team was just getting out of her car when Dennis arrived. She saw him and waited.

"Dennis, how are you?"

"Fantastic. And you?"

"Very well; this is a little late for you, isn't it?"

"Yeah, my son came home from college a day early for Thanksgiving break. He got up when I did and we ate breakfast together," Dennis explained.

"Wow, I'd think the last thing he'd want to do on his break is get up early," Kim said.

"Well, he only got up to get a drink. When he saw me making oatmeal, he had a bowl with me and went right back to bed. How is your son, by the way?"

"He's doing well. He's still playing football, but he can't decide if he wants to play in college. He's gotten a few letters from smaller colleges but nothing official yet. He said he'll decide in the spring if he wants to play or not. Other than that, he's doing very well," Kim said.

"That's good. Tell him to take his time on that decision. Also, tell him I said hi."

As Dennis and Kim headed into the office, they continued to talk about Thanksgiving and their families. Dennis took great pride in knowing about the people he worked with and their families. For Dennis and most other people, their families were the most important part of their life. Dennis hoped everyone knew he was genuinely concerned about the well-being of his employees and their families.

Because Dennis was confident that the allocation methodology he had prepared was the right one, he planned to spend the day walking around and talking to the managers, supervisors, and teams. He always found that he learned a great deal doing this, and the teams seemed to like getting a chance to talk to him. After getting to his office and checking a few emails, his first stop was the payroll area.

"Anna, how is everything going?" Dennis asked the Payroll team lead.

"Pretty good," she replied. "This is a short week, but we have everything balanced and ready to process this morning, so we shouldn't have any problems getting everything done by the end of the day."

"Do you think you'll be able to leave at 2:00 pm like everyone else, or will you have to stay a bit longer?" asked Dennis.

"We'll probably have to stay past 2:00, but it's not really a big deal. We're used to not being able to leave early on these short weeks."

"I assume you let them leave at 2:00 another day to make up for the fact that everyone gets to leave except Payroll," he said.

"Yeah, I'll probably let them pick a day next week like Thursday or Friday. We're always done processing by then, so that should work out okay."

"Sounds good. I certainly appreciate everything you and your team do week in and week out. You guys put in a lot of effort, and I'm not the only one who notices or appreciates it," said Dennis.

"Thanks, that means a lot. I'll pass it on to the team."

"I'll tell them also."

Dennis then walked around the cubicles and thanked everyone for their hard work and he wished them a happy Thanksgiving. He never liked the fact that Payroll always had to work extra hard during short weeks because they had such fixed deadlines. He knew everyone had to work hard, but it always seemed as if they had to work a bit harder during the holidays. He hoped this didn't make their holidays any less enjoyable.

He then went to the Document Management area and talked to Dolores about her team and how they were doing. He never had to worry about Dolores and her team. She was an extremely hard worker, and her team responded very well to her leadership style because she led by example. No one worked harder than she did, and she'd do whatever it took to get the job done. She was also willing to help other teams when they needed some extra work completed. She was also a very good cook and often brought in food or cookies. Although the work performed by the Document Management team was often tedious, her management style was perfect for this type of team.

"Dolores, I know you've already started preparing your Thanksgiving dinner. How's that coming?" Dennis asked.

"You're right; I did bake a few pies last night to get a head start. I'll have a lot to do tonight, but I really enjoy it." Dolores grinned.

"Yeah, well, I'm sure your family enjoys it every bit as much as you do. I've tasted your cooking," he said, smiling. "As a matter of fact, I was going to ask if my family could come over to your house tomorrow."

"Sure, the more the merrier," she said, laughing.

Dennis was sure that Dolores actually meant it. She was one of the nicest people he had ever met. If Dennis really wanted to bring his entire family over for Thanksgiving, she would be more than happy to accommodate them.

"I'm just kidding. My wife, Jennifer, is a very good cook also. If I had to cook Thanksgiving dinner though, I'd definitely take you up on your offer. I'm sure my family would insist on it," Dennis said. "How is everything going down here?"

"Pretty good," she replied. "We've been having a few problems with the scanners, but that's kind of typical. We clean them religiously every day and keep up with the maintenance, but they can be a bit finicky. It seems as if someone from IT or the scanner company is down here at least once a week. If we didn't have two scanners, we'd be in trouble, but as long as one is working, we're okay."

"Would it make sense to have more scanners?" Dennis asked.

"Not really. We keep at least one scanner going the entire day and the other one is busy at least half of the day. We have either one or two people who spend most of their time scanning. Everyone else is either indexing the images or opening or sending mail. If we had another scanner, we'd have to change our work process a bit. I really don't think it makes sense to spend so much on a scanner that won't be utilized 100 percent. And besides that, as we move more and more to EDI, we shouldn't have to scan any invoices, so we're fine with the equipment we have."

"Okay, you're the boss," Dennis said. "Just make sure you let us know if you need anything. Your team does a hell of a job, and we want to make sure they have all of the tools needed to keep doing what they do."

"I really appreciate that. I'll definitely let you know."

Dennis spent the rest of the day talking to all of the teams. Payroll wasn't able to leave until 3:30, so he stayed in his office until then. He didn't like leaving early on a holiday when everyone else wasn't able to.

He spent more time reviewing his allocation document and then walked out of the building with the Payroll team. He was looking forward to spending the next four days with his family. Although he was also looking forward to the Monday meeting with John and Donna, he decided to put all thoughts of work aside. Right now he needed to concentrate on his family.

# CHAPTER 20

# ALLOCATION DETAILS

To save driving time, Dennis went straight to the corporate office Monday morning rather than going to Shared Services first. Because he arrived about 15 minutes early, he decided to see what had been done with the space that Shared Services used to occupy before they moved to the new building. To Dennis's surprise, the space was not occupied, and it looked exactly the same as when they left it. There were still a few contact lists posted on the cubicle walls. He even noticed the mission statement and values that someone had left behind. He picked those up and put them in his computer bag. He went upstairs and waited for John and Donna. They both arrived at the same time.

"Dennis, how was your Thanksgiving?" asked John.

"Very good because I didn't cook any of it," he replied. "And yours?"

"Fantastic. I ate too much, as always, but that's what the holidays are for." John grinned.

"And Donna, how was yours?" Dennis asked.

"Same thing, very good but I ate too much. I always feel guilty this time of year."

"Speaking of guilty, the divisions certainly are trying to make us feel guilty about the allocation they're getting from Shared Services," Dennis said. "But I do think I have a good plan."

"Well, let's see it," John said.

"Before I hand this out I'll explain it a bit. First we want to make it simple but also give it enough detail so they fully understand why they are getting charged a certain amount. We also want to make sure it's not an administrative nightmare for Tanya to put together," Dennis said.

"Tanya is your controller, right?" John asked.

"Right; so what I did is use the metrics that Sara and Jerry are using to formulate their bonus program, and I broke them down by division. So, for example, in 2006 we processed 5,987 Accounts Payable invoices for Arizona. This made up 14 percent of the total number of Accounts Payable invoices processed. Therefore, they'll receive an allocation of 14 percent of the Accounts Payable team's budget. I did this for every team and every division that we are currently processing for," Dennis explained.

"Can we see the spreadsheet?" Donna asked.

Dennis handed each a copy.

"So then of the total Accounts Payable budget of $496,000, they pay $70,216," said Donna.

"Exactly. So when we talk to them about the allocation, there is really no debate about what they have received for their money. Obviously they can argue about how much it costs to run each team or even the entire center, but it's hard to debate the percentage they should pay when it's entirely based on their usage compared to every other division we're supporting," Dennis explained.

"It makes sense to me, but what do you do about the divisions that are going live in January? We don't have any data on how much their usage will be, and we've added costs to our budget so we can process their transactions. Do you make the existing divisions pay for that?" asked John.

"I personally believe Corporate should eat the additional costs for the first six months. We can start the allocation in June based on the volumes and usage at that point. It is very important though that we explain to the new divisions how it's going to work and give them an estimate of how much we think it will be when we start allocating in June," Dennis said. "They'll need this information for the budget they're preparing now."

"Can we spread the additional monies evenly until we're able to determine a usage factor?" John asked.

"We can really do anything, but I don't want to get into a debate about how much of the percentage they should take. If we do it evenly the smaller divisions will complain, and since we don't share revenue numbers among divisions, we'd have a hard time explaining an allocation based on revenue," said Dennis.

"I agree with Dennis on this," Donna put in. "It'll get a bit messy if we use one method this year and then change next year. If we just agree to absorb the first six months, we can maintain a consistency among all divisions. I think it's very important to be consistent."

"We could even give them an idea of how many transactions we think they'll do based on the size of the divisions by comparing a similar-size division that's already using Shared Services. This will make their budgeting process easier and more accurate, and it will put them on par with the other divisions this year," added Dennis.

"Are they getting a free ride for the first six months on these costs?" John asked.

"Not really because their headcount reduction won't take place on January 1. They'll need to ramp down once we get them fully engaged in the process," Dennis explained.

"Okay, let me think about that," John said. "Now, what about General Ledger? I don't understand how that is allocated."

"Since GL is not a transactional department, it's very hard to allocate based on any type of volume. What I did with GL, the managers, overhead, and administration, is allocate them based on the overall transactional percentage. So if you look at the total transactional budget of $1.8 million, Arizona, for example, gets allocated 15 percent of that total. And the 15 percent represents the total amount of actual allocation for each transactional team divided by the total transactional budget. So essentially it is a combination of Accounts Payable, Accounts Receivable, Document Management, Payroll, and Benefits, which by the way are allocated based on divisional headcount. Someone could argue that maybe they don't utilize GL as much as another division, but that argument is a bit nebulous. I wanted to create something objective."

"Okay, that makes sense. There are probably a number of ways you could do that, but your method is as good as any. Also did you consider any type of behavioral pricing?" John asked.

"I did, but I don't think we're ready for it yet. Even if we were, I'm not always convinced that it alters behavior as much as we might think it does," Dennis answered.

"Yeah, well, I know that when I return a rental car, I always fill it up myself rather than pay the price per gallon they get if they fill it up," Donna said.

"True, but you're talking about the person who is actually seeing the price that is right in front of them. In many cases in Shared Services, the person who is making a decision on the particular transaction either doesn't know the price or doesn't care," Dennis said. "Don't get me wrong, I think in some cases it can work, but when you're early in the life cycle of Shared Services, it's not a good idea to institute behavioral pricing. For one thing, the divisions can feel as if they're being punished, which is not the best way to start a relationship and, two, it can quickly spiral into a tit-for-tat situation," said Dennis.

"Why do you say tit for tat?" John asked.

"Because if we make a mistake or provide less than stellar service, they'll often make the argument that since they're punished for bad behavior, we should be punished for bad behavior."

"Is there anything wrong with that?" asked John.

"Well, it can become a bit tense as well as being very cumbersome to administer, but in some mature environments it can work," Dennis explained. "I just don't believe now is the time to institute that type of pricing. Now it's important to keep it as simple as possible yet with enough detail to eliminate the argument as to why each division pays a certain percentage."

"Fair enough," said John. "I've just read a lot about that and many companies seem to use it, but you're probably right in that it's for more mature Shared Services organizations."

"So that is really the entire methodology. I developed the spreadsheet so we can simply include all divisions as they come on board by plugging in the number of transactions. From there it's a matter of communicating to each division what their portion is and that it'll be allocated monthly," said Dennis.

"That brings up another question," Donna said. "What do we do with any overruns or hopefully underruns?"

"I think we should allocate monthly the budgeted amount, and any variances should be put to a balance sheet account until year-end. If the variance is positive, we should give the divisions a credit, and if the variance is negative, Corporate should eat it," Dennis replied.

"Why should Corporate eat it?" John asked.

"Because we report to Corporate, and ultimately it's all of our responsibilities to contain our costs. If we're unable to do that, we shouldn't punish the divisions."

"So why don't we get the credit?" Donna asked.

"That's simply a matter of relationship building. Can you imagine at year-end when a division is closing their books and we offer them a credit that would go straight to their bottom line? It would be like finding money in your pocket, which makes everyone feel good," Dennis replied.

"Good point," John said. "Now, this spreadsheet is complete and these are actual numbers, right?"

"Yes, this would be the actual allocation for the divisions that are already using our services. We can communicate this to them immediately."

"I like it," said John. "Like you said, it's simple enough to administer and detailed enough to prevent any arguments about each division's portion. They can argue the overall cost, but it'll be difficult to argue the percentages. Donna, do you have any issues with it?"

"No, I agree. We should communicate it this week and let them incorporate it into their budget. We also need to talk to the phase three divisions and explain the process and the fact that we'll absorb the first six months. We also need to give them a fairly accurate estimate so they can budget for it."

"Do we agree that we should estimate using similar-size divisions and base their potential transaction counts on that?" Dennis asked.

"Sure, it is as logical as any other way we might do it," Donna replied.

"Okay, I'll draft the communication for the existing divisions and set up a conference call with the phase three divisions so we can explain the process to them. I think all communication should come from me, which hopefully will help reduce the arguments," said John.

"You certainly will get fewer arguments than I would," Dennis said, laughing.

"Great. Send me an electronic copy of the spreadsheet and I'll send both of you a draft of the memo that will accompany the spreadsheet. I'll have Terri set up the conference calls and hopefully we can get this wrapped up by the end of the week."

"Great," said Dennis.

"Thanks for putting this together, Dennis. You did a good job," Donna said.

"I agree," said John. "Nice job."

Dennis left Corporate and drove back to Shared Services. He felt lucky to work for such easygoing and open-minded bosses. They certainly gave him the latitude to do his job, and he very much appreciated that. His week was off to a good start.

CHAPTER 21

# PERCEPTION IS REALITY

Dennis woke up early to the sounds of birds in the tree outside his bedroom window. It was not yet light outside, but obviously the birds were getting ready to get the worm, if the old saying really was true. He enjoyed the peacefulness of the mornings when the new day would sneak up like a very subtle breeze. Many times his best ideas came to him in the predawn hours when his mind was fresh and uncluttered by the events of the day. It seemed to him as if he were the only person in the entire world who was up and about.

He wandered into the kitchen to get a glass of orange juice and to start making coffee. Today he was going to eat oatmeal, which he usually did three times a week. It had been almost a year since he and Andrew ate oatmeal the week of Thanksgiving break. Last year Andrew had surprised the family by coming home one day early. This year he surprised them by saying that he wouldn't be coming home for Thanksgiving because he was going to his girlfriend's parents' home in Indiana. Dennis liked last year's surprise much more than this year's surprise, but it was something he had to get used to. Andrew was no longer a boy.

By the time Dennis finished eating and had read the newspaper, the kids and Jennifer were up and about. They didn't enjoy the mornings as much as he did. He spent a few minutes talking to the kids as they ate their breakfast and watched cartoons. He left a little bit later than usual because he enjoyed the cartoons and had a hard time prying himself away from the TV.

As he drove to work, he reminisced about all that had happened during the past year. All divisions were now using SAP and Shared Services. Not all of the divisions were happy about it, and some were being fairly vocal, especially since it was allocation time. They were happy with the allocation method, but they weren't happy with the overall cost of Shared Services or with the service. To make matters worse, there was really no way of quantifying their dissatisfaction or determining which areas needed the most improvement. Dennis needed to come up with a way to do this, and quickly. In his mind, the best way to get the information was simply to ask, but he needed to do it formally.

By the time Dennis got to work, Rosa was already there.

"Good morning, Dennis, is everything okay?" Rosa asked as soon as she saw him.

"Good morning; why do you ask if everything is okay?"

"You know I always worry when you show up later than I do," she said.

"No need to worry. I was just watching cartoons with the kids. Thanks for asking, though, I appreciate your concern. Hey, let me ask you a question. When you get a survey in the mail or someone calls you at home about a service you might have received or something like that, do you answer the survey? And if you do, are you usually honest?"

"I'm always honest, you know that; sometimes too honest," Rosa replied, laughing. "Sometimes I do. It just depends on the situation, but normally I tend to fill surveys out when something went wrong more so than when something went right. I guess that's probably not totally fair to whoever is asking the questions, but it really is human nature. When something is less than satisfactory to us, we seem to want to tell someone in charge. When something goes great, we seem to be less motivated to tell that story. Why do you ask?"

"I'm thinking of creating a survey for the divisions because I know they're less than satisfied, but I don't really have a way to quantify it. I want to know where we can improve, but at the same time I don't want to implement a survey that just becomes a tool to air gripes."

"Well, maybe on the survey you can put an area that forces people to document what areas they're satisfied with. You know, have an area for improvements and an area for successes," she said.

"Okay, so overall, though, you think it's a good idea to create a survey?" he asked.

"I don't see how it can hurt."

"All right. Set up a meeting with me, Jerry, and Sara to talk about this topic. I'd like to be able to create a survey before the year-end so we can send it out once we've closed the year. That way we could have a recap of the year. Hopefully if the divisions like the concept, we could continue to do this every year," he said. "Try to get that set up as early this week as possible. Thanks."

"Will do," Rosa said.

Dennis decided to do some research online and see if he could find any survey samples that other companies had used. He remembered that when he took his car in for maintenance or repairs, the dealership always called him a few weeks later to see if he was satisfied with the service. He had never seen a written copy of that survey, but the next time they called he might write down the questions they asked. Dennis didn't believe in reinventing the wheel.

Two days later, Dennis, Jerry, and Sara met in Dennis's office to brainstorm ideas for a survey that the divisions would complete at least annually, if not more often. Rosa brought in a flip chart, and Jerry volunteered to be the scribe. Dennis had some snacks to ensure their energy level was high and that the atmosphere was informal. There were no titles in the room when they had a brainstorming meeting.

Dennis started right in. "Okay, we need to create a survey that covers all of the areas of potential dissatisfaction or, to stay positive, satisfaction that could occur between the divisions and Shared Services."

"I did a little research on surveys so I have some information here," said Sara. "Perhaps we should start with this."

"Okay," Jerry and Dennis said simultaneously.

"This is from a service company that repairs consumer goods in the home. The major categories listed include punctuality, quality of the repair, friendliness of the repair personnel, ease of making an appointment, and overall satisfaction rating."

Jerry wrote down all of the areas Sara mentioned.

"So obviously the person completing the survey is the person who directly received the service," said Dennis.

"Yeah, I assume this would be completed by the person who owns the house or was home at the time the repair was completed," said Jerry.

"I bring that up because we need to know who our audience is. Who's going to complete this survey?" Dennis asked.

"We could have the controllers complete the survey," said Sara.

"How would we find out what the clerk in the division thinks of our service?" Jerry asked.

"The controller could either solicit feedback from division personnel, or we could send a survey to each person who has direct phone, email, or face-to-face contact with Shared Services," Sara said.

"We're kind of going away from our brainstorming the areas that need to be covered, but this is important, so first let's determine who's going to receive the survey and how often," Dennis said.

"If we have every single person complete a survey, we might get into a bashing session rather than receiving quality constructive feedback," Jerry said.

"Don't we want to receive all feedback regardless of whether it is good or bad?" Sara asked. "Since we haven't established a baseline, we can really receive any type of feedback whatsoever because we haven't even decided what we're going to do with the information, right?"

"That's true. At this point we just need to get responses that will tell us what people in the division are thinking, good, bad, or indifferent," Dennis responded.

"What are we going to do with the data?" Jerry asked.

"Hopefully get better at what we do," Dennis said. "This is nothing more than an improvement tool. We need to understand, for example, whether the divisions believe we are providing quality services. If we get responses that show the divisions do not believe we are completing quality work, then that's the perception regardless of whether it's factual.

"Unfortunately, in our business, perception truly is reality. We need to understand what they're thinking. If the facts support them, we need to take corrective action, and if the facts support us, we need to do a better job of selling ourselves and our organization. On the flip side, they could actually think we're doing a pretty good job but in reality we know based on our metric that we have significant room for improvement. Again, the results of the survey are just a tool to help identify areas of improvement. Having the divisions complete the survey gives them a say in our organization and helps create buy-in and support.

"We drifted again. Let's get back to who should receive the survey."

"I think everyone we come in contact with should get an opportunity to complete the survey, not just the controllers," Sara said.

"And why's that?" asked Dennis.

"For one, that will give us more responses, which can't be a bad thing. We can't guarantee that everyone will even take the time to complete the survey, so the more we send out, the more we will get back. Two, the controllers are probably not the people who actually have the most direct contact with our teams. It's usually a clerk in the division, a secretary, an assistant controller, or someone like that," she replied.

"Jerry, what do you think?" Dennis asked.

"I think we'll get too much griping if we send it out to everyone."

"I agree we could, but we'd be hearing straight from the horse's mouth, so to speak," Dennis said. "I like the idea of sending it to everyone, but if we do that, we need to make sure that we don't make it so lengthy and cumbersome that people won't want to fill it out."

"If you guys think it should go to everyone, I can agree with that," said Jerry.

"Okay, let's assume that we're going to send it to everyone," said Dennis. "How often do we send it?"

"I think anything more than once a year is too much," said Sara.

"Why?" asked Dennis.

"Because depending on the areas that need improvement, the corrective action might take a while to put in place. We should have enough time to evaluate the results, take corrective action, and involve the divisions if necessary. If I was in the division, I would be more satisfied knowing that we're spending time on making things better rather than asking what areas need improvement. Just sending out the survey will send the message that we value their input and that we're interested in improving. At that point, we just need to do a good job of communicating our progress. Then at the end of the year, we can send the survey again, and hopefully the results will show that our effort to improve was successful. I just think sending the survey more frequently than once a year will hamper our efforts rather than facilitate them."

"Jerry, do you agree?" Dennis asked.

"I hate to say yes because I think we should be having a bit more disagreement. Arguing is fun," Jerry responded, laughing. "But I do agree with Sara that more than once a year would probably be too much. Let's start as simply as possible. If we need to send it more frequently, we can always make that adjustment in later years."

"Okay, so right now we all agree that we should send it to all of our stakeholders in the divisions, and not just the controllers and general managers, and that we should send it once a year," Dennis summarized.

"Yep," said Jerry.

"Right," said Sara.

"Before we get into the actual content, we have a couple of more areas to cover," Dennis said. "Do we want the survey to be anonymous?"

"Do you mean completely anonymous, as in we don't even know what division it came from, or just anonymous as to the actual person who completed the survey?" Sara asked.

"I guess all of that is open for discussion," Dennis replied.

"I think we need to at least know which division it's coming from," said Jerry.

"I agree," said Sara. "If we don't do that, we won't get a true picture of the situation. Because if you think about it, you might find that a division is less than satisfied where all others are satisfied. That might point to an issue within the division rather than something we're doing here. I don't think we should know the actual person who is sending it in because people might be less than honest with us if it's not anonymous."

"Again, I would enjoy arguing, but I think Sara's right on the money," said Jerry.

"Well, that makes three then," Dennis said.

"How much time should we give them to fill it out?" Sara asked.

"Well, we want them to be able to take their time and really put some thought into it, so I would say about a month," Dennis replied.

"Sounds good to me," said Sara. "We should also probably follow up with everyone if we aren't getting the response rate we would like. We could do that at the two- and three-week point."

"Okay, now one more thing before we move into content: Do we have them complete a survey for every department, or do we just send one blanket survey for all of Shared Services?" Dennis asked.

"If we send a blanket one for all Shared Services, how would we know which departments or areas need improvement?" asked Sara.

"I don't think we would know that. Without the department breakdown, we're not going to see the whole picture, just like not knowing the division," Jerry said.

"I agree. I just wanted to ask the question. So we should break it down by Accounts Payable, Accounts Receivable, Benefits, Document Management, General Ledger, and Payroll," said Dennis.

"Do we really need to include Document Management? Remember, the divisions don't really have any interaction with them. That's really more of an internal team, isn't it?" Jerry said.

"Yeah, it really is, but I think we should include them because if we don't, the Document Management team might not feel that they're important," Dennis said.

"So it is really more for the team here than it is the divisions?" Sara concluded.

"Just in the case of not wanting to leave a team out, but correct me if I'm wrong, they do have some interaction with the divisions, don't they?" Dennis asked.

"Yes, they do," Jerry answered.

"Okay, let's leave them in," said Dennis. "Now let's recap. We're going to send it once a year to all stakeholders, we're going to request they put which division they're in, we'll give them a month to complete it, and we'll have either a survey for every team or a section for every team; correct?"

"Right," both Jerry and Sara agreed.

"Okay, that was the easy part. Now we have to determine the content," said Dennis.

"Yeah, this will be a little tougher. "How about we take a quick bathroom break before continuing?" Sara asked.

"Okay, let's take 15 minutes," Dennis said.

With that Jerry and Sara left Dennis's office. He stayed there and answered emails and snacked on chips. He was very satisfied with their progress. This was easier than he thought it would be.

# CHAPTER 22

# THE DEVIL IS IN
# THE DETAILS

Dennis continued answering emails and snacking until Jerry and Sara returned to his office.

"I'll be back in a second and then we'll get to the real fun," he said.

A few minutes later Dennis walked back into his office with a soda.

"All right, let's get down to the actual survey. Jerry, do you mind continuing as the scribe?" Dennis asked.

"No, not at all. Besides, I wouldn't be able to read either one of you guys' writing," Jerry responded.

"Good point," said Sara.

"What areas do we want to cover?" Dennis asked.

"Well, I'll start with a few," said Sara. "Quality, timeliness, attitude, accuracy, cost—"

"Wait!" said Jerry. "I can't write that fast, which is probably why you can read my writing."

"Sorry, did you get all of those?" she asked.

"I got quality, timeliness, and attitude," Jerry said.

"Accuracy and cost were the other two," she said.

"Okay, got it."

"Why cost?" Dennis asked.

"Should we be questioning the categories at this point or just getting them up there?" Sara asked.

"Okay, okay," Dennis said. "Do you have any others?"

"Well, I think that covers the basic areas, but now we need to get into much more detail," she said.

"Jerry, what about you? Do you have any other areas that we should cover?" Dennis asked.

Jerry thought for a few minutes and responded, "No, I think that covers it. We just need to add detailed questions to those areas."

"What about business knowledge? Is it important for our teams to have a good knowledge of the business?" asked Dennis.

"Definitely," Jerry replied.

"I think we should add that area because I know I hear that a lot from the divisions. They say we just don't understand what they do on a daily basis. I'd like to add some questions around that," Dennis said.

"I agree with that," said Sara.

"Okay, are there any other areas that need to be covered?" Dennis asked.

"I think that should do it, but we can always add other areas later if we come up with something else," Jerry responded.

"Okay, let's take the first area, quality. What type of questions do we want to ask, and how many do we ask?" Sara asked.

"First off, we need to provide them with a scale. I don't think the question will be very complicated; we're just asking them to rate the quality of our services. Maybe that's the exact question. Please rate the quality of our services, and then give them a one-to-five scale or something like that," said Dennis.

"Do we all agree that's how it should be done?" Jerry asked.

"We definitely need to have a scale that will allow us to compare the responses from one division to another and from one team to another. However, we should also provide them with a place to cite specific examples or to just document their thoughts," Sara replied.

"I agree with that. So each question should have a rating scale and a place to put any comments or notes. Now, what about the scale? Should we have a one-through-five scale, one-through-ten scale. . . . I'm just thinking out loud here," Dennis said.

"We should just have statements such as strongly agree, agree, disagree, and strongly disagree," said Jerry. "I think that would cover it, and it's simple. I don't think we want to be too complicated with what we're asking them to do."

"We need to be more detailed than that," Sara said. "I think there will be too much differentiation between responses. It could be discouraging to get a strongly disagree answer, but there might not be another level of response that fits."

"I don't think so," Dennis said. "I agree with Jerry that it should be very simple. We aren't asking them to give us exact answers as to what is wrong or what they don't like about our process. We're simply taking the pulse of our organization. To me this is much like someone going to a doctor and getting weighed, having their pulse taken, their heart listened to, and their temperature and blood pressure taken. Once the simple diagnosis is made that the patient has a fever, then you can go into a deeper analysis of what is truly wrong. We're just trying to get them to point us in a general direction based on their perception."

"So you're saying we should probably have one question per area and a scale of essentially one to four for each team," Sara summarized.

"Yeah, I think that pretty much covers it because it'll point out areas or teams that aren't doing as well as others, and it'll be simple enough in that it won't be a burden for the divisions to fill out," Dennis replied.

"I completely agree with Dennis," Jerry said. "If I were in a division, I wouldn't want to get a long survey that was going to take a lot of time to complete. The most important part to me would be, okay, now that I have completed the survey, what're you going to do about the areas or teams that are not doing so well? So having said that, I think we need to determine what our actions are going to be after we have analyzed the survey."

"We can't determine what we're going to do until we've seen the results," Dennis said.

"I don't mean specific actions," Jerry explained. "I'm talking more about are we going to formally communicate the results back to all of the divisions, are we going to communicate the result back to our own teams or to Corporate? Those are the types of general action items that we can communicate when the survey goes out that will probably give them more of an incentive to want to complete it. If we're specific about our plan now, they'll be more inclined to complete the survey and really give it some thought."

"I think you're right. I'd definitely be more likely to fill a survey out if I knew exactly what you were going to do with the information," said Dennis. "Do you agree, Sara?"

"Yeah, I do agree with that. I think we're still being a little simple with the survey, but I'll go along with what you guys are saying."

"I think we just need to get the process established. We can always enhance it or get more detailed as we move forward in the coming years. Right now I think it makes sense to be very simple about it," Dennis said.

"No worries, I'm okay with it," Sara answered.

"I get the feeling you're less than comfortable with it, Sara, but let's put it on paper and see what we think. We should just establish one or two questions around each area and have a notes section and see what it looks like. Besides the fact that it should be simple in substance, it should also be simple in style. If it looks complicated, people probably will be less likely to fill it out. Who wants to take a stab at putting it together?" Dennis asked.

"I'll take a shot at it," said Jerry.

"Okay, thanks. When do you think you can have it done?"

"Give me until tomorrow afternoon. I don't think it'll take that long," Jerry said.

"When you're done, just set up a meeting and we'll review it," Dennis said.

"Will do," said Jerry. He rose and went back to his office.

Sara was still sitting at the table looking at her BlackBerry. "Can I talk to you for a second?" she asked Dennis.

"Sure, what's up?"

"I think some of our teams are starting to lose a bit of motivation, and morale is probably not what it should be."

"Are you talking about the entire center or just specific teams?"

"I hear it mainly from my teams, but I also catch wind of it from other teams. For example, the feeling on the Payroll team is that the divisions only point out when something goes wrong, they're not interested in helping us do their jobs, they frequently miss deadlines, and they, to be very honest, can be hostile toward our teams," Sara said.

"Is this common at all of the divisions or just some of them?" Dennis asked.

"Well, some are worse than others and, of course, the divisions that are newest to Shared Services tend to be more hostile and less cooperative."

"What about the quality of their inputs? Do we see a big difference between divisions?" Dennis asked.

"Yeah, we definitely do."

"Well, we need to point that out to them, but obviously we need to do so in a very diplomatic and objective way. Is there any way to measure the quality of their work? For example, can we document the number of times they've sent files late for processing or how many times they request demand checks that are not really demand checks?" asked Dennis.

"We might have a hard time putting that together regarding what happened in the past, but I think we can certainly try to put something together going forward."

"That's what we need to do. In order to address this with the divisions, we need to talk facts and only facts. It's very important that we take the emotion out of the discussion because there is a lot of emotion out there. I'm sure some personnel in the divisions don't like us because in their eyes we're responsible for the change in their responsibilities and duties, but worse yet for their coworkers being laid off. Those things make for a very emotional situation, and we need to remove that from the equation as best as we can," Dennis explained.

"Okay, so if we gather all of this data, how do we present it to them?"

"We can do any number of things, such as present it to them individually or we could present it to multiple divisions with a heat chart. As a matter of fact, it might not be a bad idea to present divisional results as well as results by business unit, so for example show the West versus the Midwest and division versus division. This would create competition among the divisions, and we would probably see a bit of change in the quality of their work as well as the attitudes. Certainly this won't solve all of the problems, but it can definitely help," Dennis said.

"I just had a great idea. Check this out. We could take the survey results we're going to obtain and compare them to the inputs and results each division is getting. You would think that the divisions that provide the most timely and highest-quality inputs would also be the divisions that are most satisfied. That would make for a great conversation with the divisions," Sara said, sounding excited.

"I think you're on to something. You know, it could also show the opposite because the divisions that provide the best input might also have the highest expectations. I'm not really sure what we would see, but I definitely like the idea."

"It just came to me."

"Well, good conversations should generate good ideas, and what we're trying to do here with the divisions will certainly create good conversations. Why don't you get with the teams and try to come up with a way to track the division inputs. Try to make it as easy as possible because we don't want to overburden our teams," Dennis said. "Jerry will continue to work on the survey, and I'll work on the communication. By the time we get all of this created and then give the divisions one month to complete the survey, we should also have enough data on the divisions to get started."

Dennis paused for a few seconds, then said: "Hey, here's another idea: We could have divisional scorecards that show their satisfaction rating, their inputs, and their overall metrics such as how many transactions et cetera. We could tell the complete story of each division and their relationship and performance with Shared Services. This is good stuff. I'm excited."

"We're definitely on to something here," Sara said.

"Cool. Let's make it happen," said Dennis.

With that Sara went back to her office and Dennis started to read through a few emails. He was very excited about the direction of the conversation he and Sara had and was confident the surveys, heat charts, and scorecards would be valuable tools for Shared Services, the divisions, and Corporate.

Over the next few days, Jerry completed the survey. The three of them held another meeting to put the final touches on the work. At the same time, Dennis was working on the communication he was going to send with the survey. Sara started working with the teams to gather the information they would need to develop the divisional scorecards. Dennis waited until after the year-end to send the survey. (See Exhibit 22.1.) They all agreed that the divisions would not be focused on completing the survey because they'd be busy with year-end activities.

Capp had a successful year, setting records for revenue, gross profit, and net profit. Dennis was proud of the work the Shared Services team completed over the past couple of years. He felt that one of the reasons the company was so successful this year is that the divisions were able to concentrate on the core business. Shared Services also met their budget each year. While the divisions did not reduce all of the headcount promised with the implementation of Shared Services, they were able to drastically reduce personnel costs in the accounting departments. The administrative costs of the activities being performed in Shared Services were also much less than when each division was cutting its own checks, paying its own employees, and applying its own receivables. Capp now had the foundation needed to grow the business both through acquisition, if desired, and organically, which was certainly the goal of John Phelps.

Four weeks had passed since Dennis had sent out the survey. Responses were generally good, but a few geographic areas within the divisions had a low response rate, and a couple of areas did not submit any responses. Dennis was a little concerned and decided to call the business unit controller to see if there was an issue. With the implementation of Shared Services, Capp decided to streamline the divisional accounting functions by making one controller responsible for each business unit that went

EXHIBIT 22.1   *Customer Survey Form*

We are committed to continuously improving our services to you our customer. As part of this effort, we would like you to complete this very brief survey. We appreciate your honest and constructive feedback and will utilize your feedback to help us identify opportunities and areas of improvement.

Please complete the survey by January 31. All responses should be sent to Sara Mitchell.

| Service Attribute | Department | Strongly Agree | Agree | Disagree | Strongly Disagree | Notes |
|---|---|---|---|---|---|---|
| Shared Services processes transactions in a timely manner. | Accounts Payable | ☐ | ☐ | ☐ | ☐ | |
| | Accounts Receivable | ☐ | ☐ | ☐ | ☐ | |
| | General Ledger | ☐ | ☐ | ☐ | ☐ | |
| | Doc Management | ☐ | ☐ | ☐ | ☐ | |
| | Payroll | ☐ | ☐ | ☐ | ☐ | |
| | Benefits | ☐ | ☐ | ☐ | ☐ | |
| Timeliness | Shared Services personnel are available when needed and respond promptly to issues and requests. | | | | | |
| | Accounts Payable | ☐ | ☐ | ☐ | ☐ | |
| | Accounts Receivable | ☐ | ☐ | ☐ | ☐ | |
| | General Ledger | ☐ | ☐ | ☐ | ☐ | |
| | Doc Management | ☐ | ☐ | ☐ | ☐ | |
| | Payroll | ☐ | ☐ | ☐ | ☐ | |
| | Benefits | ☐ | ☐ | ☐ | ☐ | |

*(Continued)*

Exhibit 22.1 (Continued)

| Service Attribute | | Department | Strongly Agree | Agree | Disagree | Strongly Disagree | Notes |
|---|---|---|---|---|---|---|---|
| Accuracy | Shared Services processes transactions accurately. | Accounts Payable | ☐ | ☐ | ☐ | ☐ | |
| | | Accounts Receivable | ☐ | ☐ | ☐ | ☐ | |
| | | General Ledger | ☐ | ☐ | ☐ | ☐ | |
| | | Doc Management | ☐ | ☐ | ☐ | ☐ | |
| | | Payroll | ☐ | ☐ | ☐ | ☐ | |
| | | Benefits | ☐ | ☐ | ☐ | ☐ | |
| Customer Service | Shared Services personnel are pleasant and friendly. | Accounts Payable | ☐ | ☐ | ☐ | ☐ | |
| | | Accounts Receivable | ☐ | ☐ | ☐ | ☐ | |
| | | General Ledger | ☐ | ☐ | ☐ | ☐ | |
| | | Doc Management | ☐ | ☐ | ☐ | ☐ | |
| | | Payroll | ☐ | ☐ | ☐ | ☐ | |
| | | Benefits | ☐ | ☐ | ☐ | ☐ | |

| | | | | | | |
|---|---|---|---|---|---|---|
| **Business Knowledge** | Shared Services personnel understand our core business and display a sense of urgency toward business-critical issues. | Accounts Payable | ☐ ☐ ☐ ☐ | Accounts Receivable | ☐ ☐ ☐ ☐ | |
| | | | | General Ledger | | |
| | | | | Doc Management | | |
| | | | | Payroll | | |
| | | | | Benefits | | |
| **Management** | Shared Services Management communicates effectively to the divisions. | Accounts Payable | | Accounts Receivable | | |
| | | General Ledger | | Doc Management | | |
| | | Payroll | | Benefits | | |
| **Overall** | You are satisfied with your overall experience and interaction with Shared Services. | Accounts Payable | | Accounts Receivable | | |
| | | General Ledger | | Doc Management | | |
| | | Payroll | | Benefits | | |

live. Sam was the controller for the Midwest division, and the two areas that did not submit any responses were Indiana and Illinois.

"This is Sam," said the voice on the other end of the phone.

"Sam, this is Dennis from Shared Services. How are you?"

"Pretty good, but not as good as you down there in Florida."

"Yeah, what is the weather like in Evansville?"

"Same as every winter, gray and depressing," Sam replied. "I don't mind the cold so much; I'd just like to see the sun a little more often. We don't get to see the sun too much around here in the winter."

"Well, we need to schedule some meetings down here in the winter. I'm sure we could get everyone in the Midwest and North to attend," Dennis said with a laugh.

"Let me know when you do because I will definitely be there. So what's up?"

"I'm calling to check and see if you guys received the survey we sent out."

"Yeah, I do remember seeing that. I have it here somewhere in my email. I sent a note to everyone to ask them to fill it out, but I haven't followed up on it," Sam replied.

"Okay, do you think you could check with them today? We're trying to compile the results so we can share it with everyone, and Indiana and Illinois are the only states where no one has responded."

"Really, we're the only ones?"

"Yeah."

"Wow, that's kind of hard to believe."

"Why do you say that?"

"I just don't know how many people believe in surveys."

"Believe in surveys?"

"Yeah, meaning—are you really going to take action based on the results? It seems to me that most survey results are not really used to take action; instead, whoever is being surveyed seems to try to justify why someone might have answered the way they did, and it tends to get discounted as more of a one-off situation rather than as something that truly needs to be addressed," Sam responded.

"I don't doubt that some surveys are used that way, but I promise you that we'll pay attention to the results. I'll make sure of that. We spent a lot of time putting this together, and we want to use it to truly improve," Dennis replied.

"A long time to put it together? Dennis, it's only like ten questions long. How can that take a long time to put together?"

"It is very brief for a reason," Dennis explained. "First, we didn't want to make it too complicated or lengthy because we are appreciative of everyone's time and know how busy everyone in the divisions can be. Second, we don't expect the survey results to give us the exact answers to what needs to be corrected. We'll use the results to point to areas that need improvement, and then we'll work with our teams and the divisions to make corrections. Also, we want to be able to compare the results across our own teams because we can learn from each other. We might have departments that are better than others at producing quality work, or we might have one that truly provides fantastic customer service. If we make the survey too detailed, we'll have to get into the specifics of each team, and that will prevent us from being able to make the comparisons. And to be honest, we're also going to make comparisons across divisions and business units because we might have issues within a division that are preventing us from providing quality and timely services."

"See, that's what I am afraid of. You'll make comparisons to divisions that are satisfied and come to the conclusion that the issue is within the division and not Shared Services," said Sam.

"We're not interested in just making ourselves look good, Sam. We're here to make Capp a stronger company, and if the issue is within Shared Services, I promise you we'll admit it and do everything we can to correct it. We know we have areas we need to work on. If we didn't, I guarantee you we wouldn't even ask the questions. You have to trust us that we're trying to do the right thing for the company; just like we trust that you're doing everything in the divisions you can to create more revenue and make more profit. Our role is not about just making Shared Services look better, it's about making Capp an overall more efficient and stronger company. If you can't see that or don't believe that, then it's probably best that you don't complete the survey. I'll compile the results we have and it'll show that Indiana and Illinois chose not to participate. It's as simple as that. Anything else?"

"Look, I don't want to seem uncooperative, but I just don't think it'll help," Sam said.

"That's fine. I need to get the results compiled, so we'll just leave you out. It's your choice not to participate," Dennis replied. "I've got a meeting to go to, but once we compile the results, you'll see them just like everyone else even though you didn't participate. Look to have them in about two weeks. I'll talk to you later."

Dennis hung up the phone. He was very upset with Sam and didn't really care if he participated or not. Sam had been less than cooperative with Shared Services since the beginning, and apparently that was not going to change. Over the course of the next couple of weeks, Dennis, Jerry, and Sara compiled the results for each team and created charts to graphically show the results. (See Exhibit 22.2.) A communication was sent to each division showing the results by department within Shared Services and by division and business unit. While the results were not as satisfactory as everyone had hoped, they did show good results in some areas. It was a good starting point to develop action items. Dennis wished they had sent a survey to the divisions from the very beginning of Shared Services rather than once every division had gone live.

Dennis decided to share the results with the entire Shared Services center in one meeting. He was afraid that some teams or individuals would be discouraged by the results rather than see them as an opportunity for improvement. They held the meeting in the cafeteria; it was the only room large enough to hold the entire team.

"Good morning, how is everyone?" Dennis said. "As everyone knows, we sent a survey to our customers a number of weeks ago. We've now heard from everyone and want to take this opportunity to share the results with you. But before I go into the actual results, I want to explain what we're trying to do here. First, as you know, working in Shared Services can be pretty tough. We sit in the middle between our customers, the divisions, the vendors, the government, Corporate, and anyone else

EXHIBIT **22.2** *Survey Result, by Division, for Timely Payroll Transaction Processing Question*

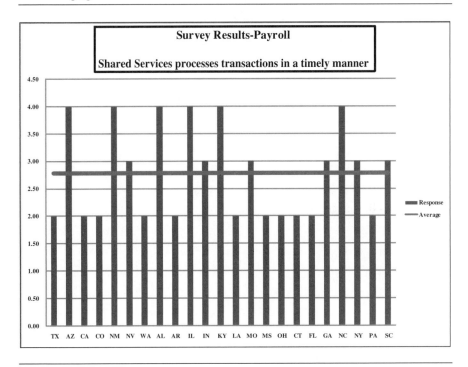

we're trying to pay or satisfy. Just the very nature of our job puts us in a tough situation in many cases, and it can be very tough to satisfy every party. Second, no matter what you're doing in life, there is always room for improvement. Sometimes we think we're doing the best we can, but in reality we can always get better. The example I always like to give is track and field. Every year someone breaks a record that was previously believed to be unbreakable. We think to ourselves how much faster can someone run or how much higher can they jump, and we find out that they can always do a little bit better. Now, they might use some artificial substances to make it happen," Dennis said, laughing, which drew a laugh from the team, "but they do get faster. The point is there is always room for improvement, and that's how we have to look at these surveys. So I know you're probably thinking the results must be horrible, but they're not. I'm satisfied with the results in many areas. Like anything, some areas need improvement more than others. So don't focus too much on individual results, just think of ways we might improve."

Dennis, Jerry, and Sara then shared the results with the entire group. Overall, the team wasn't too taken aback by the results, which probably was because the findings were presented in a very positive way rather than just pointing out the areas of improvement.

Dennis thought the meeting went well and only wished again that he had developed the survey two years ago.

# CHAPTER 23

# THE NEXT STEPS

Springtime in Tampa was much like summer in the rest of the country. The temperature was getting pretty hot, but Dennis didn't mind the heat. As a matter of fact, he kind of enjoyed it. When he was a kid, if summer days were not hot enough he made them hotter by sitting in front of the air conditioner outside the house to feel the warm air that was being removed from the house. He still did this sometimes now, except he would only do it when no one was home since he didn't want them to think he was crazy. Driving to work today, for some reason, made him think of those days as a child. He loved living in Florida and was happy Capp decided to put the center in Tampa. He wasn't sure how long he would have lasted in Des Moines.

Andrew was still in college and had decided to move back home for the summer. This was most likely going to be his last summer at home since he was finishing his junior year and was on schedule to graduate in December, one semester early. Most likely he'd get a job somewhere outside of Florida, because he told Dennis he wanted to try to live in a bigger city, either in the Midwest or Northeast. Dennis was very proud of his son's ambition and how well he was doing in school. He remembered the conversation they had prior to deciding to locate the center in Tampa. Obviously both he and Andrew had made the best of the decisions they had made.

Dennis had a meeting this morning with Donna at 9:00. She was going to drive to the center rather than have him go to Corporate. She hadn't been to the Shared Services center in a while and apparently wanted to see how things were going. As usual, Dennis was one of the first to arrive at work. He had plenty of time to read his emails and complete those tasks he had not gotten to yesterday before the meeting. He also wanted to review his notes on a subject he wanted to discuss with Donna.

Donna arrived at Dennis's office promptly at 9:00. One thing he liked about working at Capp was the fact that the culture was to arrive on time for meetings. It was considered highly disrespectful to waste other people's time by showing up late.

"Dennis, how are you?" Donna said as she walked into his office.

"Very well, and you?" he replied.

"Can't complain. You know, I don't think I've been here in about six months. I feel like I should get here more often and see how everyone is doing."

"You're welcome anytime. The team likes it when people from Corporate show up because it shows them we're important. As a matter of fact, if you have time after our meeting, it might be a good idea to walk around a bit and say hi to everyone."

"That's a good idea. I'll make time for it," Donna replied.

"You said you wanted to meet this morning but didn't really say why. Is there anything in particular you want to talk about?"

"Well, we need to talk about the next steps we're going to take in this Shared Services evolution. We're pretty happy with the results we've been able to get cost wise, and most of the divisions are basically satisfied with the services you provide, at least according to the surveys you took, which by the way was a good idea," she said.

"Thanks, but I have to be honest, while we're satisfied with many of the areas, we certainly know that we have room to improve," Dennis said.

"Well, there's always room for improvement, and I'm sure you have a plan to do that. But I wouldn't be too hard on yourself at this point regarding the level of satisfaction. Shared Services is still fairly new to most divisions, and there's going to be a certain level of dissatisfaction, especially among the most recent implementations."

"Let me ask you this, Donna: Why do you think there's a level of dissatisfaction, and do you think it'll always be there?"

"At some level, yes, I think it'll be there until the people who were personally affected by the implementation either retire or move to other companies. The mere fact that the division that you run was responsible for headcount reductions will create a level of animosity that will translate to dissatisfaction. And the truth of the matter is, your division is not responsible for the headcount reduction, John and I are. We chose the direction, and you simply executed that strategy. So there is some version of shoot-the-messenger going on here, and most likely always will be. John and I really need to do a better job of taking some of that heat off of you and your teams. If we can do that, then you and the divisions can collaborate on making Shared Services as efficient and effective as possible."

"Is there a plan to take some of that heat off?"

"Yes. We're going to visit each of the business units and review last year's results as well as the first quarter of this year. In these meetings, we're going to discuss the overall strategic direction of the company, and obviously Shared Services is a big part of that strategy," Donna explained.

"Who are you going to meet with?"

"We'll meet with the general managers and the controllers to discuss these things in detail, but we'll also meet with as many of their employees as possible. In the larger team meetings, we'll discuss the importance of our Shared Services initiative and let them know that Shared Services is here to stay and we expect them to support it."

"It's great to hear that. But I suggest pointing out that we know it's not yet perfect and obviously never will be, but we're making progress and we recognize the areas that need improvement. I think it'll carry a lot more weight if we admit some of the shortcomings," Dennis said.

"I agree. It's always a good strategy to take a bit of the wind out of their sails when talking about an issue that people are passionate about. As a matter of fact, we'll probably use some of the data from the surveys to point out the areas and also show them that we're listening to what they have to say."

"So when you mentioned taking the next steps in the evolution of Shared Services, what do mean by that? Do you have something in mind?"

"Well, we've driven a lot of costs out of the business and have automated a lot of processes, so John is kind of looking for the next big savings. Do we investigate outsourcing some of the processes or add additional services that will reduce more costs in the divisions? These are the types of questions he's asking," Donna explained

"I do have a few thoughts on those subjects," Dennis said.

Donna laughed. "I thought you might."

"I really don't think outsourcing is an option right now, and to be honest I'm not a big believer in outsourcing at any point."

"Why is that?"

"Well, in most cases, outsourcing is about lower costs, and the lower costs are generally achieved through less expensive labor or, as some would say, cheaper labor," Dennis stated. "When you chase less expensive labor, you can end up chasing it forever, and in a lot of cases that's due to wage inflation. A lot of the outsourcing firms set up shop in areas that are known for low cost of living and therefore lower wages. But as more and more companies realize this, they tend to move to these areas as well, which increases demand for the labor, and Economics 101 says that will drive the price up."

"So why do so many companies do it?"

"Because they're trying to reduce costs in the short term versus the long term, that's why. I'd rather spend my energies automating or eliminating processes rather than looking for the cheapest labor."

"Many of the business process outsourcers are very good at setting up automation initiatives or gaining compliance for these initiatives, right?" Donna asked.

"True, they're pretty good at that, but in our case, we have the automation tools configured in SAP. We just need to concentrate on getting more of our vendors, employees, and customers to participate. If we do that, we won't need to reduce our labor costs because it will take less and less labor to process our transactions."

"But we could do that too, as well as save money on the labor."

"Yes, Donna, but the time and energy needed to move to an outsourcer could be used to gain this compliance. I think if you add up all of the components and variables, you'll find that the ROI is less than you think. Remember when we initially set up shop we had this debate about Des Moines versus Tampa and we chose Tampa, which turned out okay."

"That's true."

"So I really don't think it makes sense to change that overall strategy," Dennis said. "But I do have an added service that we really should consider."

"What's that?"

"We really need to consider handling indirect purchasing for all of the divisions."

"By indirect you mean everything that we don't put into our products or resell, correct?"

"Right."

"Do you have an idea of how much money we spend on indirect materials and suppliers annually?" asked Donna.

"About $350 million, but of that number, I'd guess that about $100 million has probably been negotiated to a point that we can't save too much on it, but the other $250 million is definitely ripe for savings."

"What kind of savings?"

"Very conservatively we can expect to save 5 percent of that number, which is $12.5 million," Dennis explained. "Obviously that's more than our entire budget, so essentially we could become a self-funding division. If we could accomplish that, it would go a long way toward the divisions' perception of Shared Services and the cost of our services. We would truly become in their eyes a division that adds significant value to the business because that $12.5 million would go directly to their bottom line."

"How did you come up with these savings estimates?"

"Well, the whole thing came about because we were looking at the number of vendors that we add and the total number of vendors that we have in the system. Many of those vendors provide exactly the same product at completely different prices. So we started to investigate a bit and determined that, for example, we buy fire extinguishers from about 12 different vendors. The prices from those vendors for the exact same product vary as much as 30 percent, and in some cases the divisions that buy lower quantities actually get better prices. We are definitely not leveraging our size when it comes to purchasing these types of indirect items. Because it represents about $250 million in spend, it warrants taking a look at it."

"The savings definitely sound good, but I know a lot of companies have really struggled with these types of initiatives. I do agree, however, that we need to take a look at it. So what you're suggesting is to spend our time and resources investigating this and not focusing on outsourcing or any other types of big initiatives?" Donna summarized.

"Yeah, until we decide to either pursue indirect purchasing or not pursue it, we should put together a business case and sell it to John and his team. If we can get executive support, and I mean real support, we can realize significant savings. The companies that struggle with this struggle because they don't have true executive support, in my opinion." Dennis smiled.

"When you say true executive support, what exactly do you mean by that?"

"When we put together a national contract for, let's say, safety equipment, like the fire extinguishers, we'll have people in the business units who will say they can get a better deal from their friend down the street. And in some cases they will be able to get a better deal locally, but we can't allow that to happen," Dennis replied.

"Why can't that happen? They're getting a better deal."

"They're getting a better deal for, that particular division or plant. Nationally it will cost us more because we'll purchase less from the national vendor, and this could potentially affect our price. Also they're not thinking of the administrative portion of the transaction that includes negotiated payment terms, the lower cost of having fewer vendors to pay and maintain, and the potential pricing effect on other products that vendor might supply."

"What about the argument that we need to support local vendors where we do business?" Donna asked.

"That's important because we do want to certainly consider that," Dennis responded. "When we begin to take bids from different vendors, we'll definitely include local vendors. Also, there's nothing that will prevent us from having some regional or even local vendors. The point of the initiative is not to just have one vendor supply the entire country, the point is to have an overall strategy that is formulated nationally so that we are considering Capp when we make these decisions, not one division or even one plant."

"I have lots of questions about this that I could keep asking, but I want you to put together a business case that you and I can discuss. If we think it makes sense, we'll then present it to John and the rest of the executive team."

"Sound good."

"Okay, one last question. Who'll do the purchasing? Is that going to be done through Shared Services, or are we just going to negotiate the deals and monitor compliance?" she asked.

"That's something we'll have to discuss. It can be done either way, and there are pros and cons to each. I think that's something we should put in the business case as an option," Dennis replied.

"In your opinion, what would you do?"

"My thoughts are to make the purchases centrally except for certain items, such as office supplies, but it gets a bit complicated. The division would create a purchase requisition that indicates to us they need a certain item, and then we would ultimately make the purchase based on what they and the other divisions need," he explained.

"Okay, you're right, it's not just a black-and-white question. Put together the business case and we can go from there. "When do you think we can have that?" she asked.

"Give us a couple of weeks. I'll work on it with Jerry and his team," replied Dennis. "Do you want to go say hi to a few folks? They haven't seen you in a while."

"Sure, that's one of the reasons I came over here."

Dennis and Donna spent the next hour walking around and talking to people from each of the teams. Since Donna didn't make it to Shared Services very often, she met a number of people she did not know. It was a good opportunity for her to see some of the changes that had occurred in the center. It was also a good opportunity for the teams from Shared Services to meet one of the executives from Corporate.

Dennis could tell Donna was happy she took the opportunity to spend some time talking to the teams. And he was happy he would get the opportunity to present his indirect purchasing initiative. After he and Donna had lunch, he immediately went to Jerry to tell him the good news.

CHAPTER 24

# SMOOTH RUNNING

Nelly and Jerry were standing by Nelly's cubicle having a conversation. It looked to Dennis as if they were both a bit agitated.

"Good afternoon, Nelly, Jerry; how're you doing?" Dennis asked.

"Not bad, you?" Jerry responded.

"Good."

"Hey, I wanted to talk to you two for a few minutes. Do you have time?" asked Dennis.

"Sure, we were just talking about one of the divisions," Nelly said. "No big deal."

"Well, you didn't look happy when you were talking, but hopefully I have some good news."

"Great! We need it," Jerry said, laughing.

All three walked into Jerry's office and got comfortable.

"So what's the good news?" Jerry asked.

"As you know, Donna was here this morning, and we talked about the next big opportunities in our Shared Services center. She agreed that we should put together a business case outlining the indirect purchasing proposal we talked about," Dennis explained.

"Oh, yeah?" Nelly said.

"Now, would I lie?" Dennis smiled.

"What was her take on it?" Jerry asked. "Did she seem to be really interested, or did she just want us to put together a business case?"

"We had a long conversation about it, and I think I definitely piqued her interest. When I mentioned we could save money on $250 million in purchases, she definitely got interested. And besides that, this isn't something new we're coming up with here; too many companies have been able to generate huge savings for us to ignore this type of potential. So what I want to do is put together the business case. We need to find more examples of purchases like the fire extinguishers, and we need to think about how the entire process will work. I'll send out a meeting notice this week, and we can get started. I wanted to get you thinking about it before we have our meeting. Also, keep this under your hat for now. Okay?" Dennis said.

"We will," Jerry said.

"Definitely," said Nelly. "You're right, though, this is good news. When you walked up we were talking about Illinois and how many new vendors they request and the fact that their requests are really demands. If we can get this initiative going, it will certainly help with those types of issues."

"Those types of improvements certainly will add a lot of value and make us more efficient, so we need to make sure we put that in our business case. I want to document all of the improvements that will occur with this initiative rather than just focusing on the dollar savings from smarter purchasing," Dennis explained.

"Let me ask you this," said Jerry. "Are you leaning toward Shared Services actually doing the purchasing, or will we negotiate the deals, set up the contracts, and let the divisions continue to make the purchases?"

"That's the same question Donna asked. We'll need to discuss that. In the end, we might have to ask a few divisions to be the guinea pigs as we try this out. We can put together the pros and cons of each type of purchasing model, but we won't be able to judge the acceptance and practicality until we actually put the model into practice," Dennis said.

"So we should put together both models in the business cases?" Nelly asked.

"For now, I would. The real key to success in these types of purchasing initiatives is executive support. If Corporate does not support us when a division complains that they still need to deal with a local supplier or that they want to negotiate their own deal, we won't be very successful. It's really as simple as that. That's the reason we need to make this a very strong business case."

"Are you going to work with us to put this together?" Jerry asked.

"Of course, but I want you both to be with me when we make the presentation. It will give you an opportunity to see what it's like to make a presentation to the executives, and they'll get a chance to get to know you a bit more. Career-wise it will be very good. Assuming you put together a good presentation," Dennis said, laughing.

"Well, we'll definitely work hard on it," said Jerry.

Jerry and Nelly spent the next couple of weeks analyzing additional savings opportunities and putting together the business case. Dennis reviewed the work and met with them a couple of times a week to review and discuss. Every time they met and developed more details, it became more and more apparent that there were many opportunities to save money throughout the entire organization. Dennis was very confident that the program, if accepted, would be successful.

When the business case was complete, Dennis met with Donna to get her blessing. She would be in the meeting with John, and it made sense to have her support. While Donna had a number of questions, she supported the underlying argument that indirect purchasing was a great opportunity for Capp.

Donna and Dennis both decided it was time to pitch the opportunity to John and his team. The executive team met once a month, so Donna convinced John to put some time on the agenda to discuss this initiative. They had an hour to make their case.

Dennis, Jerry, and Nelly drove together to the corporate offices to present their case. Although Shared Services had a casual dress policy, Corporate did not, so they all were wearing suits, which was rare. They arrived at headquarters almost half an hour early, since they definitely did not want to be late. They waited outside the conference room near John's office.

"I feel as nervous as I did when I interviewed for this job," said Nelly.

"Well, don't worry now because you already have the job, you just don't want to lose it," Jerry said, laughing.

"That makes me feel better," she replied sarcastically.

"No worries, guys. We have a good case, so things will go well. There's nothing to be nervous about," Dennis told them.

Just then the conference room door opened and Donna stepped out.

"Hey, guys, how are you?" she asked.

"Good. Are you ready for us?" asked Dennis.

"Not quite yet. We got into the middle of a discussion and we'll probably be another 45 minutes or so. Just wait out here and we'll get you when we're done."

Dennis could tell that waiting was getting Nelly and Jerry more and more nervous. Also, Terri, John's assistant, was called in a number of times to bring in different documents. Dennis got the feeling that whatever subject was being discussed, it was not a pleasant conversation. After waiting a little more than an hour, it was finally time for them to make their presentation.

They entered the conference room, and Dennis introduced Jerry and Nelly to the group.

Everyone else in the room shook hands and introduced themselves if they didn't know each other. Nelly had not personally met the others in the room except for Donna. Jerry knew a few since he spent a number of years working in a division. John's team was made up of Nick, the general manager and SVP of the western division; Tom, the general manager and SVP of the Midwest division; Bill, the general manager and SVP of the eastern division; Donna, the CFO and SVP; and Sharon, the SVP of Human Resources. Once Jerry shook hands with everyone, he hooked up his laptop to the projector that was set up on the table.

"Let's get started," said John.

"Okay." Dennis stood up and went to the front of the conference room. "First I want to say thanks for letting us meet with you this morning to discuss our proposal. I'll give you a very brief background and then Jerry will do the presentation."

"Sounds good," said John.

"As you know, we started Shared Services almost three years ago and have now rolled out our services to all of Capp's divisions," Dennis explained. "And while we have done a decent job in getting this completed and gaining a good number of efficiencies from each of the processes we've implemented, we still can add significantly more value to the entire company. Obviously John realized this because he asked Donna to talk to me about the next steps in the evolution of Shared Services. One of the things we can try to do is continue to cut costs, which will have an impact, but to be honest, it would not be a quantum leap impact. The real opportunity is to streamline our current indirect purchasing process, which will have a significant impact if done correctly. We were asked to develop a plan to take us to the next level in Shared Services, and adding indirect purchasing to our services is that plan. With that, I'm going to let Jerry go through the presentation. Nelly and I will chime in when necessary and answer any questions you might have. Jerry, it's all yours."

"Thanks, Dennis. The first thing I want to do is define indirect purchasing and indirect materials. I'm sure many companies have a little different definition of indirect materials, but in our case I'll start with what indirect materials are *not*. They do not include anything that is resold or goes into the manufacture of a product. Since we don't really manufacture anything, it simply is any product that is ultimately resold. So in the simplest terms, it's anything that is not included in the cost of goods sold. So the items we're talking about include computers, cell phones, temporary labor, office supplies, safety equipment, repair parts, and those types of products," Jerry said.

"Does it include our trucks?" asked Nick.

"In our business case it does not," Jerry replied. "Some companies do choose to include fleet purchasing, but our thought is that you guys in the field forgot more about the trucks you are using than we know, so we felt we couldn't add a lot of value there. Really, the point is to take those purchases off of your plate that are not a part of the core business process. Buying, selling, warehousing, and moving the products are really the core part of the business, and we don't want to touch those things. Again, you guys are the best at doing that. We'd like to give you more time to concentrate on those things while we worry about purchasing things like office supplies and computers. I like to call the items we want to purchase toilet paper and paper clips," Jerry said, laughing.

"Well, make sure you don't cut costs on the toilet paper," said Tom. "Stick with the two-ply."

"We definitely won't reduce the quantity or probably more important the quality, but that brings up a good point, believe it or not. While that is a really goofy example, the whole point of this is to leverage our size as a company and be able to purchase the same or better quality at much better prices. We're getting a little ahead of ourselves, but we purchase about $350 million worth of indirect goods, which is a fairly large amount. That kind of size should give us leverage that will allow us to do just what I said."

"How do we buy this stuff today?" Tom asked.

"Each division buys its own supplies. Actually, in most cases, it's not just each division doing its own thing but each plant. So we're really not taking advantage of our size. In many cases we have people going to the local office supply store or cell phone carrier to buy one or two items. We are literally throwing money away, not to mention people's time," Nelly explained.

Dennis was proud that Nelly jumped into the conversation. He had been worried that she might be a bit intimidated by the people in the room, but apparently her passion for the subject made her forget all of that.

Jerry continued to go over the reasons the process of purchasing indirect materials should be changed.

"Now I want to cover the actual process we use today," he said as he advanced to the next slide. "Today each plant has someone who is responsible for making indirect purchases. As you can see from this slide, 700 users making purchases and we have about 25,000 vendors in the system, which are represented by the circles. I would have put 25,000 circles on the page, but that might have taken a while." He chuckled. (See Exhibit 24.1.)

"The sheer number of people making the purchases combined with the large vendor population creates a problem with processing and

EXHIBIT 24.1  *Current Indirect Purchasing Process*

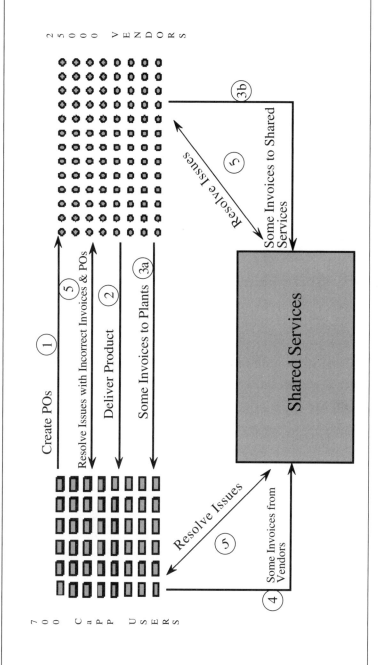

187

issue resolution," Jerry explained. "The way the process is set up today, Shared Services is responsible for resolving the issues between vendors and purchase order creators once the purchase is made. So essentially once the purchase order creators get their goods, they don't have any incentive to help resolve any payment issues. This makes it very difficult for Shared Services personnel to resolve these issues. In most cases they don't have the knowledge needed to resolve the problem, so they're forced to contact the divisions to help resolve any payment discrepancies. And no offense to the divisions, but resolving a payment issue for a product they already received is not on the top of their priority list—nor should it be."

"So how many times is this an issue?" Tom asked.

"A little more than 20 percent of our invoices block for some reason, meaning the price on the invoice does not match the purchase order, or the quantity received does not match the purchase order, or both," Nelly answered. "Of the invoices we process, about 5,000 a month are for indirect types of purchases, so that means we need to resolve issues on about 1,000 invoices a month, which is significant."

"If it's off a penny, do we need to resolve the issue?" asked Bill.

"No, we have tolerances built into the system. The tolerance is 1 percent up to $100," Nelly replied. "So the 1,000 blocks I'm referring to are everything outside of that tolerance."

"Okay, so clearly we are a bit inefficient in the processing of these invoices, but I don't think that represents the real savings opportunity we're talking about here, correct?" asked John.

"That's correct." Dennis stepped in. "Changing the process will definitely make us more efficient when it comes to paying these invoices, but the real reason we're here is to talk about the $350 million worth of goods that Jerry referred to earlier. We have an opportunity to save a significant amount of money on these purchases, and administrative efficiency will simply be a by-product of that savings effort. Jerry, go ahead with the presentation, but let's not spend too much time on the actual process of purchasing."

"Okay, so as Dennis mentioned, the real opportunity is the $350 million in purchases," Jerry explained. "There are a couple of ways to accomplish this, and they do touch on the purchasing process a bit. So having said that, we have two potential solutions: We can either have personnel in Shared Services make all of the purchases based on requisitions that would be completed in the divisions, or we could continue to have the divisions make the purchases but we could control the process through executive support and mandate and by controlling the vendor master."

"What do you mean by executive support and mandate? What would we have to mandate?" asked John.

"If we continue to allow the divisions to make the actual purchases, in many cases they'll want to use their own preferred vendors. And in some cases they might, or actually they will, be able to get some items at a lower cost than what our national agreement can provide. While this will be a cost savings for that division in that one particular case, we must be disciplined in not allowing divisions to purchase outside of the national agreements," Jerry explained.

"But if we have a good national agreement that leverages our size, how would one small division be able to purchase an item cheaper? And, if they can, why wouldn't we allow them to do that?" asked Nick.

"An example might be office supplies. In most office supply agreements, there's a standard list of products that represents about 90 percent of all of the purchases made. These items are negotiated to the best possible price for Capp as a whole. So, for example, we know that everyone uses Post-it notes. They'll be one of the preferred items that is negotiated to a very low cost, and it will be difficult for someone in a division to find them at a lower price at an office supply store or online," Jerry explained.

"However, two scenarios might come up in this case. If someone went to a 99-cent store, he might be able to get them cheaper. Or if people wanted a particular color or size that is not on our preferred list, they might be able to find that item cheaper either by walking into a store or going online. But the point is, do we want our employees to spend their time looking for these types of bargains, and do we also want to hurt our ability to leverage our purchasing power by allowing someone to go outside of the national agreement so they can save a few dollars for that one particular division? That is the question. If we decide we want to leverage our purchasing power, we need to be disciplined in not allowing these types of purchases. That's what I mean when I say executive support or mandate."

"I understand what you're saying," said John. "This looks like it's going to take a while. Let's take a break for about 15 minutes, all right?"

# CHAPTER 25

# THE MEETING CONTINUES

"As I was saying," Jerry continued once everyone was seated, "we really need executive support for this to work. Otherwise we'll put these programs in place, and we'll still have maverick buyers that undermine our program."

"You're right about that, but would you expect us to do anything different? We're paid to make our divisions as profitable as possible, and if we can cut costs for our division by buying these indirect items cheaper than you can, we're going to do it," Nick explained.

"I understand that, but we're not ultimately looking out for the good of the entire company if we do that. We need to somehow change that type of thinking," Dennis answered.

"The only way to do that is to incent the division executives to not do it," said Jerry.

"Well, you don't want to incent them to not do something," John said. "You want to incent them to do the right thing. But this brings up an issue that's bigger than just compliance with an indirect purchasing program. Since we have built through acquisition, the divisions have never been incredibly cooperative with each other when it comes to any type of issue. We have divisions that won't accept inventory from each other near month-, quarter-, and year-ends just so they can make their own inventory look better, even though the other division might have a warehouse that is bursting at the seams. Sometimes you guys act like you aren't even working for the same company."

"Our business decisions have gotten us where we are today, so I wouldn't say everything is so bad. We've done one hell of a job getting this company where it is," Nick exclaimed with a hint of anger in his voice.

"I'm not saying that you haven't, but what we've done in the past is not going to carry us to the next level in the future," John emphasized. "We need to develop an incentive plan that is going to reinforce decisions that will make us stronger as an overall company and not just at each division. We have entirely too many similarities and areas where we can help each other to not do that."

"The answer seems fairly simple to me," Dennis added. "We just need to continue to incent the divisions for their own performance while taking a portion of that incentive and applying it to the same criteria for Capp as a whole."

"You're right, logistically it's very simple. The issue is more cultural than anything, so I will handle that," John said. "Besides, that's not what we're here to discuss today. Let's continue with our discussion on indirect purchasing. I assure you that you'll have executive support for this program if we decide to do it."

"Okay, so before we got on the subject of compliance and executive support, we were talking about the actual process of purchasing and whether it makes sense to have so many people creating purchase orders. So the question is, should we purchase centrally through Shared Services or should we continue to allow the divisions to make their own purchases," Jerry summarized.

"If we do allow them to continue to make the purchases, how are we going to control the compliance?" Donna asked. "And I don't mean from the top but from someone who is actually doing the purchasing?"

"We can control it a couple of ways, but one of the best ways is through the master vendor list. We simply will not allow creation of new vendors, so they won't be able to pay the vendor they purchased from. We can shut off all nonpreferred vendors and not create new ones," Nelly explained.

"In theory that works, but what are you going to do when someone picks up the phone, orders a product, gets the product, and then gets an invoice? You have to pay the vendor. We purchased a product from them, and they have to be paid," Donna replied.

"Certainly we have to pay them, but we can measure and report our new vendor setups and noncompliant purchases by division," Dennis said. "If we create a heat chart showing these metrics, it will almost shame divisions into complying. And don't forget that if we change the incentive program to division executives, they'll enforce the behavior, especially when they see a heat chart that shows their division is not complying with the program."

"Just make sure you give us an opportunity to review these types of metrics prior to making them available to all eyes," Nick said.

"I'll make sure of that," said John. "So we really have two options here. One is to put together a team in Shared Services that will create all of the indirect purchase orders for the entire country based on requisitions created in the field. The second option is to continue to allow the divisions to create their own purchase orders but enforce the participation of the program through vendor master, executive incentives, and reporting, correct?"

"Right."

"Well, let me give you my thoughts," John said. "First off, I am confident there is a great deal of opportunity in leveraging our purchasing power for indirect items. However, I do believe it will be a bit more difficult to realize these savings than we're anticipating. The real key is to prove that we can negotiate programs that will significantly reduce the price we pay for these goods. If we put the process in place to purchase centrally but are less than effective at negotiating deals, then we won't get the ROI we're expecting. The personnel purchasing indirect goods in the divisions have many other responsibilities, so taking this away from them will not create any headcount savings. The only thing it will do is make the process a bit more efficient by increasing the quality of the purchase orders, which will make your team's job much easier, Nelly.

"And don't get me wrong, that is important, but I think we should start this off slower rather than jumping off the cliff. Having said all of that,

I'm okay with putting someone in place to begin the national negotiations, but I'm not yet comfortable putting a team in place to make these purchases centrally. What does everyone else think?"

"I tend to agree that we should take the conservative approach," Bill replied. "It will be a big cultural change for us if we were to purchase these items centrally. And as you mentioned, if we aren't able to negotiate good deals, we could put a team in place that will simply make things a bit more efficient but won't ever realize the ROI we're looking for."

"Would we hire this initial person internally or externally?" asked Nick.

"Let's not get ahead of ourselves," John answered. "Does everyone agree this is the approach we should take?"

"Yes," they all said, some more enthusiastically than others.

"Jerry, you seem a little less than enthused," said John.

"I do agree we should be conservative to start, but I would be lying if I said that I didn't want to try to purchase centrally. But I understand the reasons and I support the decision."

"Okay, so we'll go with hiring an indirect purchasing manager and maybe one other person to start looking at the opportunities we should pursue first. Dennis, put together a timeline that shows the actions we'll need to take over the next six months," John said.

"I'll post the position or positions depending on what we decide, both internally and externally. Dennis or Jerry, I just need you to get me a job posting request," Sharon told them.

"Do you think we have anyone internally who'd be interested in the position?" Bill asked.

"I'm sure there'll be a good deal of interest. We have a lot of people in the divisions who purchase either direct or indirect materials, and I'm sure they would view this as a good opportunity," said Tom. "I just hope it's not someone from my division."

As soon as the meeting was over, Dennis, Jerry, and Nelly started to drive back to Shared Services. They did not get a chance to eat lunch since the meeting got started late and their meeting took longer than expected. It was 2:00 pm and they were all hungry.

"Can we stop to get a bite to eat? I'm starving!" said Nelly.

"I'm hungry too," Dennis said. "The cafeteria is closed so we'll have to go somewhere. I don't want to eat too much though because I don't want to ruin my appetite for dinner.

"Jerry, I know you would rather have gone with the full-blown program," Dennis continued, "but I think this will be a good start. Also, I've never seen John make a decision to do something like that actually in the meeting. Usually he'll think about it for at least a few days and then make his decision. You did a good job of selling them on the opportunity. Now all we have to do is get a few good wins and I'm sure we'll be able to expand the program. To be honest, we shouldn't look at how much of the process we're involved in or controlling but rather the total dollars we're responsible for negotiating and how much we can save the company. Those will be the true measures of our success."

"That brings up a good point," Jerry said. "It's going to be very difficult to measure our savings because we're not totally aware of everything that is purchased today by the divisions and how much they pay for those items. I'm not really sure how we'll be able to measure the savings generated."

"That's true. I think we'll have to calculate it based on what we do know," Dennis replied. "For example, we probably could be very accurate for cellular phones because we can determine from SAP the dollars we pay to all cellular providers and we can also get an inventory of all phones we have in the company. Once we negotiate a deal, we can see what we pay going forward for the number of phones that we have. Sure, people can go over their minutes and things like that, but for the most part, the cost per month per phone should be much less than it is today because we have way too many providers and too many phones that were purchased individually. Obviously there is going to be a great deal of analytics that need to be completed, so I would suggest hiring a purchasing manager and a very good business analyst: one who is very good with large amounts of data, one who can work with databases and Excel, and someone who just really likes to crunch numbers.

"So items like cellular phones and temporary labor should be easy to evaluate, but office supplies is very difficult because we don't know exactly what people are buying today," Dennis continued. "We know how much we pay for office supplies, but we don't know how many pads they're using or how many reams of paper, for example. In the case of office supplies, we should just look at the amount spent per plant or division, and that overall dollar amount should go down. So I think we can come up with metrics that will show our successes, but the metrics might be different depending on the type of item."

"I agree. This is actually going to be a lot of fun. Don't you agree, Nelly?" Jerry asked.

"Fun for you but I still have to pay the bills, and I'm not sure how this process is going to help me and my team," she replied.

"Why didn't you say something in the meeting?" Jerry asked.

"Everyone was in agreement, so why should I say anything? Don't get me wrong, I know it'll be good for the company, and it's a more conservative approach, I just wish we would have gone with the model where we make the purchases for the divisions."

"This will still help your team though, because we'll have many less vendors, and we can also negotiate better payment terms and methods. In the cell phone example, we should be able to get electronic statements, automatic allocations, and those types of improvements rather than having to pay thousands and thousands of individual paper bills. We also have people submitting expense reports just for cell phone reimbursement, which doesn't add any value at all, so there are many ways this will improve the payment process. You're right in saying it won't help as much as it would if we went with the full-blown version, but this is a good start. Trust me, this is a big win for us," Dennis said enthusiastically.

Over lunch, they continued their conversation about the next steps needed to get the initiative started. Nelly seemed more and more receptive to the idea once Dennis and Jerry explained the multiple opportunities not only to save money but to improve the payment process as well. Dennis was confident that the conservative approach John endorsed was truly the right decision.

# CHAPTER 26

# BEST-LAID PLANS

It had been four months since Capp decided to hire Angie, an indirect purchasing manager, and Dave, an analyst to help her evaluate opportunities. The program was going much slower than expected for a number of reasons. John had not been able to develop an incentive plan that the division executives were comfortable with, and he was reluctant to move forward with a new plan without the full support of each division general manager. Because of this, the divisions were not as willing to participate in the program as everyone had hoped they would be. The analysis Angie and Dave completed clearly showed that multiple opportunities existed to cut costs. They had been able to negotiate a fairly successful cellular phone plan that saved over $750,000, which was significant, but there was nothing else in the works that would create a large amount of savings. Dennis could sense that Angie was disappointed with the overall support the program was receiving, and perhaps she doubted if this was the opportunity she thought it would be when she joined Capp. Angie had requested a meeting with Dennis today, and he assumed this is what she wanted to talk about.

Dennis was late coming in this morning because he had taken Danny to school today. The new school year was only one week old, and already Danny didn't like going to school. Dennis drove him so he could have a chance to talk to Danny and meet his teacher. Dennis and Jennifer had talked the situation over, and Jennifer was confident there was nothing wrong with Danny's new teacher, the boy was just having trouble getting acclimated. When Dennis arrived at work, Angie was talking to Rosa.

"Good morning," Angie said to Dennis.

"Good morning. Sorry I'm late. I had to take my son to school today and meet his new teacher. He's not having too much fun this first week, so I thought I'd have a little talk with him and meet his new teacher."

"How'd it go?" Rosa asked.

"Okay. I think he's upset because he didn't get too many of his friends in his new homeroom class and he doesn't get to see them too often, just at recess and lunch. He'll be okay. He just needs to make new friends," Dennis replied.

Dennis walked into his office and asked, "So, Angie, how are you?"

"I'm okay. Mind if I shut the door?"

"Not at all," said Dennis.

Angie shut the door and sat down in the chair across from Dennis's desk. "I want to talk to you about a couple of things."

"Okay."

"First, I'm a little worried about the success of our indirect purchasing initiative, and I'm not really sure where to take it from here. As you know, we were able to put together a good cellular deal that saved a lot of money, but other than that, we've done nothing but analysis. I don't mind doing the analysis, but the frustrating part is the analysis shows us how much opportunity we have, and yet we're not really doing anything about it."

"I agree completely that indirect purchasing has gained much less momentum than we wanted it to," Dennis replied, "and part of that reason is the lack of help from the divisions. I know we haven't yet changed the incentive structure within the divisions, but I do know that John has promised to have a plan in place by January. That is still four months away, so it won't help too much in the near future. I also think we haven't done a good enough job of communicating the potential opportunities."

"I disagree with that, Dennis. We've sent a lot of analysis to the divisions, but they always seem to shoot holes in it. They always go back to the excuse that they have a relationship with a local vendor and they don't want to damage that relationship, or they point out the instances where they can get certain items cheaper. It's not that we're not communicating, it's that they're not listening."

"So the communication has not been effective, but I don't think that's our fault. As long as they're going to continue looking out for only the best interest of the division and not Capp as a whole, we'll have these struggles. It will be difficult to change that culture," Dennis explained.

"I agree, and I guess that's why I'm here, Dennis. I get a great deal of satisfaction from saving the company money. This is what I've always been able to do at other companies, and here I feel like I am handcuffed. It's very frustrating for me and Dave. And maybe I shouldn't say this, but it's also very frustrating for Jerry. I know he feels as if he presented something that should work, but since there is really not much support, he doesn't feel like it's going to be a success. As a matter of fact, I know he's very frustrated because I've seen a change in his mood. He just does not seem like the same guy."

"I understand what you're saying, but we need to give it some time. As I mentioned, it will be difficult to be successful without an incentive plan to put every division on the same page, but I know John supports this, and in January he has committed to changing the incentive. In the meantime, I think there are some other things we can do, such as help our Information Technology department with their purchasing. I know they do a fairly decent job, but I'm sure they could use some help. We might be able to learn a lot by using our own departments as guinea pigs as we move this forward. The important thing is I want you to know that I am still fully in favor of this initiative, and I'm confident we can generate tremendous savings once we get the support we need. I'm also confident we will get that support."

"I hadn't thought about helping Information Technology. We'd love to do that. I know in the next four months we can help them do a little better job than they're doing today." Angie sounded enthusiastic.

"You said you had a couple of things you wanted to talk about."

"Well, the other one I mentioned. I'm worried about Jerry; he just seems like he's not into it anymore."

"Not into the purchasing initiative or not into Shared Services or not into Capp?" asked Dennis.

"I'm not sure which one; maybe it's all three, but I just wanted to mention it to you. Not because I'm unhappy with him as a boss, but I just need to know that my boss is committed to what I am working on," Angie explained.

"Have you talked to him about it?"

"I have and he does mention that he's frustrated. It just seems to me that it might be more than just the frustration of this particular area," Angie replied.

"Well, I'll have a talk with him and see what's going on."

"Don't tell him I mentioned anything to you."

"No, definitely not. I meet with him weekly, so I'll just see how things are going and probe a little bit. I appreciate your concern. Is there anything else you want to talk about?"

"No, that's it, Dennis. I appreciate you taking the time to talk with me, and I appreciate your patience and support for our department."

"You're welcome. Just know that I really believe in this and I'm confident we'll make it work. It might take longer than we wanted, but we will get there. If I wasn't convinced it would work, I certainly wouldn't have recommended the presentation be made to Corporate," Dennis said.

"I definitely appreciate that and thanks for listening."

Dennis was scheduled to have a meeting with Jerry tomorrow, and he would bring up the issues Angie had talked to him about.

"Rosa, I still have my meeting with Jerry tomorrow, don't I?" Dennis asked.

"Yes, and John called when you were talking to Angie. He said to call him back when you got out of your meeting."

"Okay, did he say what it was about?"

"No, he just said to call him."

Dennis picked up the phone to call John. Usually John didn't call him directly; instead he went through Donna.

"Terri, hey, this is Dennis in Shared Services. Is John available? I'm returning his call."

"Let me check. Yes, he is available. Hold on a second."

"Dennis, how is everything?" John asked.

"Not bad. How's everything in Corporate?"

"Good, very good; I need you to put together some information for me," John said.

"Okay."

"First I need you to keep this confidential. I've already talked to Donna about this, but since she's out today, I wanted to talk to you directly. We're pretty well into negotiations to buy a competitor in the northwestern part of the United States, and I'm confident we'll be able to make something happen."

"That's great," Dennis said.

"Yeah, I think this is a very good opportunity for us. What I need from you is to determine what type of time frame would be needed for us to be able to provide all of the functions in Shared Services to this new division. So obviously that would include getting them on SAP, getting them trained, and if needed getting additional staffing on your teams to make this happen. Now, obviously I hope we don't need to add anyone in order to be able to absorb this work, but I need you to do the analysis and make that determination."

"Well, there a lot of variables in that equation, so we'll need to get some clarification in certain areas," Dennis said.

"Such as?"

"Well, for example, what type of pay cycles are they on for payroll, and are they going to transition to our pay cycles? Or how many benefit plans do they have, and again are we going to require them to convert to our benefit plans? These are the types of questions we need answered before we can give a very accurate estimate," Dennis explained.

"Make the assumption that they'll convert to our business rules, processes, and procedures. This is part of the negotiation, and we have every intention of converting them to our way of doing business. Otherwise we won't be able to leverage the economies of scale that make this an attractive business to target. We're being pretty aggressive in our bid, and therefore we need to make sure we're able to cut some of their costs almost immediately."

"Okay, that won't be too hard. The only other thing I need to know is how many warehouses do they have, how many employees, and how much revenue?"

"They have just about 80 percent of the revenue of our western division, but they have 4,500 employees, which is about 500 more than we have for western," John replied.

"Obviously there is some room for improvement there."

"We definitely think so."

"Okay, let me start putting something together. When do you need this?" Dennis asked.

"By the end of the week at the latest."

"Okay, I'll let you know if I have any other questions," said Dennis.

As Dennis hung up the phone, he was very excited about the opportunity to bring in a new division. This was going to give Shared Services a real opportunity to prove the concept of volume insensitivity and showcase their ability to bring on board a new division rather quickly. Strategically it would be significant for Capp to be able to make aggressive acquisitions because they could cut administrative costs almost immediately by utilizing Shared Services for the new division. If this opportunity became reality, Dennis knew it would energize his team.

Dennis went home that night full of enthusiasm. Not only was he excited about work, he was eager to talk to Danny and see how his day at school went. As Dennis drove his usual route home, he thought back about the beginning of Shared Services three years ago. He could not believe how fast that time went. When he got home, Danny was in the front yard playing with Shorty. Dennis got out of the car carrying his briefcase.

"Dad's home!" Danny yelled into the house.

"Hey, buddy, how was school today?" Dennis asked.

"Okay," Danny answered less than enthusiastically.

"That doesn't sound too okay."

"It was okay. Can we talk about something else?" Danny asked.

"Sure, but we're going to get back to this later, okay?"

"Okay."

Dennis, Danny, and Shorty went in the house. The girls were eating at their friends' families tonight, so it was just going to be Dennis, Jennifer, and Danny having dinner. Jennifer decided to make homemade pizza tonight because Danny liked making it as much as he liked eating it.

"So, Danny, do you remember what we were talking about on the way to school and in the front yard tonight?" Dennis asked as they sat down to eat.

"Yeah," he answered.

"Well, tell me again why you don't like school this year. You always liked it before," Dennis asked.

"I don't know. It's different. I don't have any of my friends in my classes anymore."

"You should look at that as an opportunity to make new friends," said Jennifer. "And it also doesn't mean that your friends today aren't going to be your friends anymore. You can have them over to spend the night sometimes so you'll still get to see them."

"It's not the same," Danny muttered.

"Danny, I need you to do me a big favor," Dennis said. "Give it a chance, okay? I promise you'll make new friends in your class. Lots of times things change for us, and most of the times they change for the better. Change can be very good. It gives us a chance to learn new things, meet new people, and get smarter. It won't be easy, but if you just try I know it'll be okay. Why don't you have someone from your new class over to swim one night?"

"If you do that, we'll make homemade pizza again. You can have it two nights in one week. How does that sound?" asked Jennifer.

"I'll ask somebody this week," Danny said.

"Homemade pizza to the rescue," Dennis murmured to Jennifer.

Dennis was still not confident Danny would adjust quickly, but at least he was going to try.

The next morning Dennis arrived at work early as usual. He had to get started on the analysis John needed, but he also needed, to talk to Jerry.

He knew he had to make time for both. He was scheduled to meet with Jerry at 10:00. That gave him three hours to work on the acquisition analysis.

Dennis spent the next three hours gathering the statistics he needed for his analysis. Because he required the teams to be up to date in posting their metrics, he didn't have any trouble getting the information he needed. He knew he could meet John's deadline. That's one of the reasons he was excited about the opportunity. Having a shared processing center is what made this type of analysis easy, and it definitely gave Capp a strategic advantage related to acquisitions.

CHAPTER 27

# TIME FOR A CHANGE

Jerry showed up at Dennis's office exactly at 10:00 am. "Hey Jerry, what's going on?" Dennis asked.

"Same old, same old."

"How are the departments doing?" asked Dennis.

"Accounts Payable is doing okay, and so is Accounts Receivable, but Indirect Purchasing is another thing," he replied.

"I know it's going much slower than we want, but what else is going on there?" Dennis asked.

"Do you mind if I close the door?"

"No, not all," Dennis answered.

Jerry got up and closed the door. Dennis noticed that, as Angie had mentioned, Jerry did not seem to be the same guy.

"I'm really not convinced this initiative is going to work," Jerry began. "To be honest, I think we did a good job selling it, but we're doing a poor job of executing on it and we as a company are not supporting it, which to me doesn't make any sense. I know it can truly result in millions and millions of dollars in savings, but if we don't support it and put some energy behind it, I don't think it can work."

"I agree that it isn't going to work unless we have support from the top, but we *do* have support from the top. It's just that John is trying to formulate and sell an incentive plan that all of the divisions will be satisfied with. He's having a tougher time than he expected, but he doesn't want to upset the apple cart, so to speak, so he's taking his time. He'll have something in place by January," Dennis explained.

"In the meantime, we won't be able to gain much momentum for the Indirect Purchasing team, and it's going to be very difficult to keep them motivated when they don't feel the support. As a matter of fact, it's difficult to keep them motivated right now. Hell, it's hard to keep myself motivated."

"I understand that and I appreciate the position you're in. We're trying to make a change here that is definitely in the best interest of the company, but it does take time. We talked about this being a cultural change, and you know culture is harder to change than just about anything," Dennis explained.

"I understand that, but I don't know why the divisions care so much about where they buy these types of items and why they can't just embrace the program. It doesn't make sense to me," said Jerry.

"Think of it this way: Imagine that your wife lets you choose the type of car you're going to buy, but she makes you buy gas for that car at only one gas station. You are going to feel as if you've lost control. I'm sure that's how the divisions feel. It's like they have lost control, and they don't like that. To me it is as simple as that," Dennis responded.

"To tell you the truth, that's how I feel. I don't feel as if we control our own destiny. We're always dependent on the divisions supporting our efforts, whether it's indirect purchasing, a purchasing card program, a new demand check policy, or even how we process expense reports. We have to get the divisions to buy off on everything we do, and in many cases they seem to not support us because they don't have to. It's frustrating to know you have the right answer, you're looking out for the best interests of the company, and yet you don't have the power to make changes that will make Capp a stronger company."

"I have those same types of frustrations all the time," Dennis answered, "but I do know that we're gaining momentum and we just have to be patient. Eventually we won't have to fight these battles, but for now we have to. Remember, we've only been doing this for three years, and in Shared Services years that's not very many."

"I hear what you are saying, but to be honest I came in here to talk to you about more than just indirect purchasing and my frustrations. I came here to tell you that I've decided to leave Capp."

Dennis couldn't believe what he was hearing. Jerry had been with the company for many years, most of those as a controller in a division, and by leaving he seemed to be giving up on many years invested with the company.

"Are you sure this is something you want to do?" asked Dennis.

"I've been thinking about this for a long time. I don't really think Shared Services is the type of environment for me. I've always been frustrated sitting in the middle of the vendors, suppliers, and the divisions. It always seems like everything is a constant battle, and neither one of them is happy. The vendors complain you don't pay them fast enough, the divisions complain you don't pay the vendors fast enough, the divisions complain that you charge too much for your services, and we're constantly being asked to work harder, faster, and more efficiently, yet when we try to make positive changes, many times the divisions simply refuse to support our initiative. I'm tired of fighting all of the battles."

"Well, you're right about sitting in the middle. That's the nature of the Shared Services business. Unfortunately, we do sit in the middle, and therefore we take shots from all sides. It's very easy to blame us when things go wrong," Dennis said.

"Yep. I don't really want to do that anymore."

"Let me ask you this: You seemed very motivated when we put together the purchasing proposal, so did you start feeling this way after that, or has this always been something that bothered you?" Dennis asked.

"I like the concept of Shared Services and definitely believe it's in the best interests of the company, but I don't like having to sell everyone on the concept all of the time or, more important, feel like I have to defend myself every day. Having to constantly defend your existence or competence eventually wears down even the most positive person, and that is really where I'm at: I am worn out. If I were back out in a division I would definitely support Shared Services more than most controllers, but maybe that's because I understand it now. Even when I started I was a bit skeptical, but I had read a lot about it and it made sense, so I figured I would give it a shot," Jerry explained.

"So would you be interested in staying with Capp somewhere outside of Shared Services?"

"I've already accepted a position with another company."

"Is there any opportunity to change that?" Dennis asked.

"I guess there's always room to talk, but it's something I'd have to think about pretty quickly because I don't want to put these people that hired me in a bad position," Jerry responded.

"I'll have a conversation with Donna and let her know what's going on. To be honest, I put that out there, but I don't know if anything is available or even if Donna would think it's a good idea. I do know that you've done a fantastic job over the past three years here and for that matter all of your years with Capp, and I appreciate it," Dennis said.

"I would have to know something by the end of the day," Jerry told him.

"I'll talk to her as soon as we get out of this meeting. I assume you're taking a position with a local company."

"Yeah, I am. I am going to work for an automotive group that is one of the largest in not only Florida but the United States."

"Okay, we'll meet as soon as I have a discussion with Donna," Dennis said.

"All right."

Jerry got up and shook Dennis's hand. Dennis could tell by the expression on Jerry's face and his body language that this was not an easy decision for him. But Dennis knew that a Shared Services environment was not for everyone. Although he would talk with Donna, he didn't expect that anything would prevent Jerry from leaving. As soon as Jerry left, Dennis called Donna. She was in a meeting and would get back to him. In the meantime, he went back to working on the analysis John needed for the potential acquisition.

By lunchtime, Dennis still had not heard back from Donna. He decided to go to the mall and look for something to take home to Danny. He hoped Danny would be able to find a friend to sleep over this weekend. If he did, Dennis wanted them to have some kind of new game or toy to play with. Besides, browsing at the mall would take Dennis's mind off all the things that occurred so far today. It had been a fairly busy morning.

When Dennis got back to the office after lunch, Donna still had not returned his call. He decided to call her again. This time he was able to reach her. He got straight to the point. "Donna, I wanted to let you know that Jerry resigned today."

"Really? What were his reasons?"

"Well, he's pretty burned out on Shared Services for one thing. He has a hard time being in the middle between the divisions and the vendors and customers and having to constantly defend himself and his team. He really would like to be in a position where he can do his job without constantly being challenged about whether what he's doing is the right thing. I told him that a Shared Services environment is not for everyone, and he agreed with that. He said he's always struggled with that. I think what really caused him to consider leaving though was this indirect purchasing initiative. He doesn't feel it's supported by upper management, and he doubts that it will ever be successful. He feels like we're wasting a huge opportunity to save the company a tremendous amount of money," Dennis explained.

"It sounds like it is just not the place for him. Has he found another position?" Donna asked.

"Yeah, he's going to work for an automotive group here in Tampa. I asked him if there was anything we could do to keep him, and he said he would need to hear something very quickly. Obviously the only place he could really work would be in one of the divisions, and I don't think there's anything available. Besides that, unless it was in Tampa he would have to relocate, and I don't really think he wants to do that."

"There really is nothing available in the divisions right now, but even if there was, once someone has made up their mind to leave, it's very difficult to get them to stay in the long run. We're better off letting him go and finding a replacement. Over the last three years you've kept your management team in place and have done a good job managing turnover. I don't think this is the worst thing that could happen. Getting someone new into this position, whether it is an internal or external candidate, can only add new thoughts and ideas to the organization. I'm really not worried about it."

"That's easy for you to say." Dennis laughed. "But seriously, I do agree with you. I don't think it will be a hard position to replace, and hopefully we'll be able to give someone internally an opportunity. As a matter of fact, I have a couple of people in mind for the job."

"Good."

"Okay, I'll talk to Jerry and then I'll get with Human Resources and get the position posted. Also, while I have you on the phone, the analysis for John is going well, and I'll have it to him by the end of the week."

"Good, because it looks like something positive is going to happen with that," Donna said.

"Great, let's hope it does. That will be exciting," Dennis said.

"I agree. Talk to you later," Donna said.

Dennis hung up the phone and looked at the poster on his wall. He had to work on surrounding himself with good people again. He was sad to see Jerry go, but he was excited about the opportunity to find another good manager. He was also excited about the potential acquisition. That is one of the things Dennis liked about working in a Shared Services environment: Excitement was sometimes just right around the corner.

CHAPTER 28

# OPPORTUNITY

Dennis picked up the phone to call Jerry. As he was waiting for an answer he again looked at the poster on the wall. Jerry had been a very good employee, but often even good employees leave.

"Jerry, hey, it's Dennis. You didn't change your mind in the last 45 minutes, right?" he said, laughing.

"I'm not that flaky," Jerry responded.

"Well, I talked to Donna, and there is really nothing out there right now."

"That's what I figured, and besides, I'm committed to working with this new company, and I don't want to put them in a bad spot. They're kind of hurting because this position has been unfilled for a while, and I know they're counting on me," Jerry explained.

"I understand that, and that's also what makes you who you are. You're a man of your word and they're getting a good person. I know you'll do well."

"Thanks, I appreciate that. I'll type a letter of resignation and give my official two-week notice. So my last day will be not this coming Friday but the next Friday," Jerry said.

Dennis hung up the phone and started planning to replace Jerry.

"Rosa," Dennis called out of his office. "Can you come in here for a minute?"

"Jerry resigned today," Dennis said when she entered his office.

"Really? I hate to see that," said Rosa.

"He found another opportunity that's better for him. I need you to set up a meeting with myself and Clarence to talk about what we need to do to replace Jerry. Can you see if he's available today? You know what, make sure he is available today. If he has other things on his calendar, ask him to move them so we can meet."

"Okay, and I assume to move any of your meetings as well if that's the only way you two can meet," said Rosa.

"Exactly, see that poster? That's why we have to meet immediately. Anytime that you lose personnel, your number-one job has to be to get someone into that position. We can't do any of this without the right people. When you have an open position, particularly one that is so vital, your priorities have to shift to replacing that person," Dennis explained.

"So if I left, you would work on replacing me immediately, right?" Rosa said, grinning.

"Only after I stopped crying," Dennis answered, laughing.

"I'll get right on this," she said.

"Thanks."

Dennis went back to working on his analysis for the acquisition. Since today was Friday, he needed to meet with Clarence and if possible get the Financial Services manager position posted. Dennis also wanted to send out a memo to let everyone know that Jerry resigned. He decided to start working on that instead of the analysis for John. Rosa was able to arrange a 30-minute meeting with Clarence at 4:00. In the meantime, Dennis would write the memo about Jerry and then get back to the acquisition.

By 3:30 Dennis had completed the analysis for John and written the memo about Jerry. He sent the analysis to John but was waiting until he talked to Clarence before notifying everyone of Jerry's decision to leave.

Since he had 30 minutes to spare, he decided to walk around and see how everyone was doing. When Shared Services started, the team had decided to let everyone wear blue jeans on Friday. Dennis was never really sure if that was a good idea. Some people thought it made people more productive; others thought just the opposite. Either way, it would be difficult to change the policy back after three years. Besides, although Dennis did not wear jeans every Friday, he liked the fact that he didn't have to press a pair of pants when he wore jeans. He was sure others felt the same way. Even if they didn't press their own pants, it would save them a few dollars each week. For employees who often live paycheck to paycheck, that was a big deal.

As Dennis walked around, he was proud of the environment in Shared Services. It was laid back enough that most everyone enjoyed coming to work, but team members posted graphs and charts showing how they were performing. Each team took its own performance very seriously, and there was healthy competition among teams. Also each quarter they held a bowling or game night that would allow people to be on teams with employees outside of their actual work teams. Dennis felt it was very important to have fun and for everyone to get to know each other. They spent a lot of time together, and it only made sense that they should enjoy this time together as much as possible. Dennis talked with a number of people and morale seemed very high. As he walked back to his office to wait for Clarence, he wondered if that would change when they heard about Jerry.

"Clarence, how are you?" Dennis asked as Clarence walked into his office.

"Good and you? I haven't seen you all week. What's going on?"

"Lots of fun stuff," Dennis said. "Hey, before I forget, I just got done walking around talking to everyone, and morale seems real high. I noticed that some people were wearing their shirts from our last game night. You know, those types of events really help boost morale, and I appreciate you and your team working on those things. It makes a big difference."

"No problem. We like doing it, but I do agree it helps a lot. We're trying to figure out right now what we're going to do for the next event."

"Well, don't tell me what you're thinking. I like to be surprised like everyone else," said Dennis. "But that's not why I wanted to meet with you. I want to let you know that Jerry resigned today."

"Really? What were his reasons?"

"This Shared Services environment is starting to wear on him—I don't mean the environment we've created," Dennis said quickly. "He has a difficult time when the divisions don't cooperate or they fight with us and don't support us. Shared Services is not for everyone, but I'm not really worried about why he left. I just want to make sure we get his position filled as quickly as possible, and with the right person. I'm going to send a memo to all of Shared Services today letting them know that Jerry resigned. If possible, I'd like to get an official job posting out there immediately as well."

"Is he going to tell his team in person? Surely you don't want his team to find out via email, right?"

"That's a good point. I forgot about that. Luckily we haven't had any managers or team leads resign, so I'm not used to this."

Dennis picked up the phone and called Jerry. "Jerry, I have Clarence here with me, so don't say anything bad about him," Dennis said, laughing.

"I can say bad things now because I'm leaving," Jerry responded.

"He says that stuff to my face anyway." Clarence grinned.

"Seriously, we need you to meet with the team today so we can get out a memo and the job posting before everyone leaves this weekend. Can you get them together real quickly?"

"Yeah, I guess, but I really wasn't prepared to do that today," Jerry answered.

"I know, but I want anyone who might be interested to think about it this weekend. We need to get this job posted immediately. You're an important guy, and we need to replace you as quickly as possible."

"Okay, I'll get them together in about 15 minutes. Will that work?" Jerry replied.

"Yeah, that works. I appreciate it."

Dennis hung up the phone. He knew that everyone probably felt he was rushing this a bit, but they didn't know about the pending acquisition. Dennis needed to get Jerry replaced as quickly as possible and then get back to focusing on the potential acquisition. He wished he could let at least Clarence and Jerry know why he was moving this along so quickly, but it had to be kept confidential.

"Do you want me to post this to all divisions as well as outside of Capp?" asked Clarence.

"Yes, I want it posted everywhere. Obviously I'd prefer if someone internally were to get the position, particularly someone from Shared Services. As we always say, we need to promote from within as much as possible."

"I assume you feel that we have some qualified candidates internally," Clarence said.

"Sure we do, and that's why I want it posted today. If we get it out, whoever might be interested will be able to think about it this weekend and be ready to apply on Monday."

"I agree," Clarence said. "I can get it posted today. We have his job description from when we started Shared Services, and it hasn't changed too much, except for the indirect purchasing responsibilities. For that I can incorporate some of the verbiage from the posting for Angie's position. Don't worry, I'll get it out there, but I need to get started pretty quickly if we want everyone to see it. Most people leave at 5:00, especially on a Friday."

"I agree. I'll send the memo out as soon as Jerry gets done with his meeting. In that memo I mention that you'll be sending an email with the job posting," Dennis said.

Jerry called Dennis to let him know he had met with his team to tell them he was resigning. Dennis sent out the memo, and immediately his phone began to ring and the replies to his email began to roll in. He was sure Jerry was getting more responses than he was. At least the memo was doing what Dennis wanted it to do: get the word out that there was an opportunity for someone. Dennis spent the rest of the day answering emails and phone calls. Surprisingly, he hadn't heard from either Nelly or Angie. He was a little worried about that.

# CHAPTER 29

# GROWTH

It was Monday afternoon, and so far Dennis's day had flown by. He spent the morning fielding calls and emails about Jerry leaving. He also had spoken to John a few times about the analysis for the potential acquisition. Because John was asking so many questions, Dennis believed that the acquisition was probably going to happen. He still hadn't heard from either Nelly or Angie about Jerry leaving. He did, however, receive inquiring emails from Stephanie, the Benefits supervisor; Steve, the General Ledger supervisor; and Drew, the Accounts Receivable supervisor. They didn't officially apply for the job, but they did ask if the person applying had to have experience managing accounts payable or if supervisors of other areas would be considered.

Dennis was happy they were showing interest and would certainly consider someone who did not have direct accounts payable management experience. He always felt that most of the people in the world have some level of accounts payable experience, because everyone gets bills and pays them. To Dennis, that was some accounts payable experience. Sure, in a company there were a lot more bills, a lot more money involved, and more complex invoices, but essentially it is the same concept. He believed that people tended to make their jobs more complicated than they needed to be. Accounts Payable was essentially a very simple process; it just involved a lot of volume and a lot of dollars. But if it was broken down into fundamental steps, it was really not that complex, which is why he would consider management experience outside of the area.

Finally he was copied on an email Nelly had sent to Clarence that included her resume, application, and reasons for applying for the position of Financial Services manager. Dennis wondered if Angie had plans to apply. He was less confident that Angie could do the job because she currently managed only one person and her focus was solely on purchasing. Besides that, she had only been with Capp a little over four months—too brief a time to determine her true abilities, Dennis thought. He did feel that she wouldn't want to report to Nelly if Nelly were to get the job. Dennis felt that she wouldn't like reporting to someone who didn't have any purchasing experience.

By the end of the day, Stephanie, Steve, Nelly, and Drew had officially applied for the position. Clarence had also received a couple of inquiries from people within other divisions of Capp. The interest in the job was pretty high, which made Dennis feel confident they'd be able to find the right candidate. Since Shared Services had a policy of interviewing all internal candidates, Dennis scheduled interviews with everyone from Capp who applied. He did not see any reason to wait until they received resumes from people outside of the company. They could always interview those candidates, if there were going to be any, next week.

Because Dennis liked the team interview concept, he included Sara in all of the interviews. It was a little awkward for people from Sara's team to be interviewed by Sara about a job that would make them her peer, but Dennis wanted her to help evaluate each candidate. By Thursday afternoon, Dennis and Sara had interviewed all of the internal candidates. They received two qualified resumes from candidates outside of Capp and decided to interview these candidates on Friday. In order to expedite the process, they decided to choose the internal candidate who would be offered the job if one of the external candidates did not turn out to be more qualified. Sara came to Dennis's office to evaluate the candidates.

"We're moving pretty quickly on this," Sara said to Dennis as she sat down.

"Yeah, we have to. We only have three months to year-end, and you know how fast that time goes by. If we don't move on this now, the next thing you know is that it'll be November and we still won't have a candidate. You are only as good as those you are surrounded by, and if you are surrounded by no one, that's a real problem," Dennis responded.

"That's true. I think we're in good shape because I'm sure we can fill the position with Nelly, Steve, Drew, or Stephanie."

"I agree with that," Dennis said. "I still want to interview the external candidates, because you never know what you're going to find, but since I definitely want to promote from within, one of the external candidates will really have to blow us away."

"So who do you think is the one? How did you rate them?" Sara asked.

"Well, I rated both Nelly and Drew as a 4, Steve as a 3.5, and Stephanie as a 3, so in my mind it's between Nelly and Drew."

"I might be a little tougher in my ratings, but I had essentially the same result. I had Nelly and Drew as a 3.5 and both Stephanie and Steve as a 3," Sara told him.

"Okay, I don't think we need to get into the actual ratings as long as we agree that Nelly and Drew are the top two candidates."

"And Clarence never heard anything back from the candidates in other divisions at Capp, right?" asked Sara.

"No, he didn't, and they only have until the end of the day tomorrow to submit their application, so I doubt if we'll get any more."

"But if we do, we'll interview them right?"

"Not necessarily. We have a policy in Shared Services to interview all internal candidates, but Capp does not always follow that. If someone applies who is clearly not qualified, they'll tell the person they don't meet the basic requirements. I just like to interview everyone internally to Shared Services because it's an opportunity to get to know the person and talk to them about their career and those types of things," Dennis explained.

"Isn't that leading them on a bit?"

"No, because I'll let them know at the start of the interview that they are really not qualified, but I do want to give them the opportunity to tell me why they think they're qualified. Usually it results in a very good conversation, and people always seem to appreciate the opportunity. I think most people know when they're a bit of a long shot for a job."

"Fair enough," Sara said. "So between Drew and Nelly, who would you choose?"

"Like I said, I rated both of them a 4, but because Nelly is the one who knows the team and the process, and because she has been the team leader for Accounts Payable, I would choose her. The only thing I need to consider is whether I would have her manage Indirect Purchasing, because when we asked her questions related to that, she wasn't as solid with her answers," Dennis replied.

"I agree with that. She wasn't as strong when we talked about Indirect Purchasing. Don't you think it is going to be a little tough to find someone who has experience managing both of those areas?"

"Yeah, it will be tough," Dennis answered. "We definitely don't have someone in-house who has that experience. If we were to find someone from the outside, most likely they'd be very experienced and probably at a higher level than we're looking for."

"So what are you going to do with Indirect Purchasing?"

"To be honest, I was thinking about having Angie report directly to me. Indirect Purchasing has struggled a bit under Jerry anyway, which I don't think is his fault, but it probably needs a little more attention. Besides, I don't get that involved with your areas anymore, and I also don't get too involved with Accounts Receivable, Accounts Payable, or Document Management either. And there is still a potential to save the company millions and millions of dollars if we can get better participation from the divisions. I don't want to give up on it yet," Dennis responded.

"If you're going to split out Indirect Purchasing, I definitely think Nelly can do the job. I like her a lot. I think she works very hard, and her teammates really respect her and get along with her. To me she's the logical choice." Sara sounded enthusiastic.

"Okay then, she's the choice internally. If one of these people we interview tomorrow blows us away, we may have to alter our decision, but for now the choice is Nelly."

"Great," Sara exclaimed.

After Sara left his office, Dennis went back to working on other things. He was happy they chose Nelly to replace Jerry. He was confident she could do the job, and he knew that hiring internally would send a good message about promoting people from within. Luckily, since Shared Services started, there had not been a great deal of turnover. Opportunities like this did not occur very often, so it was important that when the first big opportunity opened up, an internal candidate was chosen. He didn't think they needed to interview external candidates, but since the interviews were already set up, he wouldn't cancel them. Dennis went home that night feeling pretty good. Although he hated to see Jerry leave, he felt good about giving Nelly such a big opportunity. He was sure she'd do well.

As usual, Dennis got to work early on Friday. He always felt weird interviewing external candidates on a Friday because they would usually be dressed in a suit and he was dressed casually. He wasn't going to wear something different just because he was interviewing. When he reached his office, the message light on his phone was lit. Someone had either left him a message last night or someone else was at work as early as he was. The only person who got to work that early was John. Sure enough, the message was from John, asking Dennis to call as soon as he got in. Dennis picked up the phone and called John. John answered his phone on the first ring.

"John, it's Dennis. I hope you called to tell me we made the acquisition," Dennis said.

"You're going to be happy. We finalized the deal last night. We'll close in 30 days, but we need to start getting ready to move them into Shared Services and onto SAP because we want this completed by January 1. That gives us a little over 90 days."

"Wow, that's great news, but that's also a pretty aggressive timeline, don't you think?" Dennis asked.

"Just as you put together what it would take to move them into Shared Services, Oscar did the same thing for the SAP implementation, and he said it can be done. I left a message for him as well, but I haven't heard back from him yet," replied John.

"I'm sure you will as soon as he gets in, because this will be a lot of work for him and his team."

"I agree, but they're confident they can do it. They just need to put on hold all other things they're working on right now."

"When are we going to make this public?" Dennis asked.

"Today," John replied. "Donna is out in Seattle right now working through a couple of last-minute issues, but unless something goes horribly wrong you'll see a communication later today. So until then, keep this under your hat."

"Will do, and congratulations!"

"As Dennis hung up the phone, he was extremely excited about the opportunity to add new business to the Shared Services center. They planned to be able to absorb the volume of work with very little additional headcount, which would help prove the Shared Services concept. If all went as planned, this would be a big boost for Dennis and his group. He couldn't wait to get started. Just as he was thinking through the process, his phone rang.

It was Oscar. "John just told me he talked to you about the new acquisition. Pretty cool, huh?"

"Yeah, but you guys are going to have a lot of work to do. Are you going to have to set up shop out West somewhere?" Dennis asked.

"No, other than the training of some end users, most of the work is going to be done here. Besides I'm glad to be working back in Florida and don't want to work out of temporary offices again. I like being home, so I will make it happen from here no matter what. We're going to send some people out next week to get a bit of information, but we should be able to accomplish most of what we need to do right here in Tampa. This will be a lot different from the past implementations because we're not going to have to debate the setup. They're going to be on our pay cycles, our benefit plans, and vacation cycles. According to John, we are going to set them up exactly like the western division so the configuration is simply mirrored. The real work will be the master data uploads and the training," Oscar replied.

"Speaking of training," Dennis said, "I'd like to volunteer a couple of our people to help with your end user training. I think we could help with the business process and the SAP training because our people are in it every day as an end user. They know a lot of tips, tricks, and shortcuts."

"Sure, that would be great. Once we have the training scheduled, I'll forward it on to you and you can let me know who will attend," said Oscar.

"Great. Also keep me informed of your progress on the configuration. Obviously we can talk some more once this is public. I'll set up a meeting and we'll get a project team together."

"I've got to run, but I'm looking forward to working on this. It should be fun," Oscar said.

"I agree. I'll let you get back to it. See you later."

Dennis started reading through his emails. Due to the time zone difference, he normally received a lot of emails from the West Coast once he left work, so he had a number to respond to first thing in the morning. He also looked at his schedule. Both of the interviews with outside candidates were in the morning. He was looking forward to getting Jerry's replacement announced, having the acquisition news made public, and being able to get started on bringing the acquisition into Shared Services.

As he read through his emails, he noticed one from one of the Shared Services organizations he belonged to, asking if he would like to speak at an upcoming conference about the lessons he had learned being the leader of a Shared Services organization. He was sure he could put together a pretty good list of lessons learned, so he responded yes. The conference was not being held for another eight weeks, so he had some time to prepare.

It was after lunch, and the day had flown by. Dennis and Sara had interviewed the external candidates, but they hadn't had a chance to discuss the candidates. He emailed Sara asking if she could meet with him for 15 minutes before the end of the day. During one of the interviews, his mind had drifted a bit to the upcoming conference. He decided to put together a top 25 list of lessons learned and things to do when starting a Shared Services center.

If he were starting another center, he'd certainly do some things differently right from the beginning, and he might as well pass those lessons on. What he was thinking of putting together would also help some of the more mature Shared Services centers. He was looking forward to getting started on that list as well as everything else that was going on; as he was thinking about this, Sara peeked into his office.

"Can we meet now?" she asked.

"Sure. So what did you think about the candidates?"

"You know, I liked both of them and thought that probably either one would do well, but I don't think they're so strong that we should take them over Nelly. I just think that would send a bad message because we really need to promote from within. I think if we were having problems with Accounts Payable or problems with Nelly, it would be a different story, but we're not. So having said all of that, my choice is Nelly," she responded.

"I agree completely," Dennis said. "I'll talk to Nelly on Monday morning and send a memo letting everyone know that she will be promoted to Financial Services manager, but before I send the memo I'll have Clarence talk to the other internal candidates who didn't get chosen, because I don't want them to find out via memo. Also, I decided to have Angie report directly to me at least until we get Indirect Purchasing up and running a little better. I'll put that in the memo as well. I'm excited about these changes. I know we're going to do well."

"I think so too." Sara smiled.

CHAPTER 30

# HELLO AND GOOD-BYE

Dennis spent the weekend pondering what he was going to do with Andrew's room. Andrew was adamant about the fact that he was not going to work and live in Tampa, so he told the family there was no need to keep his room. Luckily Danny, Jackie, and Samantha did not have any interest in changing their rooms, so it was up to Dennis and Jennifer to decide what should be done with the room. Dennis really wanted to turn it into a media room, where he could watch the games and the kids could watch movies. He discussed this with Jennifer and she agreed they would probably get the most use out of a media room rather than an office or a guest room. Her only concern was how much money Dennis was going to spend on a television, surround sound, and furniture. Normally he was pretty good about not overspending for items around the house, but she didn't trust him on this one.

"Honey, you know I'm going to go with you when you start looking for the equipment for the room, right?" Jennifer said.

"But you don't even like shopping for electronics. Why do you want to go along?" Dennis asked.

"Because you like shopping for electronics too much; I want to make sure you don't come home with a TV as big as a drive-in theater." Jennifer laughed.

"And what would be wrong with that? We could tear out the back wall and put the screen in the backyard."

"Now you know why I'm going!"

"I'm just kidding. We wouldn't have to tear out the back wall. We can just tear out the ceiling and have the screen sticking out of the roof," he said, laughing.

"You know, I think I like the idea of the sewing room better," she told him.

"You don't even sew. Who sews anymore?" Dennis asked.

"Well, I would rather start doing that than have to get a part-time job to pay for all of this equipment," she retorted.

"Okay, I'll be reasonable, just no sewing room."

"I'm still going with you."

Dennis still felt weird planning a new use for Andrew's room, but he was interviewing for jobs in Chicago, Boston, and New York. Andrew seemed very confident he would land an opportunity somewhere besides Tampa, and he even said that if he didn't, he was planning to move to one of the cities and work in any job just to get established. As much as Dennis hated to see him move so far away, he admired his son's determination and adventurous nature.

He had talked to Andrew two nights ago, and although it was still a couple of months away, Dennis mentioned that he would really like for Andrew to come home for Thanksgiving this year. He sensed that Andrew understood it would mean a lot to the entire family to have him come home for Thanksgiving his last semester of college. Dennis decided to not do anything to Andrew's room until after Thanksgiving, although he planned to spend a lot of time in electronic stores between now and then.

The weekend flew by as Dennis thought about the media room and did a little preliminary shopping. He read a few emails when he got in Monday morning and left a message for Nelly to come see him as soon as she got in. He hadn't been in more than 20 minutes when Nelly arrived at his door.

"Hey, Dennis, how was your weekend?" she asked.

"Fantastic, and yours?" he replied.

"Pretty good, but I wouldn't say fantastic."

"Can you shut the door?" Dennis asked.

"Sure." She looked a bit worried.

"Well, I hope what I'm going to tell you is going to at least make your Monday fantastic," Dennis said, smiling.

The look on Nelly's face changed from worried to excited.

"You probably know what I'm going to say, but I'll tell you anyway. We want to offer you the position of Financial Services manager," Dennis continued.

"Wow, I can't tell you how much that means to me!" Nelly's eyes started to tear up. "I'm sorry. It's just that I can't tell you how much I wanted to get this chance. I'm not going to let you down."

"I know you won't. Sara and I have the utmost confidence in your abilities, and we both look really forward to working with you. Now I know you probably want to know about the money," Dennis said.

"I probably shouldn't say this, but that's not the most important thing to me right now," Nelly said.

"Well, great, then your salary is going to stay the same." Dennis laughed.

"Okay, so I definitely shouldn't have said that."

"Seriously, when we looked at your performance over the past few years and the fact that you have pretty much received standard raises, we decided you deserve a pretty good increase for taking on this responsibility. When you started in Shared Services you were at $50,000 and you received the standard 4 percent increase the first year and 5 percent the second year, so today you're at $54,600 right?" Dennis asked.

"That's right."

"Well, we want to offer you $70,000 as a base salary and increase your bonus potential from $4,000 to $8,000."

"Wow, to be honest, that's more than I expected. I know we're in the service business and the divisions pay for our operation so we must hold down costs, and that's why I'm a bit surprised. Thank you very much! I accept," she said, smiling.

"You're very welcome. You deserve it. Now, do me a favor and keep this confidential until we send out a memo. Clarence is talking to the other internal candidates this morning so they don't find out via an email. Once he's done with that we'll send out the memo."

"Definitely, and again thank you very much. I've been working with Jerry the last few days, and I'll make sure I get everything from him I need before he leaves," Nelly said.

After Nelly left Dennis's office, he felt very good about the conversation and confident they had made the right decision. Besides the fact that she was the right person for the job, the move would save Shared Services a decent amount on salary because Jerry had been making a little more than $92,000. Nelly did not have nearly as much experience as Jerry, so she did not warrant that salary, but eventually she would get there. Promoting people from within always opened up this type of opportunity, and Dennis was happy it worked out. He loved giving people who had proven themselves and worked hard an opportunity to gain more responsibility and make more money. That was the best part of his job.

Dennis picked up the phone and called Clarence to ask about his discussions with Stephanie and Steve.

"They went okay," Clarence said. "I think both of them felt that Nelly was the front runner because she had been working in Accounts Payable since we started. Also, it's not like we have been having problems with Accounts Payable, and besides that the team really likes her, so they weren't surprised."

"Okay. I'm sure they'll both have opportunities some day. I'm going to send out the memo this morning congratulating Nelly on her promotion. Are we planning on doing anything for Jerry?" Dennis asked.

"Do you mean like a going-away lunch or something?"

"Yeah, we should probably do something," said Dennis.

"Okay, is he staying until Friday?" Clarence asked.

"Yes."

"All right, I'll talk to the team and set something up for Friday. We can just have some pizzas or something brought in. I'd rather do that than take him out for lunch because not everyone could go, and even if they could, it would be a logistical nightmare to get that many people into a restaurant for lunch," Clarence explained.

"Okay, set that up. Once you get the details, send out a memo and let everyone know," Dennis said.

Dennis had not spoken to John since Friday. Capp hadn't sent out an announcement about the acquisition, which had Dennis a little worried. He hoped the announcement would come out today so he could start getting the teams ready. There was not nearly as much to do on the functional side as there would be on the technical side, so Oscar was going to need as much time as possible.

In the meantime, Dennis sent out the memo about Nelly. Because some people chose to congratulate her by replying to all people on the email, he got a chance to gauge the reaction, and it seemed very positive. Nelly was very well liked, so he was confident they made the right move. Clarence also sent the memo about Jerry's going-away lunch, which was going to be held on Friday at noon.

Just as Dennis was reading about Jerry's lunch, the memo came from John about the acquisition; almost immediately people started coming to Dennis's office to ask questions. They wanted to know what the effect was going to be on Shared Services, when they would have to start processing transactions for the new division, and whether Shared Services would need to hire more people to absorb the volume. Everyone seemed genuinely excited that Capp was growing, but there also seemed to be a bit of concern about the effect on Shared Services. After three years, they were starting to get settled into more routine days. Now they had to work with a new division and go through the same pains they went through with each new division. Dennis reminded them that bringing in new divisions and acquisitions was an integral part of any Shared Services organization, and Shared Services helped make these types of acquisitions possible. He understood their concerns, but he did not feel any himself. His job over the next 90 days was to prove to everyone that they could absorb this new work without difficulty and make everyone understand this was going to add true value to Capp. This was the true strategic value Shared Services provided.

The rest of the week went by very fast, partly because there was so much talk about the new acquisition. Dennis could not believe today was already Friday. When he got dressed, he had to remind himself that it was Friday and he could wear jeans.

He spent the morning reading emails and reviewing Oscar's plan to implement SAP for the new acquisition. Oscar was going to need some assistance from a few people in Shared Services for testing, and Dennis was also including his team in the on-site training that was going to be done at each new plant. Not only would this help Oscar's team, but it would also give the Shared Services personnel an opportunity to meet the people who were going to be their customers and understand their business.

Rosa came into Dennis's office as he was reviewing Oscar's plan. "It's time for you to go to Jerry's going-away lunch," she said.

"Already? Wow, this morning has gone by quickly. As a matter of fact, this whole week has been a blur. Is the pizza here yet?" Dennis replied.

"It just got here."

"Well, I'll head over there now then. I don't want to get stuck with the plain cheese pizza. It seems all of the unhealthy stuff goes fastest, and I definitely want to eat unhealthy today." Dennis laughed.

"You can afford it, you look pretty healthy," Rosa said.

"Thank you. Let's go say good-bye to Jerry and eat some pizza."

The conference room was packed with people from every department. Either people really liked Jerry or everyone was very hungry for pizza. Free food always seemed to attract a crowd, but Dennis was sure they were there more to say good-bye. There were many conversations going on covering just about every topic imaginable. Although Dennis didn't want to disrupt the fun, he did want to say a few words about Jerry. He decided to wait 10 more minutes before getting everyone's attention. Jerry didn't like to be the center of attention, so Dennis didn't want to spend too much time making him uncomfortable.

"Attention, everyone," Dennis said loudly. "I hate to interrupt everyone's conversations, some of which I cannot repeat," he said, laughing, "but I would like to say a few words about our friend Jerry."

"They'd probably prefer to continue talking rather than hear about me," said Jerry.

"All kidding aside, I'm sure that's not true," Dennis said. "You have been a big part of our success. That is really what I want to talk about. As a group we have been very successful, and I'm confident we'll continue to be successful. While we hate to see Jerry leave, we know he's leaving us in good shape and he did a good job getting his teams ready to be able to perform without him. As a manager, that is really your ultimate goal: to eventually eliminate the need for yourself. I know that scares some people because they wonder what they'll do next. Well, don't worry because we always have plenty to do. If you're able to train and teach your teams to do their job without your input, then you have succeeded and we'll give you something else to do. In this case, Jerry felt it was best to move to an opportunity outside of the company, which is unfortunate for us, but I'm sure will be the right move for Jerry. I want to keep this brief, so I just want to say thanks, Jerry, for helping us get many divisions implemented, thanks for working so many hours, and thanks for helping to make every day a fun day. We appreciate everything you've done and you will be missed." As Dennis finished, everyone started to clap.

"Thanks for those kind words," Jerry replied. "This has been the toughest decision of my career, but for me it was time to move on. To be honest, I probably was more cut out to work in a division than in Shared Services, which as you know can be a very tough environment. It can be very stressful sitting between the vendors and the divisions, and I admire everyone in here for being able to do that day in and day out. I especially want to thank Dennis for giving me a great opportunity and for showing me how to handle that stress. I also want to say thanks to Sara for all of her help and for the support of everyone on her teams. And finally I want to say thanks to Nelly for making me look good. I know she'll do well as the new manager. You're in good hands. And by the way, good luck with the new acquisition. I know it will be difficult, but at the same time it's going to be exciting. Thanks to everyone, and I'll miss working with you."

CHAPTER 31

# THE CONFERENCE

Dennis was standing in a jetway waiting to board a flight to Dallas. He was going to the Shared Services conference, where he was going to speak on the lessons he learned in starting a Shared Services center. As he got older, he became less and less comfortable flying. Luckily Capp allowed employees at his level to fly first class, so at least he'd have plenty of legroom and be able to get a free drink or two. His flight was scheduled to arrive at 6:00 pm, and since he did not have to speak until tomorrow afternoon, he'd have time to relax, eat dinner, and get a good night's sleep. He boarded the plane, settled into his seat, and put on a pair of headphones to listen to some jazz. He nodded off a number of times before the captain's voice came over the headphones.

"Ladies and gentlemen, this is your captain speaking. We apologize for the delay, but we are awaiting our final paperwork and for a maintenance crew to come and take a look at one of the overhead storage bins. We are having trouble keeping the door closed, and we don't want the door to come open during flight and have a piece of luggage fall out and injure someone. We have a completely full flight, and all of the storage bins are full. If we are unable to repair the door, we will have to check the luggage that is in that bin. So we appreciate your patience and ask you to sit back and relax. We will be under way shortly. Again, thank you for your patience."

Dennis thought that just about every flight he'd been on recently had been delayed, but at least the music was relaxing. He nodded off a few more times, and when he looked at his watch he noticed they were now

231

45 minutes late for takeoff. After about 10 minutes the captain finally told them the problem was fixed, and they would be pushing back in just a few minutes.

As they taxied down the runway, the captain again came over the speaker. "Good afternoon, and again thank you for your patience. We are now number four for takeoff, but a band of thunderstorms is coming through, so we're going to sit tight for a few more minutes and wait for them to pass over before taking off. I know we are experiencing a few delays, but your safety and the safety of our crew is our number-one priority. We will be able to make up a little time once we are under way. Again, thank you for your patience, and we will be under way shortly." The captain was lucky enough not to be able to hear the groans and complaints from the passengers.

Finally, after another hour of sitting in the plane, the storms dissipated and Dennis was on his way to Dallas. Although the flight had arrived late, he had given himself enough time to enjoy a nice dinner and relax before going to bed. Dennis had traveled enough that he did not mind eating alone in a restaurant. Usually he read a book or newspaper, but tonight he sat at the bar and ate a steak while watching an NBA basketball game. He was looking forward to the conference and sharing his lessons learned in his Shared Services career and in particular the lessons learned in the past three and a half years.

Dennis woke up earlier than usual. He turned on the television and set up the ironing board to touch up his shirt. While ironing, Dennis remembered why he disliked travel so much.

He went down to the conference and ate breakfast with a few of the other conference participants. He had been working in the Shared Services arena long enough to know some people at every conference. He enjoyed seeing some of the same people and learning how they were progressing with their Shared Services centers. Although there were many different industries represented at the conference, the issues and challenges were very similar across almost all of the centers. These types of conferences provided great networking opportunities and gave participants a chance to learn from some of the more mature Shared Services companies. He hoped everyone would learn a bit from his 10:00 am presentation. A break was scheduled right before Dennis was scheduled to speak, so he had an opportunity to get his notes and thoughts together before everyone returned.

"We are going to get started again, so please take your seats," said the conference host. "I'll give them another minute or so before announcing you," she said to Dennis.

He did not mind giving presentations or speaking to large groups, but this group was a little larger than he was used to. He guessed there were about 250 people in attendance. With that large an audience, he knew he would have to be fairly dynamic to hold their attention. He had a few butterflies in his stomach as he waited to get started. At last the conference host announced Dennis, and with that he was ready to share three years of lessons.

"Thank you for that warm introduction. I'm sure most of you wish the room was actually that warm. I'd like to get started this morning by presenting you with my Top 25 list of things to do when starting or running a Shared Services center." (See Exhibit 31.1.)

"I've had the pleasure of working with a great CEO and a great CFO the past three and a half years, and that has been a big key to the success of our Shared Services center, which is why that is number one on my Top 25 list. You must have executive support, and I mean the highest-level executive support, not only for your Shared Services center but for the initiatives, process improvements, and changes that will come out of the Shared Services initiative. You don't need to sell them and have their support down to the actual tactical solution to an issue, but they must fundamentally agree that change is needed and that they will support the effort to make those changes. This support must cascade like a waterfall throughout your organization. This support will save you a lot of time, effort, heartache, blood, sweat, and tears; well, hopefully, not blood because I've never seen blood spilled over Shared Services, but I have seen sweat and tears." Dennis's words drew a few laughs from the audience.

EXHIBIT **31.1**   *Conference Presentation Notes–Top 25*

1. *Executive Support for Shared Services and all initiatives within Shared Services.*

   Shared Services organizations will struggle without the highest level of executive support. This support must be cascaded down through the organization into each division and particularly within the finance organization of each division.

2. *Measure everything from day one.*

   Shared Services organizations need to know if they are winning or losing on a daily basis. The volume of work processed by most Shared Services centers is tremendous, and if they are not able to keep pace with the input, they will very quickly fall behind. If you win every day you will win every week, every month, and every year.

3. *Configure automation from day one whether you will have compliance or not.*

   As an example, even if your vendors are not ready for it today, configure EDI capabilities within your ERP system so that you are ready when they are. This applies to all types of automation. Use your Shared Services organization as a guinea pig for new processes and automation. You need to "walk it like you talk it."

4. *Location does not matter as much as people.*

   I have seen successful Shared Services centers that started as green fields, brown fields, and hazel fields. They can all be successful. The right place to put a Shared Services organization is whatever place is right for your company. The most important element of any Shared Services organization is quality people, and quality people are available just about everywhere. You just need to find them.

5. *Leaders should be someone with Shared Services experience.*

   No offense to public accountants or consultants, but they should have actual experience working in a Shared Services environment as an employee not a consultant. Running a Shared Services organization is much different from running an accounting firm or a consulting organization. No one likes to hear the word *factory* because they believe it is demeaning to be associated with a factory, but factories make the world go around, and there are many lessons to be learned from manufacturing environments. Invoices and files that need to be processed are like raw materials that need to be processed to produce a final product. They must be moved throughout the process as efficiently as possible.

6. *Form process steering teams from day one.*

Process steering teams help with standardization, but the most important aspect of process steering teams is that they create buy-in from the stakeholders. The best way to create the buy-in is to have a larger number of people from the divisions than from your Shared Services center.

7. *Get buy-in from all divisions prior to implementing.*

The process steering teams will get buy-in to process changes once Shared Services is implemented, but before it is implemented it is vitally important to get buy-in from the divisions prior to starting the Shared Services center. Executive support (see number 1 on the list) is vital to this buy-in.

8. *Teach your own employees how to configure your ERP system rather than using consultants.*

As ERP systems become more popular, the demand for talent to configure these systems becomes greater and greater. Developing talent from current employees will reduce the amount of turnover and diminish your reliance on higher-priced seasoned career consultants.

9. *Do not outsource a broken process.*

Optimize current processes before outsourcing them. It is very difficult for an outsourcer to fix a broken process, especially when the correction involves changing the corporate culture.

10. *Do not chase cheap labor—chase automation.*

Cheap labor can become more expensive through wage inflation and can do so at a fairly rapid rate. Automation does not get more expensive and, once implemented, can be leveraged very quickly.

11. *Survey your customers immediately.*

At some point you are going to want to survey your customers, but this does not usually happen until they have been utilizing Shared Services for some time. Within three months of a division beginning to utilize Shared Services; you should send a simple survey to at least get a customer service baseline. The most important thing to measure at this point is customer service. The divisions must know that you are there to help them. You will make mistakes, but if you work with each division and provide excellent customer service, they will be more likely to support your efforts.

12. *Incorporate surveys into the bonus plan for all employees.*

Because customer service is so important, the customer service surveys should be incorporated into the employee bonus plan. However, it is imperative that the employees do not attempt to lobby their customers for higher scores so the bonus paid will be increased. Customers and Shared Services must have an established trusting relationship before implementing survey results into the bonus plan.

13. *Start an indirect purchasing program from day one; it will help fund or fully fund Shared Services.*

   Indirect purchasing programs offer a great opportunity to save money. They also offer an opportunity to gain more leverage from preferred vendors. Because you will do more business with the preferred vendors, you can better influence the terms and conditions of payment, which will make your accounts payable organization more efficient.

14. *Motivating nonexempt employees is completely different than motivating exempt employees.*

   Often this is why people from accounting firms fail. Many times nonexempt employees are motivated by different factors from people who choose public accounting as a career. Generally people who enter public accounting are motivated by career growth and additional opportunities, whereas some nonexempt employees are satisfied with the status quo. There is nothing wrong with employees wanting to remain in the same job as long as they are producing to the company's satisfaction. This type of employee is motivated by different factors than the employee seeking career growth.

15. *Implement a bonus program for all employees.*

   All employees should receive a bonus based on some type of performance management. If the Shared Services Center is succeeding and achieving its goals everyone should receive some level of bonus compensation tied to this success.

16. *Bonus programs should be based on the team and not individual performance.*

   No one individual can make your Shared Services center successful, so it is imperative that everyone work together as a team. Establish common goals, communicate those goals, and incent your teams when they achieve the goals.

17. *Implement a bonus program for division executives that incents them to cooperate with each other.*

   Many times companies will incent their division executives based on the performance of their division and their division only. This does not entice them to cooperate with other divisions, which can be an issue for Shared

Services. Cooperation among divisions will lead to consistency in processes, which makes a Shared Services center more efficient.

18. *Communicate your wins and your losses.*

    Mistakes made by a Shared Services center will travel quickly throughout the informal communication network of a company. Focus in the divisions will be more likely on the mistakes made rather than the successes of a Shared Services center, so you must create a formal communication process to highlight both success and opportunities for improvement. Scorecards are a good way to objectively communicate to the divisions and Corporate.

19. *Truth in allocation.*

    In many companies the divisions directly pay for the services of a Shared Services center. Regardless of the allocation methodology, be honest in the calculation and communication of the allocation. Sometimes larger divisions are asked to pay more simply because they can afford it. If you are going to implement a "luxury tax" be honest about it. If Corporate decides to subsidize some of the costs of Shared Services, be honest about that as well, because if Corporate ever decides to stop the subsidy, the allocation will increase and it will be looked upon unfavorably within the divisions.

20. *Hold town hall type meetings and roundtable discussions with your employees.*

    Communicate as often as possible with every employee in your organization. A very effective way to do this is to hold a town hall meeting, A Town Hall allows you to communicate exactly the same message to every employee. Leave plenty of time for questions and answers. Roundtable meetings also can be very effective because they are a smaller group, which can be less intimidating for many employees. Some employees are not comfortable asking questions in a town hall type of meeting, but they will ask questions in a smaller roundtable type of setting.

21. *Surround yourself with diversity (people from different industries and different backgrounds).*

    Do not fall into the trap of hiring as many people as possible from the industry you are in. There is much to be learned from different organizations and industries, and the best way to do this is to hire people from those different organizations and industries. As the old saying goes, "You only know what you know."

22. *Hire some people from the divisions you will support.*

    Your customers will be more comfortable working with your organization if you have someone on your team they personally know. Also, employees who come from a division have very valuable knowledge about past practices and processes. This knowledge will be more valuable than you can imagine. The credibility of Shared Services will also increase by having respected, knowledgeable division employees as part of the team.

23. *Document the division organizations prior to implementing Shared Services.*

You will need to know the headcount and General and Administrative costs prior to implementing Shared Services. You will need this information to show the success or failure of Shared Services. Trying to get this information after the fact is very difficult and most likely will be incorrect. Some people in the company will challenge the worth and value of Shared Services, and this information will help fight that argument.

24. *Involve the divisions in process improvement prior to the implementation of Shared Services.*

It is very difficult to change processes after Shared Services has been established and implemented. Take your time evaluating and establishing processes that will work for both the divisions and Shared Services. Let the divisions know that these are their processes, and the efficiencies gained will help make them a more successful organization.

25. *Focus on the basics.*

Just as in sports, the fundamentals will lead to your success. Do not focus on new services or opportunities until you have mastered the basics of paying bills, paying employees, and these other basic Shared Services functions. Being fundamentally sound adds to the Shared Services organization's credibility. Being very fundamentally sound will lead to other opportunities.

26. *Have fun!!!!!!*

Okay, so this is really a Top 26 list, but this is maybe the most important one and that is why it is last. Create a fun environment. Shared Services is a tough environment because you sit in the middle between the divisions and vendors, suppliers, governments, and Corporate. In some people's eyes you will be seen as the organization that caused people in the divisions to lose their jobs, and you will be blamed when things go wrong, which they will. Your employees will be challenged by this type of environment, and the best way to meet this challenge is to have fun. Laughter and smiles can make a bad day better and make your employees truly enjoy their jobs.

He continued going through his list for the next 40 minutes. When he was done, he fielded questions and comments from the other participants. He was satisfied with the presentation because it generated enough questions and comments to fill the entire 60 minutes he was allotted. He listened to the next presentation and then went to the networking lunch hosted by the conference.

"Dennis, that was a nice presentation," said a man who looked very familiar to him.

"Thanks, I appreciate that. Hopefully everyone will find it helpful as they move forward. I wish I would've had a list of 25 things to do or maybe more important a list of 25 things *not* to do when I started, because we made some mistakes along the way that we probably could have avoided. By the way, I know I've met you before," Dennis responded.

"Yeah, I'm Dave Martin. I attended a conference you were at about five years ago. I don't think you were working for Capp at the time, but you were in the Shared Services business."

"That was the conference in Orlando, right?" Dennis asked.

"Yeah, it was in Orlando."

"Well, nice to see you again. It is always good to see those people who stick with Shared Services because this can be a tough gig. It's one of the only finance or accounting areas where you end up spending a good deal of time justifying your own existence," Dennis said.

"That's funny; I was telling someone that exact same thing last week. I think we all go through that. That's why the executive support you mentioned is so important. If you are supported from the top, you won't have to worry with that too much," Dave said.

"I agree; let's go get some lunch. I hope they have some soup so I can warm up," Dennis said, laughing.

Dennis spent the rest of the day listening to presentations and networking. He enjoyed the conference and was happy his presentation went over very well. He got a lot of comments about his Top 25 list, so at least it stimulated a lot of thought and conversation. His flight back to Tampa was scheduled to depart at 7:00 pm. He was looking forward to getting home and spending time with his family. Jennifer called and told him Danny had scored two goals in a soccer game that his team won. Dennis was sorry he missed seeing Danny's game. He also didn't like it that he would get home tonight after Danny was already in bed. Again he remembered why he hated to travel.

# CHAPTER 32

# THANKSGIVING

Andrew decided to come home for Thanksgiving after all. Dennis was very happy the entire family was going to be together for the holiday. To him it seemed like forever since everyone had been home on Thanksgiving, which was Dennis's favorite holiday because it was less formal than Christmas and it involved eating and watching football. He was also glad he decided not to do anything with Andrew's room until after Thanksgiving.

Thanksgiving morning, Dennis got up early. He had convinced Jennifer to let him try to grill the turkey. A lot of people tried to deep-fry turkeys these days, but Dennis liked the idea of grilling. He purchased a nice kettle grill that would allow him to use charcoal rather than gas. Cooking a turkey on a grill was pretty easy; it involved using indirect heat and simply putting the turkey in the middle of the grill and basting it every 30 minutes or so. It seemed easy enough. Jennifer prepared the turkey, so all Dennis had to do was put it on the grill and watch it. Because the grill acted like a convection oven, the turkey could cook in only three hours using this method.

"Honey, is the turkey ready to put on the grill?" Dennis asked Jennifer.

"Just about; come in and give me a hand tying the legs together and then we'll be ready."

"This is going to be fun," Dennis said as he helped his wife finish the preparation.

"Are you sure this is going to work?"

"Of course I'm sure. I saw it on TV. This is going to be a piece of cake. All I have to do is put it on the grill and baste it. I have my chair ready, and I'm going to sit out there until it is done," Dennis replied.

"Or until you burn it," said Andrew.

"Oh, you finally can get up before noon, huh?" Dennis said.

"I've been getting up early for a long time. I made it to all my classes, you know," Andrew replied with a grin.

"Of course I know," Dennis said. "You don't get a great job in Chicago without going to class, studying, and working hard. Now all you have to do is get used to the cold weather."

"That's why I'm glad I get to start first thing in January. I figure I'll get about two or three months of the cold and then it'll start to warm up a bit. At least that will get me used to the weather without having to go through five months of it."

"So why are you up so early?" asked Jennifer.

"I wouldn't miss the chance to sit with Dad and watch him burn the turkey," Andrew said, laughing.

"Well, you better hope for the best, because this is the only turkey we have," she replied.

"That's why I'm up. I figure I can help him out if anything goes wrong."

With that, Dennis took the turkey outside and put it on the grill. The coals were burning bright, the grill smelled fantastic, and Dennis was eager to get started. Father and son spent the next three hours talking, laughing, basting the turkey, and putting additional charcoal on the grill. After three and a half hours, the turkey was a beautiful golden brown. The meat thermometer said it was done. Beaming with joy, Dennis went inside to get a plate.

"Honey, we need a plate. The bird is ready and it looks fantastic," Dennis exclaimed.

"Here you go. Everything else will be ready in about 30 minutes, so the timing is perfect. We can let the turkey cool and it will be ready to carve."

Dennis and Andrew put the turkey on the plate and took it in the house. Soon the entire family was sitting at the table with a perfectly grilled turkey in the middle of the table.

"Dad, are you going to let Andrew carve the turkey this year?" asked Samantha.

"I am," he replied.

"Hey, I want to carve the turkey," said Danny.

"Me too," added Jackie.

"Well, if they get to, I want to also," Samantha said.

"How about if we all get to carve a little bit of the turkey?" Jennifer asked.

"That's a good idea, but we need to let Andrew carve it first. Is that okay with you, Andrew?" Dennis asked.

"Sure, that way if it's carved incorrectly, I can't be the only one who gets blamed," he answered, laughing.

"Sounds good," said Dennis.

"Mom, I don't mean this in a bad way, but this is just about the prettiest turkey we've ever had," said Jackie.

"I agree," answered Jennifer.

"So how did you do it, Dad?" asked Jackie.

"I had a lot of help from Andrew and your mom. Remember what I always say, you are only as good as those you are surrounded by. And you know what: I'll bet this will not only be the prettiest turkey, it will be the best-carved turkey and, most important, the best-tasting turkey because we all had a hand in preparing it," Dennis replied.

"That was really corny, Dad," said Danny. "Can we just get started before you make us all sick?"

"I wasn't talking about corn, I was talking about turkey," Dennis replied.

"Please, you're killing us; let's just eat," Danny exclaimed.

"You got it," said Dennis while the entire family laughed.

Everyone took their turn carving a bit of the turkey. They all agreed that grilling the turkey gave it a nice smoked flavor and that they would like to cook it the same way next year. Dennis and his family spent the rest of the long holiday weekend eating leftovers, watching football, playing football, watching movies, and thoroughly enjoying their time together. Dennis got the feeling everyone sensed this would be their last holiday together for a while. Andrew was not going to be able to come home for Christmas because he had to get moved to Chicago, and he was going to start his new job on January 2. Dennis's family was certainly growing up fast, and he wanted to savor every moment with them. When the weekend was over, he looked backed and realized it was probably the best Thanksgiving he could remember since he was a kid.

Monday morning, Dennis got up early since Andrew was going back to school to finish out the semester. The entire family was going to watch him graduate in a few weeks, but his leaving today was going to be hard on everyone. Although he had not been living at home for a few years, everyone realized that he'd be venturing out on his own soon. Andrew hugged everyone and got in his car and drove away. Everyone walked into the house except Dennis, who watched his elder son's car all the way down the street. The right blinker came on and with that Andrew's car turned right and disappeared.

Dennis shook his head and wiped away a few tears. He was so proud of his son and knew he would do well. When they were outside grilling the turkey, Andrew reminded Dennis of the conversation they had had more than three years ago about where to put the Shared Services center. Andrew told him he was right when he said the college won't make you, you will make the college, and if you surround yourself with the right people everything will work out. Dennis thought about that. It had worked for Andrew at college and it worked for Dennis at Capp.

Dennis walked back into the house and got his keys. He hugged the kids good-bye and gave Jennifer a kiss. He drove to work and, like most days, his was one of the first cars in the parking lot. He walked into his office and noticed the message light on his phone was blinking. The message was from John.

"Can you do another analysis for me that will show the effect of another acquisition about half the size of the last one?" John asked. "I'll need it by Wednesday. Let me know if you have any questions."

Dennis put down the phone and smiled. He was thankful he was surrounded by not only the right people but, in his mind, the best people because "You Are Only as Good as Those You Are Surrounded By."

# INDEX